Joseph of Arimathea

BIBLICAL REFIGURATIONS

General Editors: James Crossley and Francesca Stavrakopoulou

This innovative series offers new perspectives on the textual, cultural, and interpretative contexts of particular biblical characters, inviting readers to take a fresh look at the methodologies of Biblical Studies. Individual volumes employ different critical methods including social-scientific criticism, critical theory, historical criticism, reception history, postcolonialism, and gender studies, while subjects include both prominent and lesser-known figures from the Hebrew Bible and the New Testament.

Published Titles Include:

JOSEPH OF ARIMATHEA

A Study in Reception History

WILLIAM JOHN LYONS

OXFORD
UNIVERSITY PRESS

BS
2460
.J67
L96
2014

OXFORD
UNIVERSITY PRESS

Great Clarendon Street, Oxford, ox2 6DP,
United Kingdom

Oxford University Press is a department of the University of Oxford.
It furthers the University's objective of excellence in research, scholarship,
and education by publishing worldwide. Oxford is a registered trade mark of
Oxford University Press in the UK and in certain other countries

First Edition published in 2014
Impression: 1

Published in the United States of America by Oxford University Press
198 Madison Avenue, New York, NY 10016, United States of America

British Library Cataloguing in Publication Data
Data available

Library of Congress Control Number: 2013945567

ISBN 978-0-19-969591-1 (Hbk)
      978-0-19-969592-8 (Pbk)

As printed and bound by
CPI Group (UK) Ltd, Croydon, CRO 4YY

Acknowledgements

It is perhaps only when a reluctant writer comes to write the acknowledgements that a realization sets in as to the extent of the help and encouragement received along the long and often dreary way to publication. Many of those named below are well aware how little love I have for writing books—bloody things!—and I am grateful that they have usually failed to indulge that hatred whenever I have expressed it.

Thanks are offered to Judith Anstee, Jonathan Campbell, Tim Cole, Mat Collins, Oliver Crisp, Katie Edwards, Emma England, Deane Galbraith, David Gunn, James Harding, Anke Holdenried, Andrew Mein, Robert Myles, Jorunn Økland, Mike O'Mahony, Cameron McKenzie, Chris Meredith, Jon Morgan, Lloyd Pietersen, Ad Putter, Chris Rowland, Julie Sealey, Johanna Stiebert, Beth Williamson, and Simon Woodman. Some have commented on sections of the manuscript and I am profoundly grateful to those who did, but it was a surprising few—this volume really did seem to drift alongside other more visible work for much of its gestation—and no blame can be attached to anyone other than myself for whatever infelicities remain. Your support over the years was invaluable in so many other ways.

More recently some of its ideas have been tried out in public and I am grateful to Christina Petterson and the members of the Ideology, Culture, and Translation group at the SBL Annual Meeting in Chicago, 2012, and to Susan Miller and Pete Philips and the members of the Johannine Literature seminar at the British New Testament Conference at King's College London in 2012, for the chance to try out some ideas from the book. I am also grateful to Steven A. Hunt, D. Francois Tolmie, and Ruben Zimmermann for the opportunity to write the Joseph of Arimathea chapter for their *Character Studies in the Fourth Gospel: Narrative Approaches to Seventy Figures in John* (for Mohr Siebeck's WUNT series), and to Cor Bennema who so generously supported those of us who were involved in that project.

Thanks should also go to James Crossley and Francesca Stavrako-poulou, editors for the *Biblical Refigurations* series, and to Oxford University Press's anonymous readers of the original proposal and the submitted draft manuscript respectively for their valuable construct-ive comments at the beginning and end of the project. I am also grateful for the support offered by OUP's senior assistant commission-ing editor for religion Lizzie Robottom, production editor Caroline Hawley, and proofreader Richard Hutchinson, during the production process. It is all very much appreciated.

Finally, I would like to dedicate this book to my daughter, Megan. Katie, my wife, and Hannah, my eldest daughter, have been here before about twelve years ago and I can only apologize to Megan for the length of time she has had to wait to join her mother and older sister in the dedication of an academic book written by her father. Honestly now, Meg, tell me; was it really worth waiting for?

W J Lyons
August 2013

Contents

Introduction

Exploring the afterlives of Joseph of Arimathea

In the work that you are now holding, the reception history of one of the minor characters of the biblical narrative, Joseph of Arimathea, is laid out in as much of its fullness and glory as could be fitted within this publisher's word limits. From a pious participant in the Gospels' crucifixion and burial accounts to a wealthy Christian patron, from a chivalrous grail carrier to a national political figure, from a close family member of Jesus to a patron saint, from a channelled spirit guide to a man who never even existed, the multiple faces of Joseph as seen by interpreters down through the centuries are investigated, not with a great regard for their historical veracity, but instead with a particular concern to understand their illustrative value and pragmatic effectiveness.

This book is not an exhaustive list of 'Joseph occurrences', however. Two reasons, above and beyond the word length, governed the decision to exclude many possibilities. First, the demands of operating an 'exchange' process involving the inclusion of the less well-known at the expense of the better-known means that many famous exegetes are not really included; their Josephs either lack a detailed exposition or indeed are not mentioned at all (e.g. Gregory the Great, John Calvin, Martin Luther). This is done without apology; a survey of Joseph in the works of history's 'greatest' exegetes, this is not. Second, fascinating as it might be to bring a long-forgotten but inexplicable interpretation to light, this book is intended to be a study in reception history that is shaped by two questions, not one: what has Joseph of Arimathea created, enabled, effected, and meant on his journey through two millennia of history, and why has he been able to do/be these things, aided and abetted by his many interpreters, of course? Since the availability of supporting evidence often places severe limitations on our ability to explain the why, it is inevitable that looking at both the breadth of the Joseph tradition and the how of it will not offer us satisfying answers to all of our questions. Nevertheless, it is hoped that this volume succeeds in offering explanations for many of the interpretations discussed and as an explanation for the development of the Joseph tradition as a whole.

A reception history perspective on the Bible

From the perspective of reception history, scholarship on the Bible today inhabits a situation in which the critical study of biblical texts can no longer be usefully defined in terms of a distinction between original, first-order meanings and subsequent, second-order ones. Instead it is better defined as a pragmatic activity in which a historically located investigator is attempting to understand the dynamics of an interaction between a biblical text or a biblical text as rendered in some other media, a context, and an audience's response. Since our knowledge of a context is always limited and since the text or its representation and any audience response offered to it are likely to be only partially available to us at best, biblical critics should recognize that the explanations that they offer as they struggle to grasp the implications of any given interpretive scenario are always exercises in plausibility. The incidental nature of the availability of supporting evidence also means that there is almost certainly no single approach that will work in all interpretive scenarios and thus no standard set of conclusions that are available for all texts in all times and all places. Sometimes we may be able to explain convincingly the interpretations that we find. At other times we will only be able to wonder at what we see and then perhaps choose if we wish to list them in order to ensure their continued remembrance. But it is critically important that we realize that the biblical critic who is offering an interpretation of how, say, Paul and his audience understood the text of an epistle is as fully enmeshed in this situation as the biblical critic who is attempting to account for, say, Johnny Cash's interpretation of the book of Revelation in his song, 'The Man Comes Around'. The question of whether or not the audience

under investigation is the original one is theoretically and methodo-
logically irrelevant.

Some will no doubt see this description as one entailing a situation
in which all interpretive scenarios have now become of equal value, a
situation in which terms such as 'misunderstanding' no longer have
any real currency. This is mistaken, however. While we might be able
to entertain the idea of relativity implied in the above description of
our situation, our social and historical located-ness means that we can
never truly inhabit that idea. The mores of our own native discourses
will predispose us to expressing preferences. Some readings reached
by readers/audiences will be highly amenable to their sensibilities
(they will be 'right', 'accurate', 'perceptive', 'profound'!), others will
emphatically not be (these are 'incorrect', 'misconceived', 'plain
wrong', 'absurd'!), and most will probably be somewhere in between
(they are 'noteworthy', 'reasonable', 'worthy of consideration', or
perhaps just 'dull'). Given the West's enduring penchant for historicity, these categories will often elide into notions of fidelity to what
really happened (and hence increase the hold that the idea of the
'original meaning' possesses), and interpreters might then be predis-
posed towards using the concept of historicity to make decisions
about the ordering of a particular set of Josephs. Crucially, however,
such decisions do not mean that any of the readings involved are less
worthy of investigation; interpretations that are rightly regarded as
low in value in historical terms may become important readings when
seen from a reception-historical perspective interested in how a
biblical character has developed through time. The task of the reception historian then is to read all interpretations with a degree of
empathy and a certain amount of humility. The fact that I am as
located as anyone else simply means that I have had to confront some
of my own prejudices as to value—with, I should probably admit,
some unworthy sniggering—while writing this volume. Whether or
not I have been successful in dealing with those prejudices, however,
I will let readers decide.

The shape of the book

The layout of the book reflects not just its author's temporal and
spatial location as an academic biblical scholar, but also his location in

a discipline in which the importance of historicity in determining meaning is being increasingly questioned. Still dominating the Joseph of Arimathea tradition today, however, is the widespread assumption that it is historicity that matters most; this view is to be found in the wildest claims of certain apologetic works of the Glastonbury tradition just as much as it is still found in the calm normality (?) of Gospel Studies. Indeed in an earlier draft of this book, the text began with a historical-critical depiction of the historical person of Joseph as a 'bland, but to today's Western mind-set, necessary counterpoint to the variety of interpretations that follow'. The reality of the matter, however, is that such a figure is a very modern conceit. Instead of a being a necessary counterpoint, it proved instead to be an utter irrelevance to the vast majority of the interpretations that followed it. With that experience in mind, and with the helpful suggestions of the publisher's reviewer to press home the point, the eventual shape of the book emerged. The contemporary biblical critic's image of the historical Joseph would be relegated to the final chapter of the book where it belongs, with the various church, literary, film, and spiritualist Josephs of the twentieth and twenty-first centuries. Instead, it would be the four Gospel portrayals of Joseph that eventually drove the tradition to become what it did that would be discussed first.

Chapter one: The Biblical Joseph asks the 'what' and the 'why' of the earliest traditions about Joseph, the broadly similar accounts which appear in the Gospels of Matthew (27.57–61), Mark (15.42–47), Luke (23.50–56a), and John (19.38–42). The tendency to harmonize the limited number of scenes in which the canonical Joseph appears—his request to Pilate for Jesus' body, his removal of the body from the cross, and his involvement in the entombment of Jesus—is first considered, before each text is examined individually in order to define the specific contours of each of these earliest Josephs. An explanation for the development of each text into its extant form is offered in the light of current scholarly views on the source and redaction relationships between the Gospels.

Chapter two: The Early Joseph examines the reception of Joseph's canonical scenes in the earliest oral and literary traditions with an eye to their subsequent development through expansion (in the apocryphal *Gospel of Peter*, *c.* second century), through preaching (in the homilies of John Chrysostom, *c*.390), through translation (in the Old Latin and Jerome's *Vulgate*, *c*.382–4), through harmonization (in Augustine of Hippo's *De consensu evangelistarum*, *c*.404), and through extension beyond canonical boundaries (in the *Gospel of Nicodemus*, *c.* fourth century).

Representations of Joseph in the painting traditions of the European Renaissance are considered in chapter three: The Renaissance Joseph. Here the focus is on representative examples of the four standard 'Joseph' scenes: Simon Bening's prayer book depiction of *Joseph of Arimathea before Pilate* (*c*.1525–30); Rogier van der Weyden's influential *Descent from the Cross* (*c*.1435); Sandro Botticelli's *Lamentation over the Dead Christ* (*c*.1495), a non-canonical but popular scene-type known as the 'Pietà' (Botticelli's painting is also known as *The Milan Pietà*), that was increasingly viewed in the medieval period as a separate component within the descent from the cross scene; and Michelangelo's unfinished *Entombment* (*c*.1501). The presence of the latter is taken as permission for an excursus, aimed at illuminating the secretive world of the so-called 'Nicodemites', those who hid their faith to escape persecution in the Reformation period and beyond, among whom some numbered one Joseph of Arimathea, before the chapter concludes with a consideration of A. Soudavar's recent discussion of Simon Marmion's *Ducal Lamentation* (*c*.1465) as a personality-laden allegory of fifteenth-century European political history.

In chapter four: The Glastonbury Joseph our gaze turns towards the British Isles, towards England and the Glastonbury traditions about King Arthur and Joseph of Arimathea. These traditions are traced from their origins in the interplay between Arthurian legend and the life of Glastonbury Abbey through their broadest development in the medieval and early modern periods. The political ramifications of the Joseph legend for England as a nation in the debates of the great Church Councils of the fifteenth century are examined, before the destruction of Glastonbury Abbey by Henry VIII and its current renaissance in the twentieth and twenty-first centuries as a centre of all manner of spiritualities are sketched.

The Tudor use of Joseph to prove the English Church's superiority over Rome after the abbey's destruction moved the tradition away from a narrow geographical focus on the West Country towards a

presentation of the Arimathean as a national figure, setting the
scene for chapter five: The 'Jerusalem' Joseph. In the poetic section
of William Blake's preface to some early editions of his epic poem
Milton (1804), the four stanzas now known as 'Jerusalem', we see the
political and the literary elide in a work whose value to English
nationalism and to the British Empire since being set to music by
Sir Hubert Parry in 1916 would be hard to overestimate: examples
discussed include Empire Day (24 May); the 'Jam and Jerusalem' of
the Women's Institute; English national sporting anthems (football,
cricket, and, most recently, as the official national anthem, chosen by
public vote, for the 2010 Commonwealth Games in New Delhi); its
triumphant appearance on the Order of Service for the royal wedding
of Prince William and Kate Middleton in Westminster Abbey in
April 2011; and its use in the Opening Ceremony of the 2012 London
Olympic Games.

Chapter six: The Twentieth-Century Joseph extends our range of
Joseph portrayals by considering his appearances in wider twentieth-
and twenty-first-century Western culture. His place in church-
related institutions and practices is examined, including his role as a
patron saint for tin miners, tin workers, and funeral workers. An
examination of fictional retellings of Joseph's own story—whether as
plays, novels, or poems—reveals adjustments in both pre- and post-
crucifixion Joseph lore, before two contrasting images of Joseph
presented by author Phil Rickman in his *The Chalice: A Glastonbury
Ghost Story* (1997) are examined. Brian Gilbert's *The Gathering* (2003)
provides the main focus for a look at Joseph's appearances in cinema,
alongside the works of Pasolini and Zeffirelli, and the adventures of
Indiana Jones. The development of a significant Joseph tradition as a
spirit guide channelled by contemporary mediums in England is then
considered. Finally, recent scholarly exchanges about the possibility
that Joseph never existed are discussed and an opinion is offered as to
the nature of the 'real Joseph', a shadowy historical figure who fades
into insignificance when compared with his many vital presentations
in reception history and who is powerless to force even all of biblical
scholarship to acknowledge his presence.

In the Conclusion, the bewildering complexity of themes now
associated with Joseph of Arimathea is analysed, with the myriad
strands of the tradition grouped together under two broad headings:

Joseph as an *active man*, looking at examples of his bravery, his wealth and influence, his masculinity, his sanctification, and his dominance over others; and Joseph as a *passive man*, looking at examples of his guilt, his fear, his secretiveness, his malleability, and his submissiveness to those who have appropriated him. Such a variety of developments of the minimalist Gospel accounts of Joseph into the grand figures of later tradition showcase the many available mechanisms by which multiple interpretations may become clustered around a biblical figure with any degree of depth, a process of growth which no amount of forethought by the Evangelists could have forestalled, and which no amount of effort by biblical scholars will ever be able to control. The future, it is concluded, belongs to Joseph and his interpreters, whoever and wherever they may be.

1

The Biblical Joseph

The four Gospels

Joseph of Arimathea appears in all four canonical Gospels—Matthew, Mark, Luke, and John—with each presenting roughly the same story of his involvement in Jesus' removal from the cross and the burial of his body (Mt. 27.57–61; Mk 15.42–47; Lk. 23.50–56a; Jn 19.38–42); Joseph does not appear anywhere in the Gospels outside that time frame, though he may sometimes be prefigured by earlier themes, characters, or events (e.g. the 'rich man' in Matthew's version of the 'camel/eye of the needle' saying [19.23–26]). No contemporaneous Christian or non-Christian text mentioned Joseph by name; he is known to us today only from the canonical Gospels and the details that were eventually derived from them.

Sources, dependencies, and differences

We might have expected to meet Joseph initially in Matthew, the so-called 'First Gospel' and the Church's pre-eminent 'teaching' Gospel. Though the 'Griesbach hypothesis' concerning Gospel relationships—Matthew wrote first, Luke used his Gospel, and then both were used by Mark—is reprised occasionally, however, most critics now view Mark as the earliest Gospel ('Markan priority'), with it then being seen either as a source for Matthew and Luke who worked without knowing each other's texts (the 'Two-Source hypothesis'), or as a source used by Matthew and then, with Matthew, by Luke ('the Farrer hypothesis'). For reasons of my own ambivalence, what follows will allow for either of these views.[1] The position taken on the question of John's relationship to Mark will be to accept recent arguments suggesting that John knew only Mark.[2] Joseph of Arimathea's first appearance—in an extant text at least—was in the Gospel of Mark, usually dated to the late 60s CE, with every account we now possess owing something to that text.

The four Gospel accounts are not identical. Traditionally interpreters have assumed that the variants represented complementary reports which filled out the historical figure of Joseph. Historical-critical scholarship, perhaps surprisingly, tended to adopt that assumption uncritically. In the case of W. F Albright and C. S. Mann, commenting on Matthew 27.57, for example, their choice of words made clear their belief that each Evangelist provided reliable 'information': 'All our [Gospels] give us an account of this man'; 'John...provides the additional information that'; 'Mark...asserts that'; 'and to this information, Luke adds that...'; 'We are indebted to Matthew alone for the information that....'[3]

The twin assumptions of reliability and complementarity and the practice of harmonization that has followed in their wake should be viewed with suspicion, however, because they can just as easily hide the specific contours of each Gospel's Joseph as reveal them. This comment from C. E. B. Cranfield on Mark 15.46, for example, is typical: 'That the tomb belonged to Joseph is not stated, but it is natural to assume that it did.'[4] Since this detail appears only in Matthew, however, its naturalness is less a feature of Mark's text— or indeed of Luke's or of John's—than it is a by-product of Cranfield's conflation of these two narratives. In Matthew, Joseph is a disciple and the use of his own tomb makes a certain sense, but the Markan Joseph—a non-disciple according to Cranfield himself—is simply said to have buried Jesus in a tomb cut out of rock; it is not said to be his (nor is it even said to be unused, *pace* Luke 23.53 and John 19.41). This harmonizing tendency might not have mattered if confusion had not resulted, but trying to incorporate every variant has caused significant difficulties for those who have attempted it.

Harmonization is also susceptible to a further criticism; namely, that each variant's reliability is being assumed rather than demonstrated. Since Matthew, Luke, and John all used Mark, however, it seems eminently feasible that three of Albright and Mann's sets of 'information' could have arisen from the responses of the later

Evangelists to his text rather than from any new knowledge supplied by their sources. If it can be plausibly demonstrated that each Evangelist altered Mark's account because of their own ideological concerns, it can be safely concluded that their accounts contain no independent information about Joseph of Arimathea.

Mark 15.42–47

⁴²Καὶ ἤδη ὀψίας γενομένης, ἐπεὶ ἦν παρασκευή ὅ ἐστιν προσάββατον, ⁴³ἐλθὼν Ἰωσὴφ [ὁ] ἀπὸ Ἀριμαθαίας εὐσχήμων βουλευτής, ὃς καὶ αὐτὸς ἦν προσδεχόμενος τὴν βασιλείαν τοῦ θεοῦ, τολμήσας εἰσῆλθεν πρὸς τὸν Πιλᾶτον καὶ ἠτήσατο τὸ σῶμα τοῦ Ἰησοῦ. ⁴⁴ὁ δὲ Πιλᾶτος ἐθαύμασεν εἰ ἤδη τέθνηκεν καὶ προσκαλεσάμενος τὸν κεντυρίωνα ἐπηρώτησεν αὐτὸν εἰ πάλαι ἀπέθανεν· ⁴⁵καὶ γνοὺς ἀπὸ τοῦ κεντυρίωνος ἐδωρήσατο τὸ πτῶμα τῷ Ἰωσήφ. ⁴⁶καὶ ἀγοράσας σινδόνα καθελὼν αὐτὸν ἐνείλησεν τῇ σινδόνι καὶ ἔθηκεν αὐτὸν ἐν μνημείῳ ὃ ἦν λελατομημένον ἐκ πέτρας καὶ προσεκύλισεν λίθον ἐπὶ τὴν θύραν τοῦ μνημείου. ⁴⁷ἡ δὲ Μαρία ἡ Μαγδαληνὴ καὶ Μαρία ἡ Ἰωσῆτος ἐθεώρουν ποῦ τέθειται.

[42] And when evening had come, since it was the day of Preparation, that is, the day before the Sabbath, [43] Joseph, who was from Arimathea, a respected councillor, who was also himself looking for the kingdom of God, took courage and went to Pilate, and asked for the body of Jesus. [44] And Pilate marvelled if he were already dead; and summoning the centurion, he asked him whether he was already dead. [45] And when he learned from the centurion that he was dead, he gave the body to Joseph. [46] And he bought a linen shroud, and taking him down, wrapped him in the linen shroud, and laid him in a tomb which had been cut out of the rock; and he rolled a stone against the door of the tomb. [47] Mary Magdalene and Mary the mother of Joseph saw where he was laid.⁵

In Mark, Joseph appears only in the words of the narrator. He never speaks and no one else speaks of him. He is identified as being 'from Arimathea' (ἀπὸ Ἀριμαθαίας). Although often identified with Ramathaim-Zophim (1 Sam. 1.1) and said to be located not far from Jerusalem,⁶ the only contemporary clue to either its whereabouts or its civic identity comes from Luke's description of it as a 'city of the Jews' (πόλεως τῶν Ἰουδαίων; 23.51).

Joseph is also described as a 'councillor' (βουλευτής). Though sometimes taken to indicate membership of a 'council' (βουλή) rather than membership of the Jerusalem Sanhedrin (συνέδριον), these terms tended to overlap in contemporary Jewish texts; Josephus, for example, called the Sanhedrin a council (e.g. *Ant.* 20.1.2; *War* 2.15.6; 2.16.2). Mark's readers would presumably have understood the term as indicating his membership of the Sanhedrin (as Luke clearly does), and—with 'the whole Sanhedrin' (ὅλον τὸ συνέδριον) explicitly implicated by Mark in Jesus' death (14.55; 15.1; cf. 14.64)—seen it as implying that Joseph was personally culpable.[7] Luke certainly worked very hard later to avoid drawing that conclusion from Mark's account (23.51).[8]

The persona of 'Joseph the councillor' is qualified twice, with an adjective, 'respected' (εὐσχήμων), and a phrase, 'who was also himself waiting expectantly for the kingdom of God' (ὃς καὶ αὐτὸς ἦν προσδεχόμενος τὴν βασιλείαν τοῦ θεοῦ). Joseph was 'of high-standing', 'respected', or 'esteemed' (cf. e.g. Acts 13.50, 'devout women of high standing' [τὰς σεβομένας γυναῖκας τὰς εὐσχήμονας] and 17.12, 'a few respected Greek women and men' [τῶν Ἑλληνίδων γυναικῶν τῶν εὐσχημόνων καὶ ἀνδρῶν ... ὀλίγοι]. Describing a Sanhedrin member thus, of course, begged an obvious question; respected by whom? Rather than implying that he should be respected by his Gospel's audience, however, Mark's description of Joseph as an esteemed member of the Sanhedrin responsible for Jesus' death was more probably intended to help illuminate Pilate's decision to grant his request for the body.

The description of Joseph as one awaiting the kingdom of God has led some to assume that he should be seen as a disciple in Mark. For W. L. Lane:

[Joseph's] earnest expectation of the coming redemption had apparently attracted him to Jesus and his teaching concerning the Kingdom of God. His request [for the body] was daring because it amounted to a confession of his commitment to the condemned and crucified Jesus.[9]

R. E. Brown pointed out, however, that the 'also' suggests an element of comparison with 'others awaiting the kingdom', a phrase likely indicating 'a common Jewish anticipation covering many others beyond the disciples of Jesus'; he offered the wise scribe in Mk 12.28–34, the centurion at the cross (Mk 15.39), the blessing in the *Rule of the Congregation* (1QSb 5:21), and the Qaddish prayer as suitable examples.[10]

D. Senior offered an intriguing comparison between Joseph and the wise scribe:

Joseph is 'waiting for', 'expecting' the kingdom of God. This suggests that he was not yet a disciple, but is someone open and responsive to the message Jesus proclaimed. In similar language Jesus had blessed the Scribe who instinctively understood and accepted Jesus' teaching on the primacy of the love command.... In both instances, a person from the ranks of those who seem to be Jesus' unyielding foes—the scribes and the council—is stirred by Jesus and in so doing *moves closer to the Kingdom they seek*.[11]

Yet there was no evidence in Mark that the scribe ever became a disciple, that Jesus' view of the kingdom was one that he finally embraced. Should Joseph be viewed differently? Though Brown claimed that the remembrance of his name indicates his later conversion, ascribing Matthew's temporal 'error' in seeing Joseph as a disciple at the crucifixion to pedagogical concerns, his argument did little justice to the essentially ad hoc nature of Mark's limited use of names; were Jairus, the synagogue leader (5.22), the blind beggar Bartimaeus (10.46), and Simon the Leper (14.3) also remembered for their conversion as the logic of Brown's argument demands?[12] It is more likely that Joseph's name was simply attached to a pre-Markan tradition. Acknowledging Joseph's lack of belief would also lead us to properly acknowledge the meaning that Mark apparently intended to ascribe to verse 47; it is the two Marys alone among the followers of Jesus who see where his body was laid and it is only they who would have been able to function as the witnesses to his later resurrection by testifying that the corpse had not been mislaid or stolen: '[they] saw where he was laid' (ἐθεώρουν ποῦ τέθειται).

If Joseph did not believe, why did Mark present a Jewish leader responsible for Jesus' death with so little hostility? Why not leave him nameless or perhaps remove him altogether? The answer probably lies in Mark's way of dealing with Jesus' disciples. C. C. Black has suggested that in Mark the disciples' 'special status...is indirectly compromised by the presence of a larger motley cast of characters, who in many ways exhibit the sort of exemplary behaviour that one might justifiably expect of the twelve'.[13] He provided 17 examples of this use of compromising contrasts, including Peter's mother (1.31), the Syro-Phoenician woman (7.25–28), and Jairus, the synagogue leader (5.22–23), alongside Joseph of Arimathea. Rather than a strange feature requiring explanation, the description of Joseph is part of a significant Markan motif. The Arimathean fulfilled his role precisely as a 'pious Jew' awaiting 'the kingdom of God in the sense that he sought only to obey the commandments, much as the scribe of 12.28' (so Brown).[14]

How then to explain Joseph's action in boldly asking Pilate for Jesus' body? The injunction in Deut. 21.23 to avoid the defilement of the land by burying executed criminals before nightfall made the Roman practice of leaving crucified bodies to rot deeply problematic. Commenting on the Idumeans' failure to bury their dead, Josephus noted that 'the Jews are so careful about funeral rites that even those who are crucified because they are found guilty are taken down and buried before sunset' (*War*, 4.5.2). That Gentile authorities gave crucified bodies back for burial is attested by Philo of Alexandria (*c.*20 BCE–*c.*50 CE) who wrote of the giving of bodies to 'relations' and castigated Flaccus, Governor of Egypt, for failing to do so (*In Flaccum*, 83). The crucified skeleton found in an ossuary at Giv'at ha-Mivtar in 1968 shows that at least some bodies were recovered. As J. D. Crossan has rightly pointed out, however, these examples do not demonstrate a Roman policy,[15] and Brown has noted that bodies may even have been removed by stealth, citing as evidence the later ban on such thefts in *Semaḥot 2.11*.[16]

Crossan has suggested two motives for why a non-family-member who was a respected member of the group partly responsible for Jesus' death might have asked for the body. First, he could have been acting out of personal piety. The Jewish literary hero, Tobit, stated that if 'I saw the dead body of any of my people thrown out behind the wall of Ninevah, I would bury it' (Tob. 1.17; also 2.4 where he recovers the body of a strangled Jew and buries it at sunset; Lane also cited 2 Sam. 21.12–14 and Sirach 7.33, 38.16 as support).[17] Second, a communal sense of duty could have motivated Joseph, with an obligation being placed upon anyone who was able to prevent defilement of the land.[18]

In either case, the 'they' of Mark 16.6—'the place where *they* buried him'—would indicate the involvement of unimportant accomplices. In contrast with the elaborate rites of John 19.40, Mark's burial is rushed. The corpse is not washed and anointed for burial—Jesus' female followers bring 'spices' (ἀρώματα) the following day to do that—but is simply wrapped in a 'linen cloth' (σινδών), and placed in a tomb nearby. Though Mark later mentions the difficulty of removing the entrance stone (16.4), he does not use that detail to emphasize the tomb's expensiveness; nor does he say that the tomb belonged to Joseph (cf. Mt. 27.60). For Brown, it may just have been a nearby grave intended for the burial of crucified criminals; the trench aside, burial probably did not get any simpler.[19] A stranger to Jesus, the Markan Joseph acted out of either a sense of personal piety or of communal responsibility in going to Pilate. He would have lived and—in all likelihood—died a pious Jew.[20]

Matthew 27.57–61

[57]Ὀψίας δὲ γενομένης ἦλθεν ἄνθρωπος πλούσιος ἀπὸ Ἀριμαθαίας, τοὔνομα Ἰωσήφ, ὃς καὶ αὐτὸς ἐμαθητεύθη τῷ Ἰησοῦ· [58]οὗτος προσελθὼν τῷ Πιλάτῳ ᾐτήσατο τὸ σῶμα τοῦ Ἰησοῦ. τότε ὁ Πιλᾶτος ἐκέλευσεν ἀποδοθῆναι. [59]καὶ λαβὼν τὸ σῶμα ὁ Ἰωσὴφ ἐνετύλιξεν αὐτὸ [ἐν] σινδόνι καθαρᾷ [60]καὶ ἔθηκεν αὐτὸ ἐν τῷ καινῷ αὐτοῦ μνημείῳ ὃ ἐλατόμησεν ἐν τῇ πέτρᾳ καὶ προσκυλίσας λίθον μέγαν τῇ θύρᾳ τοῦ μνημείου ἀπῆλθεν. [61]ἦν δὲ ἐκεῖ Μαριὰμ ἡ Μαγδαληνὴ καὶ ἡ ἄλλη Μαρία καθήμεναι ἀπέναντι τοῦ τάφου.

[57] When it was evening, there came a rich man from Arimathea, named Joseph, who also was a disciple of Jesus. [58] He went to Pilate and asked for the body of Jesus. Then Pilate ordered it to be given to him. [59] And Joseph took the body, and wrapped it in a clean linen shroud, [60] and laid it in his own new tomb, which he had cut in the rock; and he rolled a great stone to the door of the tomb, and departed. [61] Mary Magdalene and the other Mary were there, sitting opposite the sepulchre.

The shortest of the four accounts, Matthew's text is considerably shorter than that of Mark. Joseph's boldness, Pilate's interaction with the centurion, and the day of Preparation are omitted. Pilate orders the body to be given to Joseph, whose act of retrieval and burial is described with different verbs from Mark's account (λαμβάνω for καθαιρέω, ἐντυλίσσω for ἐνείλεω); the choice of λαμβάνω is less suggestive of a role for Joseph in removing the body from the cross. The cloth for the body is 'clean' (καθαρᾷ), but is no longer bought at the time. The tomb is described as 'his... tomb' (τῷ... αὐτοῦ μνημείῳ) and as having been cut in the rock by Joseph's own hand; it is sealed by a 'great stone' (λίθον μέγαν). Its emptiness is emphasized by the addition of 'new' (καινῷ); the Matthean Jesus' body could not possibly be confused with any previously interred members of Joseph's family. In Matthew, Joseph is no longer described as a councillor. Instead he has become a 'rich man' (ἄνθρωπος πλούσιος). He is also explicitly described as 'one who was also himself discipled to Jesus' (ὃς καὶ αὐτὸς ἐμαθητεύθη τῷ Ἰησοῦ). It is almost as though, as R. Gundry put it, once 'dissociated from the council, Joseph is . . . free to be made a full-fledged Christian disciple',[21] a wealthy man whose believing presence demonstrates perfectly Jesus' maxim that 'with God all things are possible' (cf. Mt. 19.23–26). In this context, the description of 'his new tomb' with its 'great stone' serves to emphasize the grandeur of both the wealthy Joseph and Jesus' burial place. In contrast with the Markan account of the *women* of faith who watched the body as it moves between cross and tomb, it is now the *man* of faith Joseph who is to be the witness to the resurrection par excellence; Mary Magdalene and Mary are said to be just 'there, sitting opposite the sepulchre', and Mark's statement that they 'saw where he was laid' is omitted.

The Matthean Joseph's rich status may owe something to Mark's use of 'εὐσχήμων', but both his wealth and his discipleship are much more likely to be due to Matthew's deep interest in seeing the events of the life and death of Jesus Christ as prophetic fulfilments of Scripture, a pattern extensively deployed in his text (e.g. 1.22; 2.15; 12.17; 13.35; 21.4; 27.9). The quotation of Isa. 53.4 in Matthew 8.17 makes explicit his interest in relating Jesus' life and death to the 'suffering servant song' of Isa. 53.1–12. In verse 9 of the song, the following appears: 'I will give the wicked man for his burial and the rich man for his death' (LXX). That Isaiah's 'rich man' (πλούσιος) was understood by parallelism to be also wicked did not particularly bother Matthew. In Gundry's words, 'his use of the [Old Testament] easily surmounts such obstacles.'[22]

Matthew's linking of Jesus' burial with Isaiah 53, however, did create a tension with the Markan Joseph. How could a pious Jew's hurried burial of an executed corpse be reconciled with the rich Joseph's decision to put Jesus in his own elaborate tomb? In an example of 'prophecy historicized', Matthew could best explain Joseph's behaviour if it were that of a wealthy disciple caring for his master's body. If the historical truth was something different,

Matthew and his audience would have been blissfully unaware of it, Joseph probably having been long dead by the time of writing.

Luke 23.50–56a

⁵⁰Καὶ ἰδοὺ ἀνὴρ ὀνόματι Ἰωσὴφ βουλευτὴς ὑπάρχων [καὶ] ἀνὴρ ἀγαθὸς καὶ δίκαιος ⁵¹ – οὗτος οὐκ ἦν συγκατατεθειμένος τῇ βουλῇ καὶ τῇ πράξει αὐτῶν – ἀπὸ Ἀριμαθαίας πόλεως τῶν Ἰουδαίων, ὃς προσεδέχετο τὴν βασιλείαν τοῦ θεοῦ, ⁵²οὗτος προσελθὼν τῷ Πιλάτῳ ᾐτήσατο τὸ σῶμα τοῦ Ἰησοῦ ⁵³καὶ καθελὼν ἐνετύλιξεν αὐτὸ σινδόνι καὶ ἔθηκεν αὐτὸν ἐν μνήματι λαξευτῷ οὗ οὐκ ἦν οὐδεὶς οὔπω κείμενος. ⁵⁴καὶ ἡμέρα ἦν παρασκευῆς, καὶ σάββατον ἐπέφωσκεν. ⁵⁵Κατακολουθήσασαι δὲ αἱ γυναῖκες, αἵτινες ἦσαν συνεληλυθυῖαι ἐκ τῆς Γαλιλαίας αὐτῷ, ἐθεάσαντο τὸ μνημεῖον καὶ ὡς ἐτέθη τὸ σῶμα αὐτοῦ, ⁵⁶ᵃὑποστρέψασαι δὲ ἡτοίμασαν ἀρώματα καὶ μύρα.

[50] Now there was a man named Joseph, a councillor, a good and righteous man,—[51] this man had not consented to their purpose and deed—from Arimathea, a city of the Jews, who was looking for the kingdom of God. [52] This man went to Pilate and asked for the body of Jesus. [53] Then he took it down and wrapped it in a linen shroud, and laid him in a rock-cut tomb, where no one had ever yet been laid. [54] It was the day of Preparation, and the Sabbath was beginning. [55] The women who had come with him from Galilee followed, and saw the tomb, and how his body was laid; [56a] then they returned, and prepared spices and ointments.

Luke's account is closest of the canonical Gospels to Mark. Nevertheless, a number of Markan elements do not appear: Joseph's courage; Pilate's surprise and his enquiry made via the centurion; his giving of the body; the mention of the tomb's 'stone'; and the purchase of the shroud. The phrase 'day of Preparation' (ἡμέρα . . . παρασκευῆς) is positioned later in the account, with Mark's 'evening' rendered with the equivalent phrase, 'the Sabbath was beginning' (σάββατον ἐπέφωσκεν). A different verb is used for wrapping the body (ἐντυλίσσω, like Matthew, for ἐνείλέω). Added is a comment emphasizing that the tomb was unused, presumably intended to remove the potential ambiguity of Mark's account as to the presence of other bodies, and the detail that the women—nameless and described as being from Galilee—leave the burial site to make preparations to anoint the body.

In contrast with Matthew's 'rich man', the Lukan Joseph is still described as a 'councillor' (βουλευτὴς) 'who was waiting for the kingdom of God' (ὃς προσεδέχετο τὴν βασιλείαν τοῦ θεοῦ). The term 'esteemed' is absent, however, and in its place two new asides qualify the basic Markan description. First, Joseph is described as 'a good and righteous man' (ἀνὴρ ἀγαθὸς καὶ δίκαιος). For Luke, he is included in what Brown has called 'the pattern of pious Jews described at the beginning of the [Gospel]' (e.g. Zechariah and Elizabeth [Lk. 1.6] and Simeon [Lk. 2.25–35]).[23] Second, since the Markan Joseph is clearly a member of the Sanhedrin that condemned Jesus, readers of a Lukan recasting of Mark which did not explicitly address that issue might legitimately have asked just how a man described as good and righteous could have been part of that plot. Luke's pre-emptive response was an explicit attempt to exonerate him from complicity in the plot of the Sanhedrin; his text reads: 'this man had not agreed to their purpose and deed' (οὗτος οὐκ ἦν συγκατατεθειμένος τῇ βουλῇ καὶ τῇ πράξει αὐτῶν).

For Mark, the question of complicity was not significant because Joseph was guilty as charged. By identifying the Arimathean with his understanding of pious Jews rather than simply repeating Mark's use of him for positive comparative purposes, however, Luke put himself into a position where he had to try to see the 'good and righteous man' in Joseph in order to explain the resulting conundrum of how such a pious Jew could have condemned Jesus. Luke's answer was to edge away from Mark's bold Joseph in the direction of depicting the councillor as what we might today politely call 'ineffectual'. With his piety defended at the cost of his effectiveness, the Lukan Joseph remains open to the kingdom offered by Jesus, but that was as far as Luke was apparently prepared to go; as with Mark, his account does not include a believing Joseph. It was the women who thus remained the witness-guarantors of the resurrection story ('[they] saw the tomb, and how his body was laid' [ἐθεάσαντο τὸ μνημεῖον καὶ ὡς ἐτέθη τὸ σῶμα αὐτοῦ]; Lk. 23.55a), their testimony aided and strengthened by Luke's added description of the tomb as one 'where no one had ever yet been laid' (οὗ οὐκ ἦν οὐδεὶς οὔπω κείμενος; 22.53c).

John 19.38–42

³⁸Μετὰ δὲ ταῦτα ἠρώτησεν τὸν Πιλᾶτον Ἰωσὴφ [ὁ] ἀπὸ Ἀριμαθαίας, ὢν μαθητὴς τοῦ Ἰησοῦ κεκρυμμένος δὲ διὰ τὸν φόβον τῶν Ἰουδαίων, ἵνα ἄρῃ τὸ σῶμα τοῦ Ἰησοῦ· καὶ ἐπέτρεψεν ὁ Πιλᾶτος. ἦλθεν οὖν καὶ ἦρεν τὸ σῶμα αὐτοῦ. ³⁹ἦλθεν δὲ καὶ Νικόδημος, ὁ ἐλθὼν πρὸς αὐτὸν νυκτὸς τὸ πρῶτον, φέρων μίγμα σμύρνης καὶ ἀλόης ὡς λίτρας ἑκατόν. ⁴⁰ἔλαβον οὖν τὸ σῶμα τοῦ Ἰησοῦ καὶ ἔδησαν αὐτὸ ὀθονίοις μετὰ τῶν ἀρωμάτων, καθὼς ἔθος ἐστὶν τοῖς Ἰουδαίοις ἐνταφιάζειν. ⁴¹ἦν δὲ ἐν τῷ τόπῳ ὅπου ἐσταυρώθη κῆπος, καὶ ἐν τῷ κήπῳ μνημεῖον καινὸν ἐν ᾧ οὐδέπω οὐδεὶς ἦν τεθειμένος· ⁴²ἐκεῖ οὖν διὰ τὴν παρασκευὴν τῶν Ἰουδαίων, ὅτι ἐγγὺς ἦν τὸ μνημεῖον, ἔθηκαν τὸν Ἰησοῦν.

[38] And after this Joseph of Arimathea, who was a disciple of Jesus, but secretly, for fear of the Jews, asked Pilate that he might take away the body of Jesus, and Pilate gave him permission. So he came and took away his body. [39] Nicodemus, who had at first come to him by night, also came bringing a mixture of myrrh and aloes, about a hundred pounds weight. [40] They took the body of Jesus, and bound it in linen cloths with the spices, as is the burial custom of the Jews. [41] Now in the place where he was crucified there was a garden, and in the garden a new tomb where no one had ever been laid. [42] So because of the Jewish day of Preparation, as the tomb was close at hand, they laid Jesus there.

John also altered the Markan account. A vague 'after this' replaces Mark's 'evening', with the 'day of Preparation' moving to the end of his account. Mark's verb for the 'taking down' of the body (καθαιρέω) is omitted; as with Matthew, a different verb for 'taken' is used (αἴρω) which perhaps implies that others have already removed the body from the cross. The tomb is said to be nearby, in the 'garden' (κήπῳ) where Jesus was crucified. It is also described as 'new' (καινὸν; as with Matthew and, by implication, Luke), but it does not belong to Joseph himself (*pace* Matthew). The singular 'cloth' (σινδόνα) becomes the plural 'clothes' (ὀθονίοις).

Like Matthew and Luke, John does not mention Joseph's boldness or Pilate's surprise at Jesus' death. Indeed in his account of events Joseph is not even the first to ask Pilate for the body; 'the Jews' (Οἱ . . . Ἰουδαῖοι) do so in 19.31; Pilate orders his men to break the legs of those crucified long before the man from Arimathea comes to him. Far from bold and active, the Joseph presented in John merely follows a path previously trodden by a group whose role in the Gospel is largely constructed in terms of their (initially fragmented) opposition to Jesus and his mission.[24] This co-equivalence with regard to actions probably created some ambiguity for John's audience about Joseph's relationship to 'the Jews'.

Unlike Luke, but as with Matthew, John omits Mark's description of Joseph as a councillor, but, *pace* Matthew's 'rich man', the status of the Arimathean is left unspecified. Though John's text does agree with Matthew's that Joseph is a 'disciple of Jesus' ($\mu\alpha\theta\eta\tau\dot{\eta}s$ $\tauo\hat{v}$ $\text{'}I\eta\sigmao\hat{v}$), it adds the phrase 'but secretly, for fear of the Jews' ($\kappa\epsilon\kappa\rho\upsilon\mu\mu\acute{\epsilon}\nuos$ $\delta\grave{\epsilon}$ $\delta\iota\grave{\alpha}$ $\tau\grave{o}\nu$ $\phi\acute{o}\beta o\nu$ $\tau\hat{\omega}\nu$ $\text{'}Io\upsilon\delta\alpha\acute{\iota}\omega\nu$), thus providing a sharp contrast to the Matthean Joseph's apparently open declaration of his faith.

Although Joseph asks for and receives the body, it is another man, Nicodemus, returning for a third time in the Gospel (following his appearances in 3.1–21 and 7.45–52), who dominates the burial. Because Nicodemus brings along a 'mixture of myrrh and aloes weighing about a hundred pounds' ($\mu\acute{\iota}\gamma\mu\alpha$ $\sigma\mu\acute{\upsilon}\rho\nu\eta s$ $\kappa\alpha\grave{\iota}$ $\dot{\alpha}\lambda\acute{o}\eta s$ $\dot{\omega}s$ $\lambda\acute{\iota}\tau\rho\alpha s$ $\dot{\epsilon}\kappa\alpha\tau\acute{o}\nu$), and Joseph passively acquiesces in its use, the Johannine burial is an elaborate, albeit still quick affair, with John stating that Jesus was buried 'according to the burial custom of the Jews' ($\kappa\alpha\theta\grave{\omega}s$ $\ddot{\epsilon}\theta os$ $\dot{\epsilon}\sigma\tau\grave{\iota}\nu$ $\tauo\hat{\iota}s$ $\text{'}Io\upsilon\delta\alpha\acute{\iota}o\iota s$ $\dot{\epsilon}\nu\tau\alpha\phi\iota\acute{\alpha}\zeta\epsilon\iota\nu$). No other canonical Gospel has Joseph share the limelight in this way or portrays him as being so passive in his actions. Even the impact of Matthew's use of the male disciple Joseph as the prime witness to the burial instead of the two Marys is lessened in the Fourth Gospel's presentation of its secret disciple; though the women have disappeared and Joseph remains a witness, he is only one of the two male witnesses required (cf. Jn 8.17).

For some, the Johannine burial's grandeur means that, although Joseph is explicitly described as a secret disciple who lived in 'fear of the Jews', such a description no longer fits either him or Nicodemus by this point in the Gospel. As R. E. Brown has put it, 'we are left with the expectation that the public action of Joseph and Nicodemus will lead them to bear witness to Jesus after the resurrection'.[25] Even the most charitable of interpretations, however, should not go beyond 'expectation'; the actions of Nicodemus and Joseph do not add up to the Johannine 'ideal' of the future disciple who would openly proclaim Jesus in the manner envisaged by Jesus in the farewell discourses of John 14–17. True, their actions at the tomb can be understood as a moment of hiatus before the spirit, the *Paraclete*, is given in John 20.22, but the Johannine Joseph of Arimathea and Nicodemus are both presented as characters in transition, their futures defined only by possibilities. Yet even Joseph's 'possibility' is a powerful illustrative tool for John. If the Johannine Joseph had remained Mark's pious Jew and had given Jesus' body a hurried simple burial, Nicodemus would not have had an occasion to reappear, fading into obscurity. John's interest in relating the final scene of Nicodemus' story, even though it remains incomplete, probably compelled him to draw upon an additional Johannine motif, the fear of the Jews and of expulsion from the synagogue (cf. 9.22, 12.42), in order to cast a peripheral figure, the Johannine Joseph, as a secret disciple. Joseph in John is exactly the passive sort of person who would not object to the Pharisaic leader's anointing of Jesus' body with an inordinate quantity of myrrh and aloes, allowing Nicodemus to reappear once more in the text. It is harder to imagine the Markan Joseph being quite so obliging.

John's act of conversion was motivated by reasons very different from those of Matthew. When all was said and done in both cases, however, there was just no pressing need for either Matthew or John to leave him in his Markan state of unbelief.

Harmonization refocused

Despite the temptation to see the Gospel variants about Joseph of Arimathea as complementary, accurate, and eminently harmonizable, they can be easily understood as arising from the interaction of Mark's account with the ideologies and needs of the three Evangelists who used his Gospel. This being so, it seems perfectly reasonable to suggest that any who wish to search for the Joseph behind these texts must begin and end with the portrayal in Mark, explicitly discarding the uncritical harmonizing tendency assumed by so many scholars. If we turn to examine the development of the Joseph tradition, however, we will find that the harmonizing tradition will continue to be of great interest to us, though as we shall see, that particular treatment of the texts is only one of the many ways in which the afterlives of Joseph were to be expanded during the next two millenia.

2

The Early Joseph

The earliest echoes of the canonical Josephs

Having discussed the content, development, and interrelatedness of
the four Gospels, it is now time to turn to the earliest recorded layers
of the canonical Joseph's reception history, to look at important
examples of the *mechanisms* by which the Joseph tradition began to
develop in the first millennium or so of the Common Era. We will
look in turn at an *expansion* of the canonical tradition, the *Gospel of
Peter* (*c.* second century), an *exposition* of parts of that tradition, John
Chrysostom's *Homilies on Matthew* and *on John* (*c.*390), the *translation* of the four Greek Gospel texts into Latin, the Old Latin, and
Jerome's *Vulgate* (*c.*382–4), a *harmonization* of Matthew, Mark, Luke,
and John, Augustine's *De consensu evangelistarum* (*c.*404), and finally,
an *extension* of Joseph's story way beyond its canonical boundaries, the
Gospel of Nicodemus (*c.* fourth century [earliest elements]). These
examples and the modes of development which they embody certainly do not share equal responsibility for the variety of Josephs that
were to follow, but each in its own way helped to enhance the shape of
the canonical Joseph tradition in significant and myriad ways.

The *Gospel of Peter*

Lost to history for over a thousand years, the *Gospel of Peter* (*c.* second
century) was rediscovered in Egypt in 1886–7 when an incomplete
manuscript was found in the ninth-century grave of a Christian
monk. Narrated by Peter the Apostle, the recovered text begins
with the closing moments of Jesus' trial, details the crucifixion, and

ends with the build up to a now-lost but probable resurrection appearance of Christ.[1] It was the use of Peter as narrator that led scholars to identify the Egyptian text with the 'Gospel of Peter' mentioned by Eusebius of Caesarea in his brief discussion of Serapion of Antioch's work, *Concerning what is known as the Gospel according to Peter* (*Ecclesiastical History*, VI.12.1–6). Serapion, Bishop of Antioch from *c.*190 to *c.*210, had initially given permission for the church in nearby Rhossus to continue using the Gospel, before deciding, upon closer examination, that parts of it were susceptible to docetic interpretations (i.e. Jesus only 'seemed' [δοκέω] human); these sections he then listed for the audience of his work. Because Eusebius ended his excerpt of Serapion's work with the fact of the list, and not with the list itself, however, we do not know the content of the passages that troubled the bishop. If we accept the identification of his text with the recovered Egyptian text, however, one probable example would have been *GPet.* 4.10: 'And they brought two wrong-doers and crucified the Lord in the middle of them. But he was silent as having no pain.'[2] Ironically, scholars today argue that, whatever its potential openness to a docetic interpretation, this passage fitted easily into the ideology of martyrdom that was current in the period. Nevertheless, the charge of heterodoxy stuck and the text faded from historical view.

In the incomplete text available to us, Joseph of Arimathea appears first at the close of Jesus' trial, an event described as having taken place before Herod and the judges of Israel, with Pilate merely being on hand.[3] Joseph is described as 'the friend of Pilate and of the Lord' (2.3) rather than as a councillor, and his request to Pilate for the body is redirected by the apparently unimportant Roman to the one who is in real charge, King Herod (2.4). It is this latter figure who then explicitly links the body's removal from the cross to what was written in the Law (2.5), with Joseph dropping out of view altogether as the crowd's taking, mocking, and crucifying of Jesus between two criminals is narrated (2.5c–4.11). The actions ascribed to Roman soldiers in the canonical Gospels become those of the Jews; they gamble for his garments (4.12) and give him vinegar to drink (5.16). In the midday darkness, their concern that the crucified might not die before nightfall proves unwarranted as Jesus breaths his last (5.15–19). The nails from his hands are removed by those who had crucified him and his body is laid on the ground as the earth shakes and the Temple veil is torn (5.20–6.21). As the Jews rejoice, Joseph returns into view; though he has not removed the body from the cross, he is given the body to bury, because, we are told, 'he was one who had seen the many good things he did' (6.23), a hint perhaps suggestive of an earlier role in the complete *Gospel of Peter*. Joseph takes the body and washes it, ties it with a linen cloth, and puts it in his own tomb, which is called the 'Garden of Joseph' (6.24). With that Joseph disappears from view.

In studying the text's relationship with the canonical Gospels, R. E. Brown has noted that common elements link the text to Matthew (13 elements), Luke (nine elements), and John (10 elements), but not to Mark (no elements). He concluded that vocabulary differences suggest that direct literary relationships are highly unlikely, however; the 12 elements unique to the *Gospel of Peter* could not simply be creative additions to a 'literary' rewriting of three canonical Gospels. Instead Brown offered a different view of its origins:

> I doubt that the author...had any written Gospel before him, although he was familiar with Matthew because he had read it carefully in the past and/or had heard it read several times in community worship on the Lord's Day, so that it gave the dominant shaping to his thought. Most likely he had heard people speaking who were familiar with the Gospels of Luke and John— perhaps travelling preachers who rephrased salient stories—so that he knew some of their content but had little idea of their structures. The spoken background of [the *Gospel of Peter*] is echoed in the fact that about one third of its verses are in direct discourse.... Intermingled in the...author's mind were also popular tales about incidents in the passion, the very type of popular material that Matt had tapped in composing his Gospel at an earlier period. All this went onto his composition..., a gospel that was not meant to be read in liturgy but to help people picture imaginatively the career of Jesus.[4]

Using certain ideological markers, Brown then reconstructed its setting. First, he noted the high Christology implied by its preference for 'Lord' (14 times) and 'Son of God' (four times) rather than the absent terms 'Jesus' and 'Christ'. Second, the text is strongly anti-Jewish. Herod and the Jewish leaders refuse to wash their hands of Jesus' blood (*GPet.* 1.1), they mock/assault him (2.5c–3.9), complete 'their sins on their own heads' (5.17), guard his tomb to prevent his resurrection (8.28, 32–33; 10.38), and ensure Pilate's silence even though they knew how greatly they are sinning in denying that Jesus is the son of God (10.38–11.49). Third, an implicit knowledge of the Scriptures is apparent, despite only one text being explicitly referenced (a paraphrase of Deut. 21.22–23 in 2.5, 5.15). Fourth, insensitivity to Jewish festivals and Sabbath observance suggests that the author had little familiarity with Jewish practices. Finally, Christian observance of Sunday as the 'Lord's Day' is mentioned (9.35, 12.50).[5] Noting parallels with other mid-second-century texts (e.g. 5.16 with *Epistle of Barnabas* 7.5: 'gall with vinegary wine'), Brown placed the text earlier than 150 CE, but—citing as evidence Herod's anachronistic portrayal—not before 100 CE.[6] Syria, he suggested, was the most likely place of origin. The author, he surmised, wrote a text reflecting a popularized Christianity, which included material echoing the entertaining stories already added to the Jesus story, especially by Matthew (e.g. Pilate's wife's dream [27.19]). Composed apart from the canonical traditions, the author's imagination was allowed a freer rein.[7]

Certain features of the Joseph presented by the *Gospel of Peter* echo aspects of the canonical Josephs, the request to Pilate and the use of his own tomb for the burial being obvious examples (see also Brown's long lists of linking elements).[8] But there are also significant differences. Joseph's actions pre-crucifixion are given an explicit shape; he was apparently present during Jesus' ministry and saw him doing 'good things'. Joseph is also present during the trial itself. Though this potentially leaves him shouldering a greater culpability because the *Gospel of Peter* sees Jesus condemned at a Jewish trial and not at a Roman one, his relationship to the actions of Herod and the Jewish leaders is explicitly framed in terms of his friendships with Jesus and with Pilate, serving to exonerate him. With the request for the body also now being made before the crucifixion and with Pilate lacking the authority to order that Jesus' body be given to Joseph, the Arimathean is forced to take a back seat as Herod takes charge of the removal of the bodies, a period of inactivity which extends—*pace* the explicit canonical accounts of Mark and Luke at least—to Jesus' body being removed from the cross by someone other than Joseph. Only when the body is on the ground is Joseph able to prepare it for burial.

Though indebted to the canonical texts, this second-century account introduced a subtly different Joseph into the tradition. The anti-Jewish tone, which led to a greater and, in historical terms, deeply anachronistic role for Herod in Jesus' trial, produced in turn a much diminished role for Pilate and, hence, for his 'friend' Joseph of Arimathea, who no longer even removed the body from the cross. But Joseph's disappearance during the trial and the insertion of a rationale to allow him to reappear—his earlier experience of Jesus' ministry—also served to extend his role. Such shifts generated additional Joseph details for later audiences to replicate or exploit for their own purposes, though, of course, we would be right to question how much influence changes made in this soon-to-be lost gospel could have had.

The homilies of John Chrysostom

John Chrysostom was born at Antioch in Syria around 349 CE. Completing his elementary education at age 12, he began his rhetorical studies with a professional orator, probably the renowned pagan, Libanius. An exceptional student, Chrysostom was most likely destined for the law courts or the civil service, but at 18, his commitment to Christianity led to his entry into the service of the Church. Following his baptism in 368, he worked as an aide to the pro-Nicene Bishop of Antioch, Meletius. Intensive studying of the Scriptures and of the interpretive method of the Antiochene School was accompanied by instruction on the beliefs and practices of the Church.[9] In 371, Chrysostom was made *lector*, an office that involved reading the Old Testament and the Epistles during worship services. Following a brief dalliance with asceticism, John became deacon in 381, and priest in around 386;[10] in a city which had recently had four bishops with differing theological persuasions (Arian, Apollinarian, Nicean [times two]), his talents served well those who followed the Nicene version of the faith. A prolific preacher, his written legacy would eventually extend to over nine hundred homilies—and that is certainly not everything that he preached!

The death of Nectarius, Bishop of Constantinople, now the second city of the Roman Empire, in 397 led to a major change in John's life, however. Attending a meeting outside Antioch, Chrysostom found himself bundled off to Constantinople and consecrated as Bishop, the unwitting choice of a powerful patron, the eunuch Eutropius.[11] After five and a half years of ministry in Constantinople's politically charged atmosphere, some monks in dispute with the Bishop of Alexandria, Theophilus, arrived in the city. Accused of the heresy of 'Origenism', they asked for Chrysostom's support. Theophilus was summoned to stand trial, but found himself instead a member of the 'Synod of the Oak' that was formed to try Chrysostom in turn.[12] Found guilty of ignoring the charges against him, John's banishment was initially rescinded following rioting. In 404, however, his opponents forced Chrysostom into exile. In 407, John died on the Black Sea coast.[13]

The two homilies discussed here were delivered during two long series of homilies, on the Gospels of Matthew (90 in total) and John (88), with both homily 88 on Matthew 27.45–48 and homily 85 on John 19.16–18 being delivered in Antioch around 390.[14] Since their contents do not allow us to order them chronologically, we will deal first with the least developed exposition, that on the Matthew text.

In the homily on Matthew 27.45–48 Joseph of Arimathea is described as neither obscure nor unnoticed; instead he is a councillor and highly distinguished. A believer who has hidden his faith before the crucifixion, he is now courageous and bold, a character development which the preacher clearly believes to be all the more laudable because his high status exposes him to retribution; his persistence in requesting Jesus' body combined with his costly burial preparations and the use of his own tomb all serve to highlight Joseph's faith and courage. Moreover, the homily concludes, these actions also have a greater purpose; the donation of Joseph's tomb ensures that no suspicion could exist about the resurrection.

In Chrysostom's homily on John 19.16–18, Joseph is described as one of the 'seventy' sent out by Jesus as he journeyed up to Jerusalem for his final Passover (Lk. 10.1–20). A distinction is drawn between the 12, whom the homily sees as the more distinguished disciples, and Joseph and Nicodemus, however. That the former—present at the cross in the person of 'John', the 'beloved disciple' (Jn 19.26–27)—do not ask for Jesus' body is not to do with their fear; Joseph is also afraid. Rather it is the latter's status which allows him to procure the body from Pilate. After all, how could the Roman refuse a request from a man of such high social standing? The actions of Joseph and Nicodemus in preparing the corpse so lavishly for burial gains them credit for their honouring of Jesus' body, the preacher goes on to suggest, but it also reveals their limited understanding of what is about to happen to Jesus' soon-to-be risen body; it does not need the spices that 'they'—rather than just Nicodemus as the Fourth Gospel has it—have brought to anoint it. The tomb is not at any point described by Chrysostom as Joseph's own, however; the focus at the end of the homily is on its location. With evening approaching, speed is of the essence, and the new tomb, so conveniently—and, once again, so providentially—available, allows everyone present to witness the body's entombment, whether they are the disciples or the 'guards' who have been set on watch (Mt. 27.65–28.4). Christ himself, the sermon concludes, wanted both the burial and resurrection to be as public as possible. In such circumstances, no later charge of theft could convince. The Markan use of the watching women as the guarantors of the link between Jesus' corpse and Christ's resurrection body has been left far behind as Joseph and the crowd take their place in the mind of the homilist and his audience.

A tendency towards conflation is apparent even in the shorter exposition of Matthew (though obvious links could also be left unexpressed; e.g. Nicodemus is not mentioned in that sermon). Matthew's rich man is given his Markan and Lukan role as a councillor. Burial preparations are not detailed in Matthew's Gospel, but are described by Chrysostom as costly, something which may perhaps have derived as much from the Johannine description of Nicodemus's lavish contribution to the burial as from the Matthean emphasis on Joseph's wealth. Joseph's boldness in approaching Pilate—explicit only in Mark—is also highlighted. Each of these elements was used by Chrysostom to stress the dangerous risk that Joseph as a high-status individual was taking in pursuing the body. Significantly, that risk was further amplified in the homily on the John text through the addition of a new detail—Joseph's 'persistence' in seeking the body—which introduced a character trait wholly absent from the Joseph of the canonical Gospels. For Chrysostom, demonstrating to his audience that Jesus' body had been under the control of believers from the cross to the grave was an essential part of securing for them the idea of the resurrection itself and he was not afraid to develop a non-canonical notion such as Joseph's persistence to help him attain it. Indeed, John believed that providing that security was the very purpose behind Joseph's involvement.

As a preacher, Chrysostom did not see his day-to-day task as requiring the systematic harmonization of the four Gospel accounts of Joseph of Arimathea. Instead, he appeared to have assimilated their individual details with ease while making the theological and pastoral points in which he was interested. Even the most obvious harmonization could be left unuttered—and perhaps even unthought—if Chrysostom's homiletic purpose did not explicitly require it; the Matthew homily makes it very clear that he thought the tomb was Joseph's, but someone hearing only his John homily would not have known that from its content. From this small sample, it is not possible for us to know exactly how Chrysostom thought the four canonical accounts of Joseph were interrelated, though it seems likely that he would have seen them as complementary. If ever asked, he would also no doubt have thought that his use of the 'persistence' of Joseph was wholly legitimate. What his homilies make readily apparent, however, is that the various Joseph details that make up the canonical Gospels were being reproduced, intermingled, and omitted in homilies aimed at a Christian audience while at the same time the canonical traditions were being supplemented in order to support the lessons being preached.

Jerome of Stridon's *Vulgate*

Another prolific author from antiquity, Jerome was born in Stridon in 347, a now-lost town in the Roman province of Dalmatia (somewhere near the border between modern Slovenia and Croatia). Well educated, the young Jerome was sent to Rome for advancement and began his lifelong acquaintance with the ruling classes of the Roman Empire. His eventual move to Trier, an important imperial residence and administrative centre in Gaul, accompanied by a friend, Bonosus, coincided with the arrival there of the imperial court of Valentinian I (321–75) in 367.[15] Jerome's prospects must have seemed promising. Around 370, however, he experienced a religious awakening. S. Rebbenich has noted the ingenious hypothesis of P. Courcelle (1968) that the conversion story of two young unnamed court officials

encountering the asceticism-oriented *Life of St Anthony* in Augustine's *Confessions* (8.6) referred to Jerome and Bonosus, but settled for
viewing it as a picture of what probably happened to him.[16] Jerome
left for Aquilea, capital of Venetia and Istia, and a centre of both
Nicene orthodoxy and ascetic forms of piety; a monastery was
founded there in 374, with wealthy patrons in northern Italy being
known to embrace such teachings.[17] Jerome flourished, making influential acquaintances, and becoming well read in Christian texts.[18]

When disputes arose among the city's Christians about asceticism,
however, Jerome left for the East, taking his library with him. One of
his patrons in Aquilea, Evagrius of Antioch, who had translated the
Life of St Anthony into Latin, was returning to his home in Syria;
Jerome appears to have accompanied him, intending to go onwards to
Jerusalem.[19] Illness, however, meant that he remained in Antioch,
eventually spending many years exploring ascetic practices at Evagrius' nearby country estate. Jerome corresponded widely, acquired
books, added Syriac and Hebrew to his Latin and Greek, and became
involved in church disputes, not always successfully. He particularly
aligned himself with Evagrius in supporting Bishop Paulinus, an
opponent of Chrysostom's favourite, Bishop Meletius, the two leaders of the Nicene factions in Antioch, and was ordained by him.[20]

In Constantinople in 380, Emperor Theodosius issued an edict
supporting Nicene Christianity. Jerome travelled there, meeting
Christian leaders such as Gregory Nazianzus and Gregory of
Nyssa. He updated Eusebius of Caesarea's *Chronicon* and translated
both it and Origen's *Homilies on Isaiah* into Latin, an increasingly
necessary task as knowledge of Greek waned in the West. Jerome's
advocacy of asceticism in his own publications won him admiration in
the imperial court.[21] In 382, he left with Bishop Paulinus for a synod
in Rome, staying on after his companions returned home. His knowledge of the Eastern Church now came to the attention of Damasus,
the Bishop of Rome; Jerome became involved in Church correspondence with the East and continued to translate Greek theologians into
Latin. Soon Damasus was asking him to revise the Church's Latin
translations of the four Gospels in the light of the Greek texts, a task
that was completed before the former's death in 384.[22] Though
Jerome would eventually fall from grace in Rome, and end his days
in Bethlehem, dying in *c.*419, it is with this commission for a

revision—and not a completely new translation—that his work on what would become the *Vulgate* began. The Old Latin Gospels exist today in around 30 manuscripts, some fragmentary.[23] In the Old Latin of Mark 15.42, '$\beta ov\lambda \epsilon v\tau \acute{\eta}s$' was translated with '*decurio*', a term whose possible meanings we will return to below.[24] The Markan adjective '$\epsilon \mathring{v}\sigma \chi \acute{\eta}\mu \omega v$' ('respected') was rendered either by '*dives*', 'rich' (e.g. manuscripts *Colbertinus*, *Bezae Cantabrigensis*, *Corbeiensis*, and *Monacensis*) or by a near synonym, '*locuples*', '(a person of) substance', 'wealth' (*Sangallensis*). In Luke 23.50, '$\beta ov\lambda \epsilon v\tau \acute{\eta}s$' was again translated as '*decurio*', with the Lukan adjective '$\mathring{a}\gamma a\theta \grave{o}s$' rendered as '*bonus*', 'good' and '$\delta \acute{\iota}\kappa a\iota os$' as '*iustus*', 'just'. Manuscript *Colbertinus* lost '*iustus*' altogether and used simply '*bonus homo*', 'good man'.[25]

The *Vulgate* of today includes a number of revisions of Jerome's work, including those of Alcuin of York in the late eighth century for Charlemagne, and the 'Clementine' version commissioned by the Catholic hierarchy in the 1590s. Our best witness to Jerome's original translation is therefore the early eighth-century *Codex Amiatinus*.[26] There we find that the Old Latin rendering of '*decurio*' was retained by Jerome for '$\beta ov\lambda \epsilon v\tau \acute{\eta}s$' in both Mark and Luke, and that Luke's adjectives were left unchanged.[27] In fact the only change made to the Gospel accounts of Joseph was the replacement of the Old Latin Gospel of Mark's adjectives rendering '$\epsilon \mathring{v}\sigma \chi \acute{\eta}\mu \omega v$' as wealth—'*dives*' and '*locuples*'—with '*nobilis*', 'noble' or 'renowned'. Jerome thus moved away from the Old Latin Mark's explicit affirmation of Joseph's wealth, made perhaps under the influence of Old Latin Matthew's '*homo dives*' (for '$\mathring{a}v\theta \rho \omega \pi os \ \pi \lambda o\acute{v}\sigma \iota os$'),[28] a translation reproduced in the *Vulgate*,[29] towards a translation which instead emphasized the 'noble' and 'renowned' status of Joseph, the '*decurio*' from Arimathea.

So what would Jerome have understood the term *decurio* to indicate? Strictly speaking, a *decurio* was a 'member or representative of a group of ten'.[30] Of the numerous specific meanings for the word listed by C. Gizewski, however, two are particularly relevant: the first is that of the *decurio* as an unsalaried honorary member of the *curia*—the 'city council'—in *municipia* and *coloniae* under Roman law; the second is that of the military *decurio*, a Roman officer in command of a group of ten riders, though that ratio varied over time and place.[31]

With regard to the *curia*, membership was restricted to citizens of a city, usually over 25 years of age and of independent financial means (the wealth required depended upon the city's size). The role of a *decurio* involved taking turns in public office, and provided those involved with considerable status. Some legal privileges applied, but financial obligations were also entailed. In theory, those accorded such status were personally liable for the 'entire city's fiscal and financial conduct', which could lead to such excessive demands that some would try to avoid the obligation altogether; the right to relinquish this status was eventually abolished altogether.[32]

Jerome's Antiochene patron, Evagrius, was of the *curial* class. M. H. Williams summarized Evagrius' background: '[he] was the son of an Antiochene curial class of middling wealth and standing; they descended from a third-century general, likely a Latin, who defeated the Palmyrene Zenobia under [E]mperor Aurelian'.[33] R. Pack has suggested that Evagrius subsequently managed to avoid the demanding obligation of the *curia* by obtaining 'two appointments secured for him in 363–4 by the prefect Salutius',[34] an evasion which the descent of the *curiae* into 'a hereditary and compulsory guild' encouraged.[35] As F. Gilliard has also noted, 'throughout the Empire in the fourth century, if you scratch a bishop you will most likely find a *curiales*'; Evagrius, eventually elevated to Bishop of Antioch in 388, was one such.[36] Though his patron did not himself act as a member of the *curia*, Jerome would surely have understand his retention of the Old Latin's *decurio* for Joseph the βουλευτής in the light of his benefactor's social status.

It is possible, though less likely, that the military use of *decurio* also influenced Jerome; Evagrius came from a military family, though he did not serve in the legions. Regardless of that possibility, however, the word's polyvalence would have allowed later audiences deeply familiar with the *Vulgate* to impute a military aspect to Joseph the *decurio*. One example in which at least the beginnings of such a transfer of meaning is visible is that of a twelfth-century English nobleman, Harscuit Musard. In the *Liber Eliensis*, a contemporary monastic chronicle, the abbey's monks described this donor of land to Ely Abbey as a:

bonus decurio...greatly favoured by the king, praised for his honesty, and if not greater than the nobles of the country, at least their equal, having knights (*milites*) under him; but unlike other men of this kind, he was not caught up in vice, boasting, and excitement, but rather devoted himself to honesty and freedom, troubled no one and did no one any injury, and managed all according to the things of salvation (3.38).[37]

According to J. Paxton, such plaudits would have made an audience 'steeped in the Vulgate' think of Joseph, Scripture's only '*decurio*', and have led to the abbey's benefactor being labelled with Mark's '*nobilis*' and Luke's '*bonus et iustus*'. Musard's 'having knights under him' would also, Paxton argued, have created echoes with the centurion of Matthew 8 and Luke 7.[38] As Musard, the commander of numerous soldiers, was being compared to the noble, just, and good man who had buried Christ, however, so Joseph of Arimathea was being compared in turn to a very powerful 'man-at-arms', a linkage which would surely have informed a twelfth-century audience's understanding of Jerome's '*decurio*', quickly removing any need for them to think about the centurion at all. Indeed, Paxton may have been overcautious in suggesting that such echoes were still required in Musard's day.

Ironically, Paxton concluded her discussion of Ely by noting that 'there is...no genuine basis for the character sketch of...Musard'. In the *Liber Eliensis*, she wrote, he was mentioned during a literary attack on the Bishop of Ely, Hervey le Breton, who was said to have stolen the lands donated by Musard. Historical documents prove, however, that Musard had donated the land to King William II, who had then granted it to le Breton ten years before he took office at Ely. In the Chronicle's creative but demonstrably false account of events, '[Musard] has been elevated to the type of the ideal noble patron to serve as a counterweight to the bad behaviour of the monastery's enemies.'[39] Joseph of Arimathea, of course, was available to 'fill out' such figures, whether they were real or otherwise.

Augustine of Hippo's *De consensu evangelistarum*

Augustine was born to a pagan father (who died when his son was 15) and a Christian mother, Monica, in Thagaste in North Africa in *c.*354.

Despite his family's relative lack of wealth, he was classically educated, largely thanks to the financial support of Romanianus, a 'local dignitary'.[40] Sometime around 370, Augustine began a 13-year relationship with the woman who would bear his son, Adeodatus (b.372). At the age of 19, influenced by an unfavourable comparison of the rhetoric of Cicero with the Bible, he decide to devote his time and energies to the Manicheans, a group who followed the teaching of Mani (third century BCE), that human beings consisted of 'rational and spiritual beings created by a supreme God...unhappily bonded to a material body created by an evil demi-urge';[41] this belief he held for some nine years before discarding it as unsatisfactory. He taught rhetoric in Thagaste and Carthage before eventually travelling, in 385, across the Mediterranean to Italy, to become professor of rhetoric in Milan.[42] Though Augustine would only stay in Europe for four years, resigning his post with little notice on the grounds of ill-health, his life was heavily influenced by his time there. On hearing the preaching of Ambrose, the Bishop of Milan, Augustine was impressed, and was eventually baptised by him at Easter 387.

Returning to North Africa two years later, Augustine initially intended to establish a monastic community with his son and some friends in his hometown. (His mother died as they were about to embark for the sea-crossing home.) In 391, however, and in the aftermath of the untimely death of his son and a friend, Nebridius, he was popularly acclaimed as priest while in Hippo, a city then dominated by Donatist Christians. The 'orthodox' Bishop of Hippo, Valerius, encouraged him to preach regularly, and on the bishop's death in 395 Augustine was made bishop, a post he was to hold until his death some 35 years later. During his years at Hippo, Augustine preached often, settled lawsuits in ecclesiastical court, and wrote many works including his *Confessions* (397–400), his *On Christian Doctrine* (begun in 397 but only finished around 425), and his *City of God* (begun after the sacking of Rome by the Goths in 410 and taking some 10–15 years to complete). At the heart of Augustine's huge body of published work was his desire to understand and appropriate the biblical texts, all of which was worked out in the context of his interaction with three sets of ideas—Manichaeism (the dualist heresy of his youth); Donatism (an ecclesiological heresy prominent in North Africa); and Pelagianism (a developing heresy related to the role of human striving in the work of salvation).[43] We might also add to the mixture of ideologies against which Augustine was writing, a critical pagan milieu and a brief flurry against a resurgent local form of Marcionism around 420.[44] Augustine died of a fever in 430, just before Hippo was sacked by the Vandals.

Augustine's treatise, *De consensu evangelistarum*, is an extended piece of apologetic writing which was composed around 404. It was intended to rebut pagan and Manichean criticisms of the canonical Gospels on account of contradictions, both within an individual work and between the four texts (and the other Christian Scriptures). Because those criticisms were focused on supposedly factual errors, Augustine was forced to respond on a level which meant that he was unable to invoke the more figurative methods that he might use elsewhere to resolve textual tensions. This requirement became particularly difficult for him when he was dealing with the passion accounts since the ascription of doublets of a particular story to repetitions of actual events were obviously ruled out. Behind his method of working, however, was the view—previously employed by Tyconius (d. *c.*390) as the first of his seven rules of interpretation[45]—that the Pauline analogy of head and body applied to scriptural interpretation. As C. Harrison has put it: '[i]f Scripture is an organic whole, the body working and writing in unity at the instigation of the head, then one might expect it to be harmonious in its witness and to have no disagreements or discordances.'[46]

Composed in four books, *De consensu evangelistarum* consists of a long series of answers to critical questions. It includes quotations of large parts of the Gospels generally; for the section in which we are interested, for example, Augustine quotes all of the relevant texts, interspersing his own comments among them. Book I tackles general questions about the Gospels that were typical of those posed by pagan critics. Books II and III use Matthew—the first Gospel according to Augustine—as a base text against which to compare the other Gospels synoptically, the former up to the preparations for the last supper and the latter from that point onwards. Book IV considers passages that occur only in Mark, Luke, and John. These, Harrison has suggested, were more typical of the criticism arising from the Manicheans.[47] Since Joseph accounts occur in all four Gospels, it is the two questions in book III that are specifically addressed to the post-crucifixion narratives in which he appears that concern us here: Question 22: 'Concerning [Of] Joseph who asked Pilate for the body of the Lord, how all agree, and how John does not by himself disagree' (*'De Joseph qui corpus Domini petiit a Pilato, quomodo omnes consentiant, et quomodo a seipso Joannes non dissentiat'*); and Question 23: 'Of his burial, how the three [Gospels] have no disagreement with John' (*'De sepultura ejus, quomodo tres a Joanne non dissentient'*).[48]

Concerning Joseph ('Q. 22'), Augustine presents Matthew's text first, followed by Mark's and Luke's. Before John's text is recounted, however, Augustine notes that John precedes an account that is similar to that of the other Evangelists with a unique depiction of the breaking of the legs of those crucified alongside Jesus and of the piercing of his side with a spear. He then concludes—without indicating the existence of any textual difficulties—that there is no antagonism between the four accounts. He does allow, however, that some people might question John's account on the grounds of internal inconsistency because he has set the shared story of Joseph before Pilate alongside his singular statement that Joseph 'had been a disciple of Jesus secretly for fear of the Jews'. It would be a reasonable question to ask how this fearful disciple could have been courageous enough to go to Pilate and ask for the body, Augustine writes, the very thing that Jesus' disciples were too afraid to do. The answer lies in Joseph's dignified status which allowed him to presume confidently in expectation of Pilate's good favour, he concludes. Furthermore, he suggests, it would also be allowable for readers to assume that the legitimate need for someone to bury Jesus would itself have left Joseph much less concerned about leaving himself open to the enmity of the Jews. With concerns about his fear deflected, Augustine's harmonized Joseph could more easily approach Pilate.

On Q. 23, the issue at hand is once again to do with John's account, but this time it relates to the potential irreconcilability of that text with the first three Gospels. Augustine again repeats the accounts of Matthew, Mark, and Luke in that order. Once again he asserts, without offering any explicit justification, that the harmonious nature of these three could not be questioned. Augustine does note, however, that the Gospel of John had introduced the figure of Nicodemus into the story of Joseph, and he includes the story as John presents it.

Even this gives little grounds for suspecting a discrepancy, he declares, however, if the four accounts are understood correctly. The first three Evangelists did not choose to mention Nicodemus, but they did not explicitly claim that Joseph buried Jesus alone either. Nor, to Augustine's mind, did their statements about the singular 'linen burial cloth' preclude the use of other linen cloths at the same time. With the various cloths used for the head and body all made of linen, it seems feasible, he concludes, that the three Evangelists can each talk truthfully of a single linen cloth because all the cloth used was made of linen, while the multiple nature of the pieces also made it possible for John to be accurate in using the plural form.

Augustine's purpose in writing answers to such questions was to show that 'not one of these Evangelists contains anything either at variance with other statements in his own Gospel, or inconsistent with the accounts presented by his fellow historians' (*De consensu evangelistarum*, IV, I).[49] Comparing the answers to Q. 22 and 23 offered by Augustine with the discussion of these texts in chapter one of this volume, however, it is clear that there was no great desire on his part to deal with the issues that might arise from a comparison of these texts. Indeed as a Latin-speaking author with little knowledge of Greek, Augustine was ill-equipped to undertake such a task. By stating that the four Gospel accounts agreed in Q. 22 and that the first three Gospels were unquestionably coherent in Q. 23 alongside verbatim reproductions of the four texts themselves, Augustine emphasized their harmony while limiting his discussion of their potential disharmony to the issue of fear and boldness in the former, and to the issue of the role of Nicodemus in the latter.

The possible tension between fear and action in the Johannine Joseph's approach to Pilate was assuaged by Augustine's recourse to two 'historical' arguments:[50] first, that a person of high status would have had an important role in civic life; and second, that the need for someone—anyone!—to remove the bodies would have lessened the danger of Joseph going to Pilate. The potential difficulties attached to the appearance of Nicodemus in John were resolved by Augustine's recourse to an argument that the inspiration of each of the Evangelists did not mean that they were thereby bound to include every detail in their accounts; they could select material in line with their own recollections and these would then be expected to complement each other;[51] this is the position taken with regard to the issue of cloth/ cloths. For Augustine, disharmony was not a property that the Scriptures possessed. The reality of the matter was that, regardless of any appearance to the contrary, the four canonical accounts of Joseph of Arimathea had to be in complete agreement with one another, and the diverse elements that made up the Arimathean were to be compressed by interpreters into a single individual.

The *Gospel of Nicodemus*

The popularity of the works of Chrysostom, Jerome, and Augustine would have undoubtedly given their treatments of the Joseph story through homily, translation, and harmonization a quite considerable influence. The same cannot be said for the narrative offered by the *Gospel of Peter*, however; it was soon lost to history. The *Gospel of Nicodemus* (*c.* fourth century), however, supplies us with a significantly larger extension of the Joseph story which was to become influential in the medieval West. The *Gospel of Nicodemus* would eventually grow to contain three interlinked sections: the trial, crucifixion, and burial of Christ; the story of Joseph of Arimathea; and an account of Christ's descent into Hell. Though traces of the earliest sections of the *Gospel* exist in 'Greek, Coptic, Arabic, Ethiopic, Syriac, Palestinian Aramaic, Armenian, Georgian and Slavonic',[52] the later Western vernacular translations—in, for example, Catalan, Italian, Old English, Dutch, German, Irish, and Welsh—all derive, not from the Greek original, but from its Latin translation. Combined with that translation—and its many summaries and retellings in Latin—these vernacular *Gospels* had such an influence on later works in so many geographical locations—the Low Countries, Scandinavia, the British Isles, the Iberian peninsula, France, and Germany—that the *Gospel* could be comfortably described by Z. Izydorczyk as possessing a 'commonplace status'.[53] Two examples of its reuse that were to prove highly influential in turn were Vincent of Beauvais' *Speculum historiae* (*c.*1260) and Jacobus de Voragine's *Legenda aurea* (*c.*1267).[54] In some manuscripts, the text was even presented as a fifth Gospel, inserted between John and Acts. That influence would only wane with the text's rejection by the sixteenth-century Reformers.[55]

Despite its widespread use, however, the origins of the *Gospel of Nicodemus* are shrouded in mystery. The earliest identifiable references to the text come from the fourth century, and occur in the context of a dispute about the timing of Easter. Though some were using a text akin to the *Gospel*'s opening section to set the date, Epiphanius of Salamis (*c*.310–403) informed the readers of his *Panarion* (completed *c*.378) that he knew of other versions of that text which suggested a different date (50.1.5,8), perhaps indicating a degree of diversity in the *Gospel* early on.[56] Though hints of ideas found in the medieval text can be seen in earlier second-century works of Justin Martyr—who suggested his opponents inspect Pilate's records (*First Apology*, 35.9)—and of Tertullian—who referred to a report of Jesus' death debated by the Senate (*Apologeticum*, 5.2–3; 21.42)—these are more suggestive of an early belief in the existence of an official record than direct evidence for the early existence of sections of the *Gospel of Nicodemus*.[57]

When Eusebius of Caesarea echoed the idea of an official report in the early fourth century ('Pilate communicated to the Emperor Tiberius'; *Ecclesiastical History*, 2.2.1) it was partly in response to certain anti-Christian Pilate texts that were in circulation.[58] It seems likely that the *Gospel of Nicodemus*, first referenced by Epiphanius some 50 years later, was one of a number of Christian texts written in a milieu in which an official report from Pilate would have formed an almost essential element of any narrative retelling of the story of Jesus; a conversion-oriented re-examination of the Roman would also have been an obvious development. With a developing interest in transforming Pilate from sinner into saint from the fifth century onwards,[59] the *Gospel* would have both helped to generate further pro-Pilate works and then gained popularity as those ideas took hold in popular Christianity, eventually becoming part of an extensive Pilate cycle of texts.[60] With Gregory of Tours in the sixth century, we find a description of a text including the opening two sections of the medieval text, the passion, and the story of Joseph.[61] Only later would the 'descent into hell' section finally be added, forming the medieval text as we know it.

The text begins with an extended narrative about the trial and crucifixion of Jesus (I.1–IV.4).[62] Against Pilate's wishes, Jesus is taken away and crucified between two thieves (X.1), with the governor washing his hands of events (IX.4). On subsequently receiving a report from the centurion about Jesus' death and the striking events which accompanied it, Pilate is vexed, and refrains from food and drink (XI.2). With the disciples absent, it is Joseph who now comes to him and asks him for the body—his first appearance in the story. Joseph is described as 'a counsellor, of the city of Arimathaea, who also himself looked for the kingdom of God', and—with no inquiry to the centurion needed or made—he is given permission to remove the body, wrapping it in 'a clean linen cloth', and putting it in an empty stone-cut tomb (XI.3).

Hearing that Joseph has taken the body, the Jews look for him and for the disciples and for those, including Nicodemus, who had defended Jesus before Pilate. Nicodemus, when found, boldly agrees with their charge that he is to be counted with Jesus' followers. When Joseph appears, he tells them what he has done with the body, but then charges them with false dealings with 'the just one'; they had pierced Jesus' body with a spear! He is seized and threatened with death, his body to be given to the birds. Likening his captors to the boastful Goliath, he compares them unfavourably to Pilate, described positively as one 'circumcised in heart', who washed his hands of guilt, whereas they embraced it for themselves and their children. Enraged, the Jews imprison him in a windowless house, seal it up, and set guards on the door (XII.1). But the next day, after they have decided to kill him, he is not to be found there. The seals remain and Caiaphas has the key, but Joseph has vanished. Afraid, the Jews leave the other followers of Jesus alone (XII.2).

The 'miracle' of Joseph's disappearance is followed by reports of another strange event; Jesus' body has also vanished, with the guards swearing that they saw an angel announce that the body had been raised to life to a group of women. Aware of Joseph's disappearance, the guards respond to the Jews' disbelief with the retort that if they produce Joseph, the guards will produce Jesus. When the Jews reply that Joseph has left for his hometown, the guards respond by claiming that Jesus has gone to Galilee! Afraid once again, the Jews buy the guards' silence, promising to protect them if Pilate should hear of events (XIII.1–3).

A report of Jesus' commissioning of the disciples and his ascension in Galilee is then brought to Jerusalem by three visiting rabbis. Their story is rejected, however, and they are sent back to Galilee, with food, drink, and a pay-off (XIV.1–2). The Jerusalem leaders reconsider what they have heard, but still decide that they will not accept the veracity of the claims that they have heard (XIV.3). Nicodemus intervenes, gaining their agreement for a search across the land for evidence that Jesus has risen. Though the search for Jesus eventually proves unsuccessful, Joseph is discovered living at his home in Arimathea (XV.1–2). After some thought, the 'elders, priests, and Levites' in Jerusalem write to Joseph, via seven of his friends, and request a personal account of what happened to him. They admit their fault and acknowledge that the Lord saved him (XV.3); will he come to speak to them?

Joseph travels to Jerusalem and is welcomed with great reverence by 'all the people', who are astonished to see him. At Nicodemus's house, he is feasted along with, among others, 'Annas and Caiaphas and the elders and the priests and the Levites' (XV.4). The following day, he sits before the council, between Annas and Caiaphas, and answers their inquiry truthfully. After a brief rehearsal of events, Joseph is asked to explain what happened in the sealed and guarded house. He begins by saying that at midnight on the Sabbath he was praying when a bright light appeared. Falling to the floor, he was raised up by someone who kissed him and told him to look at who was speaking to him. Doing so, Joseph saw a figure that he did not recognize; it was Jesus, the one whose body he had buried, who then identified himself to the stricken Arimathean. (Here the account added further burial details, including a napkin-covering for the face and a great stone for the tomb entrance.) The still unsure Joseph was taken from the sealed house to the tomb and, seeing the grave clothes himself, believed that it was Jesus who was with him. He was then taken to his own home, blessed—'Peace be to you', said Jesus—and instructed him not to leave the house for 40 days, during which time Jesus would go to Galilee and then ascend to heaven. On hearing these words, the rulers fall down like the dead. Nicodemus and Joseph comfort them and send them home after prayer, food, and drink, to prepare for the coming Sabbath (XV.6–XVI.1).

A discussion about Jesus takes place on the Sabbath, with a teacher of the law, Levi, and Simeon testifying in his favour. A decision is taken to summon the three rabbis who had testified to Jesus' actions in Galilee, and the three willingly agree to attend. Again they recount their story about Jesus' ascension, even when questioned separately. The council accepts their testimony: 'It is in the Law of Moses: At the mouth of two or three shall every word be established.' Annas and Caiaphas conclude that evidence exists for the events of Jesus' life, death, resurrection, and ascension. The people praise God and depart to their homes (XVI.2–8).

At this point, the focus of the *Gospel of Nicodemus* turns away from Joseph towards an account of Christ's harrowing of Hell, as witnessed by two of the souls saved, Karinus and Leucius, the sons of Simeon and residents of Joseph's hometown (XVII.1–XXVII). The texts are linked by the simple expedient of having Joseph, Nicodemus, Annas, Caiaphas, and Gamaliel travel to Arimathea to enquire of the two men—known to have died but now very much alive—what happened to them as they shared in Christ's resurrection. Taking them back to Jerusalem, the two ask for paper and testify in writing to the events that took place, each providing a separate description of Jesus' battle with Satan and Hell. The narrative culminates with the two men being transfigured and vanishing from sight, the writings left behind being found to be identical. Joseph and Nicodemus speak of these events to Pilate, who then writes an account of all of the events concerning Jesus for his official records (XVII).

That the *Gospel of Nicodemus* owes much to the canonical stories of Joseph cannot be doubted. The text reminds us of Mark and Luke (Joseph as 'councillor', 'awaiting the kingdom of God') and John ('Nicodemus') and Matthew (Pilate 'washes his hands' of the blood of Jesus). No attempt was made at an inclusivity of each Gospel's details, however; Joseph is not described as a rich man, nor is the tomb in which Jesus was laid said to belong to him; Nicodemus does not help Joseph with the burial.

Where the *Gospel of Nicodemus* added significantly to the traditions about Joseph is in its narration of the events which take place *after* the burial, not only allowing the character of the man to develop but also allowing him to speak for himself. Hints about the Johannine Joseph's fear are expanded into a fulsome narrative of imprisonment and victimization at the hands of those upset at his temerity in requesting the body, of the appearance of the risen Christ to free Joseph miraculously, and of his highly effective testimony to the council in Jerusalem. These new additions did not require significant changes to the canonical portrait of Joseph, however; rather, they developed organically from it, becoming part of an extended reverie in which the canonical limits were cast to the four winds.

In the *Gospel of Nicodemus*, Joseph became the witness to Jesus par excellence. His action in recovering the body and his resulting imprisonment led directly to a transformative encounter with the risen Christ and his miraculous release. After the 40 days leading up to the ascension and the short period of time before his discovery in his own house by the searchers from Jerusalem, Joseph became a witness whose personal account of the Christophany that he has seen would bring the entire Jerusalem council to faith. With Nicodemus, his account of these events and of the written testimony of Karinus and Leucius about the harrowing of Hell would become the trustworthy source for the report recorded in the official documents of the Roman governor. The *Gospel of Nicodemus* thus portrays itself as an accurate account of the passion and subsequent events; in one sense it may be apocryphal and secondary, but in another sense, it partakes of the authoritative aura of Joseph himself. It is no wonder that Z. Izydorczyk has described it as almost an equal to the canonical Gospels.[63]

Available in a populist and dramatic format, the influence of the *Gospel of Nicodemus* may have even rivalled that of the canonical Gospels for a period, especially when summarized as part of a popular collection such as Jacobus de Voragine's *Legenda aurea*:

> It is said that Jesus was also seen on the same day [the day of the resurrection] by Joseph, as we read in the *Gospel of Nicodemus*. When the Jews heard that Joseph had asked Pilate for the body and had placed it in his own tomb, they were indignant, and took him and shut him in a small room that they had carefully locked and sealed. They intended to kill him after the Sabbath, but the very night of the resurrection the house was lifted up by the four corners and Jesus came into him, dried his tears, embraced him, and, leaving the seals intact, led him out and brought him to his house in Arimathea (*Legenda aurea*, vol. 1).[64]

The beginnings of a diverse and growing Joseph tradition

Doubtless more could be said about the figures of Joseph of Arimathea who appeared in evermore significant numbers in the literature of the first millennium of the Christian era. Even this brief look, however, shows the diversity of the earliest examples of his literary afterlife. The five examples outlined here show that the differences between the four Gospel portraits of Joseph were important factors in the creative development of the Joseph tradition. Discussions of wealth and status, boldness and fear, discipleship and secrecy, Joseph's relationship to Nicodemus or Pilate or the Jews, and even the material elements of the burial itself all derived from the interplay between the different nouns, verbs, adjectives, and adverbs that had been used to describe events between cross and grave. In their turn, these discussions generated further alternative Josephs which could then influence subsequent interpreters. The influential commentary of a Chrysostom, an Augustine, a Jerome, or a vastly popular and increasingly authoritative apocryphal gospel such as that attributed to Nicodemus, could, and did, spread those possibilities far and wide.

The textual variants of the canonical accounts of Joseph rarely seem to have been discussed openly, however. Even Augustine's explicit and (relatively) systematic attempt at harmonizing them was occasioned, not by particular Church concerns about the Joseph stories, but rather by the critical questioning of Gospel passages by those outside the Church. In practice then, the textual differences were sidelined by our 'authors'. The details of the four accounts were either used individually or combined as and when required by the interpreter's requirements. In even so few samples, these ranged from rebutting outside polemic (Augustine) to strengthening a theological doctrine such as the resurrection (Chrysostom), or from responding to changing language skills in an audience (Jerome) to generating a new historical report of the events of the passion (*Gospel of Nicodemus*). In achieving these goals, the interpreters did not hesitate to add new elements to the Joseph balance sheet.

The two narratives examined exhibit the impact of ideological traits on the Joseph presented. The *Gospel of Peter*'s anti-Jewish stance and the *Gospel of Nicodemus*' pro-Pilate position both significantly altered Joseph's persona, changing his description (e.g. 'friend of Pilate'), altering his actions (e.g. removing his involvement in the body's removal from the cross), giving him a voice (e.g. allowing him to describe his miraculous escape from imprisonment in his own words), and even adjusting the timing of his entrance into the story (to pre-death of Jesus rather than post-death), and of his exit (e.g. providing him with a role in delivering the account of events claimed to underlie Pilate's records). The figure that appears is recognizably that of Joseph—there are clearly some constraints supplied, if unevenly, by the four Gospel accounts—but the adaptability of that figure and its easy availability for later development is impressive nonetheless.

The tensions within the canonical Gospel accounts, their lack of a definitive characterization of Joseph, and the gaps created by his abrupt appearance and unexplained disappearance left him wide open for literary development. His early life is hinted at unevenly in the canonical texts (his 'wealth' [Matthew], his role as a 'councillor' [Mark/Luke], his hometown of 'Arimathea' [all four]), and his pre-passion participation in the Jesus movement itself is introduced suggestively but without any detail by both Matthew and John. Intriguing questions and possibilities are raised, with plenty of space being left within which later interpreters could provide their own answers; he was one of the 70, for example, with Chrysostom. But even more openness is left by his abrupt disappearance from the four Gospels. Where did he go to and why did Christian audiences hear no more of him? The *Gospel of Nicodemus* acknowledged these questions and answered them by having Jesus himself tell Joseph to remain in his own house until he had ascended to heaven. But what then of the period covered by Acts 1–7 and the activities of the Church in Jerusalem? As we shall see, later developers of the literary tradition would also worry about Joseph's absence from the early Church and create ways of assuaging that difficulty, thus extending the tradition even further.

| 3

The Renaissance Joseph

The paintings of the European Renaissance

On the basis of the discussion so far, one could be forgiven for thinking that the afterlives of Joseph were developed and extended only by oral and literary means. Visual representation of the foundational elements of the Christian story began quite early, however, and Joseph's involvement in three of the pivotal events in the Gospel accounts of the passion—his request for the body, the deposition (or descent) of the body from the cross (in Mark and Luke at least), and the entombment (or burial)—led to a significant number of representations of the man being produced in the West in the medieval and Renaissance periods. In what follows, representative examples of each of these three images will be discussed; no pretence at comprehensiveness is thus being claimed, though a number of important developmental strands will become apparent.

A large number of renderings of Joseph from the Renaissance period do not portray one of these three events, however. Instead they show his involvement in a scene that does not occur within the canonical Gospels, but which is nevertheless set within the brief time-period when Joseph is centre stage in those texts, namely, the 'Pietà' ('pity' in Italian) or lamentation. While discussing Caravaggio's *The Entombment of Christ* (*c*.1600–1604), M. A. Graeve has helpfully distinguished between 'the fundamentally separate themes' of the entombment and the Pietà 'both in their literary origins and in their artistic form'. According to her:

The older theme, the Entombment, is based on the laconic and concordant account in the Gospels... None of the four Gospels mentions the Virgin as present at these last rites, only the Magdalen and another Mary. Thus told, and as consequently pictured in art from the ninth century on the Entombment is a busy extroverted event, concentrated on the action of burial, with Christ's body the center of interest. The Pietà, on the other hand, refers to the compassion of the Virgin as she weeps over her dead Son. Emphasis on the Virgin's sorrow developed as a result of ninth- and tenth-century apocryphal accounts of Mary as chief mourner in an interlude of lament over Christ's body between the cross and the tomb. The Pietà, a relatively late artistic outgrowth of this tradition, crystallized into a definitive type in the early fourteenth century: a representation of the Madonna, seated alone, with Christ across her lap. The title Pietà need not be restricted to scenes which show the Virgin isolated, but if other mourners are present as she cradles her Son, they remain a background chorus, subordinate. In sum, the Pietà is a sorrowful brooding subject, often given to subjective piety and symbolism, with the Virgin equal to Christ in importance.[1]

A fourth extra-biblical scene needs therefore to be added to the three biblical scenes that we shall have to consider. Graeve's Pietà's typology, however, has already warned us that, in contrast to the centrality of Joseph to the request, deposition, and entombment scenes, the Joseph of the Pietà will, instead, be part of a passive 'background chorus, subordinate' to the mourning Virgin and the dead Christ.

The four examples chosen for discussion are as follows: Simon Bening's *Joseph of Arimathea Before Pilate* (*c*.1525–30); Rogier van Der Weyden's *Descent from the Cross* (*c*.1435); Sandro Botticelli's *Lamentation over the Dead Christ* (*c*.1495), also known as the *Milan Pietà*; and Michelangelo Buonarroti's *The Entombment* (*c*.1500–1501). A brief excursus will take advantage of this chapter's discussions of the Pietà and Michelangelo to introduce an idea which invoked Joseph for support, that of 'Nicodemism', the hiding of one's faith for fear of persecution, as illuminated by the issues surrounding his *Florentine Pietà* (*c*.1547–55), also sometimes called *The Deposition*. The chapter concludes with a discussion of A. Soudavar's 2008 interpretation of Simon Marmion's *Ducal Lamentation* (*c*.1465) as an allegory of the high politics of fifteenth-century Europe.[2]

Simon Bening's *Joseph of Arimathea Before Pilate*

Of the four scenes in which Joseph figures, the least plentiful are those which depict him requesting Jesus' body from Pilate. C. Hourihane has noted that images of this scene, though common in the East from the ninth century onwards, are comparatively rare in the West. When describing the earliest extant Western image, that of the twelfth-century *Canterbury Psalter* now in the Bibliothéque Nationale in Paris, he pointed out the scene's iconographic similarity to Christ's appearance before Pilate, before describing a bare-headed, youthful, and seated Pilate who is being addressed by a behatted, elderly, and standing Joseph.[3] In typical medieval portrayals of the scene, both men are expensively dressed, with Pilate confronting, in some sense, a man approaching and even equalling his own high status. Nevertheless, the scarcity of the scene suggests that patrons wishing to commission such an image and ecclesiastical settings for its usage were both limited in Western Christianity.

Simon Bening (1483–1561) was a renowned Flemish painter, who was born in Ghent but moved to Bruges as a youth. A scion of a painting dynasty, patronized by wealthy individuals and royalty from all over Northern Europe, Bening specialized in the illumination of expensive books.[4] The image of Joseph of Arimathea before Pilate that we are considering comes from a work of his now known as *The Prayer Book of Cardinal Albrecht of Brandenburg*, a parchment volume that contains 62 devotional prayers, many of which are focused on Jesus' passion, and which is now in the J. Paul Getty Museum in Los Angeles (as MS. LUDWIG IX 19).[5] Beautifully illustrated with 41 full-page (approx. 16.8 × 11.4 cm) miniatures of Christ's life and passion, the book is a 1525 copy of a printed text with 35 woodcut images created by a student of Albrecht Dürer known as the Petrarca Master, which was published in Augsburg in 1521. The miniatures differ markedly from the woodcuts in both subject matter and style.[6] According to the writer of the Getty Museum website commentary, Bening's images were 'designed to evoke an intense empathic response as the viewer contemplated Jesus' suffering'.[7] That viewer, of course, was originally intended to be a wealthy individual, Bening's patron, Cardinal Albrecht of Brandenberg (1490–1545); despite its potential public display in the Getty Museum (it was not on display in 2012), it is

ironic that the institution in which the *Prayer Book* now resides bears
the name of a wealthy American oil man and contains his personal
art collection.

Of the House of Hohenzollern, the dynastic rulers of Brandenberg
(and much else besides), Albrecht was ordained priest in 1513, then
Archbishop of Magdeberg and Administrator of Halberstadt, before
taking up the position of Archbishop-Elector of Mainz in 1514, rising
to Cardinal in 1518, all by the tender age of 28.[8] A devoted patron of
the arts, he is perhaps best known to history as the 'Most Reverend
Father in Christ, Most Illustrious Sovereign' addressed by Martin
Luther in a letter attacking the sale of indulgences by Albrecht's
man, Johann Tetzel, in October 1517;[9] the indulgences were author-
ized by Pope Leo X to raise funds for the construction of St Peter's
in Rome, and the responsibility for their sale in the region was given
to Albrecht. It was not just the question of the 'theological impro-
prieties' that led to Luther's nailing of his 95 theses to the door
of Wittenberg's All Saints Church that would have mattered to
Albrecht, however. Suspicions were also voiced that the moneys
raised were intended to defray the costs of his climb up the political
ladder and to help fund a profligate lifestyle.[10] A painting by
Lucas Cranach the Elder entitled *Cardinal Albrecht of Brandenburg
as St Jerome in his Study* (*c.*1526) suggests a strong desire on its subject's
part to appear scholarly, pious, and ascetically minded. It thus seems
likely that Albrecht's use of Bening's work from the same period in
his devotions would have involved his contemplation of its numerous
portraits of the influential men involved in Christ's life and death.

In picture order, Bening's miniature of *Joseph before Pilate* (fol. 311v)
appears after an image of Jesus' side being pierced with a spear
(fol. 302v), but before two further images in which the man from
Arimathea also appears: a lamentation scene (fol. 317v) and an
entombment scene (fol. 328v). It is significant, however, that the
book's choice of pictures meant that the iconography of the image
could be compared by Albrecht, not only to Bening's painting of
Christ before Pilate (fol. 138v), but also to those of Christ appearing
before three other powerful figures: Annas (fol. 119v), Caiaphas (fol.
128v), and Herod (fol. 143v). Without doubt, the format of a series
of images in the 1521 book was a major enabler for Bening's inclusion
of *Joseph before Pilate* in the 1525 prayer book, but the fact of his

inclusion of Joseph as a wealthy man who *kneels* alongside other images of influential men who are *seated* or *standing over* Christ would—intentionally or otherwise—have offered his patron a figure of status eminently worthy of contemplation or even emulation. After all, as hard as it might be for a rich man to enter the kingdom of heaven (Mt. 19.23–24), the Matthean Joseph had managed it with ease.

In the lower-left of the miniature, an aged, grey-bearded Pilate stands facing three-quarters to the front, at the top of three steps in front of a large building, styled after a medieval church, which extends up out of the frame. He is elaborately dressed in a decorated dark blue and gold garment, over a blue long-sleeved satin tunic, and wears on his head a green turban wound around a central red spike. In his right hand he holds a thin switch, held straight up, and his left hand is placed on his hip. By his side, behind a low buttressed wall, are three colourfully dressed, behatted, and stern-looking men. Below him, in the cobbled medieval street, the balding, white-bearded Joseph is bent down on his left knee, his arms held out in supplication, and his eyes lifted towards Pilate. Though his clothes are not as extravagantly coloured as Pilate's, his fur-lined green outer garment is worn over a purple long-sleeved tunic. He is bareheaded, his grey hat held in his left hand. Behind him stand two official-looking figures, both holding hats. Two further figures stand in the distance, in front of a set of medieval town buildings, built of yellow stone with blue and red tile roofs.

The muted background colours of the light-tan streets and the darker greys of the building behind Pilate serve to foreground and highlight the colour garments of the main figures. Pilate's authority is clear from his attire and is further emphasized by his physical eleva-tion over Joseph. He is in control of events as a whole, and of the body of Jesus in particular, and Joseph is portrayed as showing him due deference. For Bening, there was little sense of equal standing between the two men—his Pilate is hardly being forced by a powerful local figure to accede to his request—and yet Joseph's clothing still marks him out as someone whose status is well above the ordinary. The scene's conclusion, that Pilate would grant Joseph's wish, is held in abeyance, however. The outcome remains uncertain as Joseph pleads on bended knee for the body, his arms raised towards the governor. Any Markan boldness therefore does not appear as an arrogant assertion of rank. Working for such a patron, Bening was unlikely to have had complete freedom to choose the book's scenes. Nor would the images necessarily have been representative of his own theological leanings even if he had done so. Nevertheless, his vibrant depiction of the two actors in this scene does emphasize the difficulties facing Joseph as he appears before the powerfully rendered Pilate, contrasting his own high status with his bending of the knee to plead for Jesus' body; his boldness is that of the weaker man who dares to petition the stronger. Joseph's triumph in eventually succeeding in persuading the domineering Pilate to release the corpse is thus made all the more full. For a man of the social status of Albrecht of Brandenburg, this twin affirmation of Joseph's piety and his wealth within the covers of his personal prayer book would surely have not gone unnoticed.

Rogier van der Weyden's *Descent from the Cross*

The twin concepts of wealth and status were already present in the Gospel accounts and had been developed further in the earliest literary developments of Joseph's story. But the positivity of the pictorial affirmation of pious wealth that was created for Albrecht's private devotions in the form of Bening's *Joseph of Arimathea before Pilate* was also being exhibited before all and sundry in the visually rich societies of medieval and Renaissance Europe. It appeared before priests and worshippers in the adornments of ecclesiastical buildings, and it appeared to both residents and visitors in the decorations of the dwellings of the rich and the powerful. And, as local and national museums came into existence in the modern era, it was also placed on public display for perusal by the masses. Our next painting, Rogier van der Weyden's *Descent from the Cross* (c.1435), now in the Museo Nacional del Prado in Madrid, has functioned in each of these three settings during its near 600 years of existence.

Rogier van der Weyden (1400–64) was a Flemish painter, born in Tournai, but who moved as a young man to Brussels where he established himself as one of the best known and most sought-after painters in Europe. Around 1435, Louvain's Guild of Crossbowmen—a group dedicated to the Virgin Mary and known as the 'Sixty' because of its fixed size—commissioned him to paint a large rectangular altarpiece with a raised square central section, 220 × 260 cm in size, for its chapel on the edge of the city, Our Lady of Ginderbuiten ('Outside the Walls').[11] Such guilds or brotherhoods had a significant role in the life of the medieval city; they not only had feasts, festivities, and religious observances for members, they also wined and dined local dignitaries at those feasts and organized public tournaments as part of their festivities. Guild chapels were sometimes established within city churches, but the wealthier guilds could get permission to build and staff their own chapels; if granted a bell tower to summon people to worship, these even had a semi-parochial status which would have required negotiations with other churches nearby.[12] If not exactly on public show, the Guild of Crossbowmen would have expected the painting to be seen by non-members.

The guild's role as patron for the *Descent* was indicated, not by donors painted among the figures in the painting,[13] but by the tiny crossbows that hang from the tracery in the upper corners of the painting. It may, perhaps, also be indicated, as A. Powell has suggested, by the bow-like shape of the dead Christ, a shape then echoed by the Virgin, collapsed in grief in the foreground;[14] the relationship between Christ and Virgin here has been much discussed in terms of a *co-redemptio* motif.[15] Set prominently above the high altar, Powell has noted that the painting would have not been seen in isolation; rather worshippers would have seen it accompanied by nearby images and, during the celebration of the Mass, by the raised 'body of Christ'.[16] Nevertheless, the painting soon attracted specific attention. In 1443, a copy was made by a now-unknown artist for the burial chapel of the family of William Edelheer in the Church of St Peter in Louvain. This triptych is the only copy known to have wings, each of which portrays members of the commissioning family kneeling at prayer, watched over by two patron saints.[17]

A hundred years later, Mary of Hungary (1505–58) purchased the original from the Guild of Crossbowmen in exchange for 1500 florins, additional funds for a new organ, and a copy for its chapel, to be painted by Mary's court painter, Michiel Coxcie.[18] Born in Spain and daughter to the King of Castile, Philip I, Mary had been briefly married to King Louis II of Hungary and Bohemia. Widowed in 1526, she became Stadtholder of the Low Countries five years later, ruling the region as the representative of her older brother, Charles V, the Holy Roman Emperor. The *Descent* was moved to the chapel at Mary's castle at Binche in Wallonia. In 1551, a visiting dignitary, Vicente Alvárez, wrote of it:

> In the chapel, there was a painting showing the deposition from the cross; it was the best painting in the entire castle and even, I believe, in the entire world, for I have seen many fine paintings in these regions but none that could match this one in verisimilitude and piety. All who have seen it have this same opinion.[19]

Some five years after Mary's death, in 1564, the painting was moved to Spain, as the possession of Philip II, the King of Spain, newly in charge of the Netherlands following the death of his father, Charles V, and ruler over a Spanish empire containing numerous colonies around the world including the Philippines, which were named after him. Though its transport ship managed to sink on the way, the painting was recovered undamaged. Philip initially sent the picture to El Pardo, his hunting lodge near Madrid, before it was moved ten years later to San Lorenzo de El Escorial, a monastery which he had established some 30 miles northwest of Madrid; Coxcie produced a second copy for the lodge.[20] Despite its relocation to Spain, however, the copies made in the Low Countries were still being copied and their influence continued to grow. Only in the seventeenth century would painting styles move on significantly enough for the image to lose its influence, de Vos offering Peter Paul Rubens' *Descent from the Cross* (c.1615) as its first worthy Netherlandish successor.[21]

In 1936, the painting was exhibited in Geneva before being moved to its current location, the Museo Nacional del Prado in Madrid; Coxcie's El Pardo copy, in the Prado's collection at that time, took its place at the Escorial monastery.[22] The painting is one of 14 recently made available as part of the 'Masterpieces of the Prado Museum with Google Earth' online collection, photographed in such high definition (14 giga-pixels) that 'delicate tears on the faces of the figures in *The Descent from the Cross*' are visible.[23]

Set against a golden ground reminiscent of a gilded wooden case, van der Weyden's *Descent* is dominated by five flattened spatial planes, evident in the image's centre; each stands out in sharp but compressed relief from the others. To the front is the swooning Virgin Mary (plane 1), her knees touching the grassy foreground, but with her upper body held aloft. The body of Christ appears next (plane 2), supported by Joseph of Arimathea with a white burial cloth (plane 3), behind whom stands the unrealistically rendered cross (plane 4). The final layer is supplied by the man on a ladder leant against the rear of the cross (plane 5), who has released Jesus' body and then broken the separation of planes, first by holding the bloodied nails in his right hand placed over the cross, and then by holding Jesus' left arm with his left hand.[24]

The Virgin with tear-stained face swoons backwards and her brilliant blue dress, white scarf, and headcovering are contrasted vibrantly with the pale skin of the near-naked thorn-crowned Christ. He is covered only by a white loin-cloth, stained with blood from the wound in his side (the wounds in his hands and feet are also visible) which flows on down his leg; he is laid against a burial sheet, a stark white amongst the rich colour and dark hues of the garments of those around him. The echoing of the body shapes certainly begs the question of the relationship between the suffering of these two central figures for viewers.

Joseph is depicted as an influential, wealthy Jew, an elderly, white-haired, balding man with a heavily lined brow, solemn face, and forked grey-white beard. He is dressed in a black velvet mantle lined with fur, over a 'carmine tunic' with golden trim on the sleeves and hem elaborately decorated with gold-set rubies and sapphires interspersed with pearl couplets and a beaded edge. His ensemble is completed with 'vermilion hose', black, silver-clasped shoes, and a crimson hat.[25] The symbolic cross behind means that Joseph's reception of the body as it is lowered is not realistically shown.[26] Rather his lower body position seems to suggest movement to the right of the painting, a suggestion that is supported by the twisted body and outstretched left foot of Nicodemus, who holds the lower legs of Jesus against the burial cloth to the right of the picture.[27] In contrast to Joseph's portrayal, Nicodemus stands shaven, but stubbled, head tilted downwards, and is elaborately dressed in gold fur-lined coat with a purplish pattern, worn over dark blue clothes, and with a black head-covering. Tear-less, Joseph gazes over and along the line of the body of Jesus, but makes little connection with any of the image's elements, an intriguing contrast with the reciprocated gaze assigned to the tear-marked Nicodemus, across the hands of Christ and Virgin to the skull of Adam on the grassy floor by the Virgin's right hand. (It is noteworthy that the gaze was not always reproduced later, even in those paintings meant to be copies; in the Edelheere Tryptych, for example, the skull has been moved to the right, into Joseph's line of sight, but it has also been made to look out of the image to the right, towards the donors in the wings.)

Mary Magdalen, behind Nicodemus with hands together, stands contorted over the feet, reminiscent of what churchmen had long seen harmonistically as the wiping of his feet with her hair in the Gospels (cf. Mk 14.3–9; Mt. 26.6–13; Lk. 7.36–50). At the back, an unidentified bald-headed, bearded older man stands, holding her jar of ointment. To the left, stand two women: the first, Mary Cleophas, is weeping in the background, eyes covered; and the other, Mary Salome, supports the swooning Virgin, right hand holding her head and left hand under her upper left arm, with the help of the young, bare-headed, bare-footed, and clean-shaven figure of John the Evangelist, dressed in red, who leans in from the left of the frame. B. Ridderbos concluded his description of the overall image thus:

> The intensely expressive mourners form a single wave of grief around the dead Christ and the swooning Virgin, whose frontal poses command the believer's attention...The chapel of Our Lady of Ginderbuiten was dedicated to Mary's sorrows, and the prominent display of her suffering in the painting must express the wish of the chapel's ecclesiastical authorities and the patrons, the crossbowmen.[28]

The portrait of Joseph, created by van der Weyden and then reproduced by both himself and the many copyists of his work, placed him firmly as a controlling presence in descent scenes for centuries to come and promoted a specific typological image of Joseph which was widely adopted. (Compare this portrait of Joseph, for example, with van der Weyden's *Entombment of Christ*, possibly commissioned by Cosimo de Medici, c.1460, and now in the Uffizi, Florence, or the portraits of copyists, especially the pair *Joseph of Arimathea* and *Nicodemus in Prayer* attributed to Albrecht Bouts (d. 1549), and now in the Egerton Collection at Tatton Park, Cheshire.) Joseph is depicted as the aged Jew, well dressed and solemn in appearance, supporting the upper body of Jesus, with the younger Nicodemus placed slightly lower, holding the legs. Though capable of being portrayed as plainly dressed (for example, the simple black garments in Bout's *Prayer* image), the opulence of van der Weyden's pearl, emerald, and ruby-laced, gold lined, velvet-clothed, and fur-lined mantle served to emphasize Joseph's wealth and status among the group at the foot of the cross, with only Nicodemus even approaching his finery. It can be no surprise to us that such a painting found favour with the Guild of Crossbowmen and the civic dignitaries who were its guests, nor that it found favour in the eyes of the ruling classes represented by Mary of Hungary and Philip II of Spain. Once again, the wealth and status of Joseph combined with his piety and position in the passion narrative to offer a figure both worthy of contemplation by the powerful and worthy of being shown by them to any subject or foreigner who visited their palaces.

Sandro Botticelli's *Lamentation over the Dead Christ*

With the burial cloth already wrapped around the body and the implied physical movement of the group to the right, the Prado *Descent* hints ahead to the next 'biblical' scene, the entombment. Though this tantalizingly offers us the possibility of 'skipping' the Pietà altogether, we should recall that van der Weyden himself painted a number of such images, and so it is to the mourning Virgin and Christ, with their attendant background figures, that we now turn. In so doing, we will also be moving from the northern Flemish Lowlands towards the European south and Italy.

Alessandro di Mariano Filipepi (1445–1510), better known as Sandro Botticelli, was a highly successful Florentine artist, frequently commissioned by that city's wealthy Medici rulers, its other important citizens, and by the pope in Rome, to produce paintings of biblical, historical, and mythological subjects. In his painting of the *Adoration of the Magi* (1475), his Medici patrons and their families appear among the Magi and the crowd, with Cosimo de Medici

(d. 1464) himself kneeling before the Christ child; a self-portrait appears to the right.[29]

Our interest in Botticelli's work relates to the fact that his painting style underwent a fundamental change towards the end of his life, however. As H. T. Goldfarb put it:

[I]n the 1490s, Botticelli experienced the radical religious exhortation of the Dominican visionary Girolamo Savanarola (1452–98), and in his late compositions his figures reflect a concern for clear, direct, sermon-like communication, becoming more agitated, moving with a compulsion and a theatrical directness of emotion. The atmosphere of courtly grace and the softly modelled and idealized forms of his earlier style are gone, replaced by an impetuous intensity of feeling and a passionate expressiveness of figures.[30]

Two Pietàs, painted by Botticelli in the early to mid 1490s, helpfully illustrate both the change in the artist and a notable alteration in the presentation of Joseph of Arimathea. The first, *Lamentation over the Dead Christ with St Jerome, Saint Paul and St Peter* (140 × 207 cm, tempura on wood), dates to *c.*1490–92 and was painted for a church in San Paolino, Florence; it is now in the Alte Pinakothek in Munich (and is now often called the '*Munich Pietà*'). The second, *Lamentation over the Dead Christ* (106 x 71 cm, tempura on wood), dates to *c.*1495, and was painted for the Church of Santa Maria Maggiore in Florence; it is now in the Museo Poldi Pezzoli in Milan (and is therefore referred to as the *Milan Pietà*).

As noted earlier, Graeve argued that these images focus on the relationship between the suffering Virgin and the dead Christ, encouraging 'subjective piety and symbolism, with the Virgin equal to Christ in importance.'[31] Some images included only these two, whereas others included one or more people set around the central couple. But these bystanders were always peripheral, were mere background for the Virgin and Christ, she insisted.[32] In the *Lamentation over the Dead Christ with St Jerome, Saint Paul and St Peter*, set against the opening of the tomb with a sarcophagus behind, the two central figures are framed by four figures who were traditionally associated with the scene: St John and Mary Magdalen standing behind the Virgin, with the former reaching around to hold the burial cloth of Christ and the latter's arms crossed high over her chest, nails in her left hand and her cloak covering her lower face, and two Marys, bowing low and holding the corpse's head and feet. To the rear right stands St Peter, key to Heaven in hand, and to the rear left is stood, first, St Paul—San Paolino's patron saint—with sword, and St Jerome, present perhaps as the donor's patron saint, but symbolically linked to the Pietà by the stone in his hand, with which, or so tradition had it, he would strike his chest in an act of penitence (so R. Lightbown).[33]

Nowhere does Joseph appear, but it is not his absence that is significant to us here; background figures were usually chosen either for compositional reasons (St John, Mary Magdalen, the two Marys) or for reasons of patronage and piety (St Peter, St Paul, St Jerome). Rather, what is important to us is Lightbown's description of the painting's style as 'chastened', 'courtly', 'chilly', and as 'suggesting satisfaction in a well-wrought artefact rather than any deep urge of feeling'. It represents, he suggested, 'the more coldly ornate aspects of Botticelli's art from around 1489 and 1492'. The *Lamentation over the Dead Christ*, in which Joseph does appear, represents something different altogether.[34]

In 1492, Lorenzo de Medici died. Power in Florence soon passed to Savonarola, a Dominican friar who took advantage of various portents of disaster (including a lighting strike on the cathedral), of the flight of Lorenzo's son Piero before the advancing army of French King Charles VIII, and of his own success in keeping the French out of the city, to seize control between 1494 and 1498. Famed for his powerful preaching, Savonarola viewed the Medici family as tyrannical, corrupt, and worldly. He and his followers (known as *Piagnoni* or 'wailers') argued instead for a state founded on religious principles and moral reform, for a New Jerusalem. J. Hankins has described how the opening up of the city's politics for wider participation in civic life was balanced by increased legislation aimed at closing taverns, banning gambling, inhibiting blasphemy and sodomy, and controlling excessive consumption and public festivities. Tougher penalties and a more rigorous enforcement regime culminated in the 'Bonfire of the Vanities' on 7 February 1497, when a wide variety of vice-related items were publicly destroyed by fire. When Savonarola lost political control of the city, however, this wave of piety quickly dispersed. He was arrested, savagely tortured, and hanged for heresy on 23 May 1498.[35]

According to Giorgio Vasari, the well-known contemporary commentator on Renaissance artists, Botticelli produced a print—'of which there is no trace', wrote Goldfarb[36]—that was supportive of the friar. Vasari also wrote, incorrectly, that the artist's partisanship with regard to the *Piagnoni* was so strong that he gave up painting altogether, and would have died destitute had his old patrons not supported him.[37] Nevertheless, indebted to this fierier religious ethos, Botticelli produced the second of our two paintings, *Lamentation over the Dead Christ* (or the Milan *Pietà*), a vertical image destined for an altar at the foot of a pier in Florence's Chiesa di Santa Maria Maggiore. It was commissioned by Donato di Antonio Cioni, a book illuminator, at least two close relatives of whom were also deeply devoted followers of Savonarola; Botticelli's brother Simone was similarly committed.[38]

Set against the tomb entrance and the sarcophagus within, the identity of the foreground group matches that of the *Lamentation over the Dead Christ with St Jerome, Saint Paul and St Peter*. The Virgin and Christ are surrounded by St John (in near-identical pose but with his head placed directly over that of the Virgin), Mary Magdalen (now on the left of the image, with her face fully covered), and the two Marys at the feet and head of the body. Swathes of dark cloth, red, green, and blue, contrast with the lighter flesh tones of a Christ, held in a near-seated position rather than the traditional curve, and the linen cloth (decorated, not white) beneath him, with the foreground sloping upwards forcing the viewer's eye towards the group of faces above the mid-line of the work. For Lightbown:

[t]he whites of [the two Marys'] headdresses help to divide the middle ground from the final apex of the composition, one of the most dramatic in all of Botticelli's art—the deep blazing yellow robe and agonised wrinkled face of Saint Joseph of Arimathea standing in the entrance to the tomb holding the Crown of Thorns and the Three nails, silhouetted against the black darkness above the sarcophagus, his shadow falling on the right of the entrance.[39]

Beardless, with long wavy hair under a crimson hat and well dressed rather than lavishly so, this Joseph stares heavenward, holding aloft the items—the crown of thorns and the nails—that tradition so often placed in his hands. Now the only figure overlooking the scene, his visible emotions replacing the impassivity of the trilogy of saints that formed the backdrop to the *Munich Pietà*. In dramatic contrast to that painting, the religious passions of a more extreme and heart-felt piety are unleashed by Botticelli in the *Milan Pietà*, with Joseph's grief and anguish at the death of Jesus bursting forth. Lightbown concluded that 'in [this great picture] the courtly and decorative elements that accompany the passionate feeling are transfigured . . . and colour and composition attain a climax of expressiveness within the rational premises of Florentine naturalism.'[40] Gone is the restrained tearless and expressionless Joseph of van der Weyden, centrally located within the painting; here instead is the dramatic expression of the troubled soul of a man who had loved Christ deeply, who had begged Pilate for his body, who had removed it carefully from the cross, and who was now about to lay it in the tomb. Though still marginal as the Pietà-style demands, Botticelli nevertheless set the bereft Arimathean alongside the Virgin and Christ, and provided an exemplary figure for those who were similarly moved by the sight of their suffering.

Though certainly no beggar, Joseph's status recedes as his visible response to events demonstrates his deep love for Christ. Set against Savonarola's Florence, this Joseph reflects the mores of a city focused on visible personal faith and heart-felt religious observance. Staring heavenward, he exemplifies a different kind of faith at the end of the fifteenth century, one that valued enthusiasm over coldness, the inner man over the surface flesh.

Excursus: Nicodemism and Nicodemites

Before moving to our final representative image, *The Entombment* (1500–01) by Michelangelo Buonarroti (1475–1564), a brief consideration is required of a later sculpture by that artist, a Pietà dated to 1547–55 and now in Florence Cathedral (sometimes called *The Deposition* or the *Florentine Pietà*). This work usefully exemplifies the development of the pictorial traditions of Joseph of Arimathea in two ways: first, it shows the confusion that has arisen between representations of Joseph and Nicodemus; second, it hints at the development in the Reformation period of a type of religious action given the name of 'Nicodemism', with both practitioners and opponents seeing

Joseph as an exemplar of that mode of behaviour (cf. Jn 19.38). Nicodemism was defined as the honourable or dishonourable (depending
upon your viewpoint!) withholding of information about one's personal
beliefs when the open espousal of those beliefs would bring opposition
and even persecution upon the person(s) concerned.

Michelangelo's reputation as a sculptor was well established
by his twenty-fifth birthday, with the completion in 1500 of the
Pietà sculpture that now resides in St Peter's Cathedral in Rome.
Returning to Florence, he carved his *David* (1501–04) and began the
never-to-be-finished *Matthew*, before being called to Rome by Pope
Julius II and given the commission to paint the vaulted ceiling of the
Sistine Chapel (1508–12). Following his experience of the siege and
capture of Republican Florence in 1529–30, Michelangelo abandoned
the city for Rome. The *Florentine Pietà* was one of his later sculp-
tures, presenting Virgin and Christ accompanied by a small figure of
Mary Magdalen to Christ's right, with a towering hooded, bearded
male figure standing behind and looming over the three, right hand
on the shoulder of the Magdalen and left hand supporting the body
of Christ. It was begun in about 1547, abandoned in 1553, and then
badly damaged, apparently by the sculptor himself in late 1555; some
limbs were broken off before an assistant persuaded him to relent.
Both Vasari and Michelangelo's early biographer, Ascanio Condivi,
stated that the male figure was intended to be Nicodemus, with the
former also describing it as a self-portrait intended to adorn the
sculptor's own tomb.[41] Many scholars have accepted this, arguing
that Nicodemus was placed at the head rather than at the feet of
Christ in some pietà- and entombment-style groupings and that a
medieval tradition which held that Nicodemus himself was a sculptor
might also have encouraged Michelangelo to include him. Others,
however, have continued to doubt that identification, instead seeing
the *Florentine Pietà*'s fourth figure as Joseph of Arimathea. Though
J. Kristof eventually identified the figure as Nicodemus, she helpfully
listed the wide degree of variety in the representation of these two
men in the period, before acknowledging that:

> it must be admitted that strong arguments can also be made for Joseph
> of Arimathea, based on his traditional prominence and seniority in Depos-
> ition and Lamentation scenes. Having offered his own intended tomb to

Christ, he would also be an especially appropriate model for the contemporary tomb owner.[42]

Even if we accept Vasari and Condivi's claims, invoke the tradition of Nicodemus as sculptor, and agree that Michelangelo intended to carve Nicodemus, it is abundantly clear that sufficient ambiguity remained for later viewers to see the figure as Joseph of Arimathea.

In the heavily charged political and religious atmosphere of the sixteenth century, the combination of dissident religious views and the repression that awaited those who held them led to situations in which dissimulation about one's beliefs was widely practised. C. M. N. Eire's argument that the application of Nicodemus and terminology reflecting his name to such situations was not the result of calm theoretical reflection, but rather the result of off-the-cuff responses to external pressures means that 'labellers' in different contexts were almost bound to view the various connotations attached to the term quite differently.[43] Kristof noted that as early as 1521, Otto Brunfels (1488–1534) had written, without any overt condemnation, that one of his correspondents could be categorized as 'a Lutheran but secretly, [just as] Nicodemus and Joseph [of Arimathea] hid themselves for fear of the Jews'.[44] Reformers such as Ulrich Zwingli (1484–1531) and Johannes Brenz (1499–1570) followed suit, likening the dissembler to an honourable Nicodemus, who was not to be castigated for failing to profess faith openly, but rather to be seen as a potential source of help to the non-dissembling faithful.[45]

The existence of alternative responses for Nicodemus-like believers to their circumstances—escaping into exile or professing faith openly and enduring persecution on the Protestant side, or abandoning heterodox views altogether on the Catholic side—meant that not all would view dissembling so positively, however. On the Protestant side, it was John Calvin (1509–64) who popularized the pejorative sense of 'Nicodemite' in a 1544 polemical work addressed to the 'Messieurs les Nicodemites' of the Catholic-dominated areas of Europe, especially France. His view of their behaviour is summarized in a letter sent a year later to Martin Luther (1483–1546):

When I saw that my French fellow-countrymen, as many of them had been brought out from the darkness of the Papacy to the soundness of the faith, had altered nothing as to their public profession, and that they continued to defile themselves with the sacrilegious worship of the Papists, as if they had never tasted true doctrine, I was altogether unable to restrain myself from reproving so great sloth and negligence, in the way I thought it deserved.[46]

Kristof and V. Shrimplin-Evangelidis have argued independently that Michelangelo's decision to add the hooded figure of Nicodemus to the *Florentine Pietà* reflects the sculptor's social links through his close friend Vittoria Colonna—according to Kristof, 'his spiritual mentor, the Beatrice to his Dante'[47]—to a group of Italian Catholic 'Nicodemites', the *Spirituali*; initially followers of the Spaniard Juan de Valdes, they formed a circle of some political and religious influence at Viterbo after his death in 1541.[48] Under increasing pressure after the establishment of the Roman Inquisition in 1542, some group members would go quickly into exile (for example, Peter Martyr Vermigli who left for Geneva that year), while others chose to willingly take upon themselves the designation of 'Nicodemites', seeing themselves as being well-placed to bring unity to the Church, situated as they were within the Catholic fold and yet sympathetic to Protestant ideas.

When the Catholic Church's response to incursions of Reformation ideology into Italy hardened in the 1550s, the resulting difficulties for these self-professed practitioners of Nicodemism did not in actuality touch Michelangelo himself. Nevertheless, Kristof and Shrimplin-Evangelidis have both suggested that it was a fear of persecution that drove Michelangelo to try to destroy the *Florentine Pietà*, to escape its linkage of him through Nicodemus to those being designated and persecuted as heretics. The comparative ease with which the figure's identification could change from Nicodemus to Joseph, noted above, however, has led M. Arkin to reject such an explanation for the damage; after all, he pointed out, Michelangelo could simply have claimed that the figure was Joseph.[49]

Calvin eventually stopped using the term 'Nicodemite', arguing that the biblical Nicodemus did rather more than secretly visit Jesus at night and then dissemble about his religious views. Since he had openly professed his faith later through his public actions in burying Jesus, it was inappropriate to use his name to label those contemporaries whom Calvin was now attacking for dissembling; the 1549

Latin translation of his polemic work against the Nicodemites titled *Excusatio ad Pseudonicodemos* makes clear his view that any such person was in fact a false Nicodemus.[50]

Calvin's reluctance to use the term without a prefix did little to lessen its popularity in its prefix-free form, however. Nor indeed did the practice itself disappear, with Tudor England especially being the setting for many who found that they needed to practise forms of Nicodemism. In a review of J. Schofield's *Philip Melanchthon and the English Reformation* (2006) in the journal *Renaissance Quarterly*, S. Wabuda noted recent scholarly work on what she described as 'the survival tactics of English Nicodemites, evangelicals who temporized, or made accommodations, with Mary Tudor and survived her reign', before going on to criticize Schofield for claiming that Queen Elizabeth I was 'a Lutheran queen'; 'for anyone who recognizes Elizabeth as the ultimate Nicodemite, this will not do', she concluded.[51] Similarly, S. D. Snobelen has outlined Isaac Newton's adoption of a form of Nicodemism a century or so later, creating a way of life for himself built upon scriptural texts that enabled dissembling (including Joseph's secret belief as mentioned in John 19.38) and allowed Newton to reconcile his outward observance of the rites of the Church of England with a belief in the non-Trinitarian doctrines of the Socinians.[52]

According to the Third Edition of the online *Oxford English Dictionary* (2012), the term is to be firmly located in the Reformation period itself, with a Nicodemite being described as: 'a person who resembles Nicodemus; a secret or timid adherent; *spec.* a Protestant living in a Catholic country in the 16th cent. who concealed his or her faith to escape persecution. Nicodemus was afraid of being seen with Jesus and visited him at night (John 3:1ff.)'. Nicodemism itself is defined as '[t]he practice and beliefs of Nicodemites; *spec.* the view held by certain 16th-cent. Protestants during the Counter-Reformation that outward conformity with the Catholic state was acceptable if one's true faith continued to be inwardly professed'.[53] This authoritative definition could be held to suggest that the word is basically an archaic one. It is not too hard, however, to find more recent usages in cultural contexts where the open profession of Christian beliefs might have brought the certainty of persecution and even of death.

In a work from 1924, *The Law of Apostasy in Islam*, S. M. Zwemer recounted a description offered by a pre-First World War German missionary, travelling in Sudan and Palestine, of a number of '"hidden" disciples who dared not openly confess Christ'.[54] The German described one such person as:

[a] Nubian Sheikh of high position [who] has been coming regularly to our Mission. He is very anxious to know more about the Gospel, and has even acknowledged some of the essential doctrines; but he is a 'Nicodemus-soul' who does not dare confess Christ openly, as he would lose caste.[55]

Zwemer wrote of such 'Nicodemus-souls' without condemnation: 'In all mission fields, the experience has been similar. In the days of persecution, of intolerance, and of open hostility toward the religion of Christ, those who were afraid to confess Him before men, and yet believed in Him secretly, came by night.'[56] Instead, he offered the following argument, published in the proceedings of a 1906 Conference in Cairo on evangelization in Muslim lands, as a justification for their secrecy in belief:

To baptize publicly in Damascus or Teheran or Morocco when the government is purely Mohammedan and the population ignorant and fanatical would be a serious mistake. In countries under Christian rule, English, French, German, or Dutch, it may be both safe and wise to advise a convert to profess Christ boldly in baptism, as a proof of his sincerity and a testimony to others. The battle for religious liberty must be fought and won at some time, but no one can decide for another when that time has come.[57]

Should the context require it, Nicodemism is alive and well, with Joseph of Arimathea remaining a prominent example for any who choose to hide their faith out of fear.

Michelangelo Buonarroti's *Entombment*

Now in the National Gallery in London, Michelangelo Buonarroti's *Entombment* (161.7 × 149.9 cm, oil painting on wood) is unfinished and shrouded in considerable mystery. Absent from contemporary accounts of the life and works of Michelangelo, the painting has been connected with documentary evidence, discovered in 1971, that suggests the artist was commissioned to paint an altarpiece for

Rome's Basilica di Sant' Agostino in 1500–01, subject unknown, and that he failed to complete the work, returning the money involved. If so, the unfinished piece was then lost until the 1640s when an inventory of the Farnese collection mentioned a painting by Michelangelo of Christ being carried to his tomb by 'Mary, St James and Simon of Cyrene'.[58] (Such a description also reminds us of the confusion, already noted, between Joseph and Nicodemus and adds yet another name, Simon of Cyrene, to the potential uncertainty about the identities of the figures in some of these scenes.) In poor condition, thrown out, and destined to be made into furniture, the painting was bought in the nineteenth century for a pittance by a Scot, Robert Macpherson, and taken to Britain; in 1868 he sold it to the National Gallery for a very handsome profit (£2000).[59] Despite attempts to attribute the painting to other artists and the glaring gaps in its history, a recent thorough sifting of the evidence by P. McCouat led him to accept that Michelangelo was the most likely painter of the piece.[60]

Unusually for an entombment scene, the group of figures is seen from the front, as they ascend a set of steps backwards, the tomb's unfinished entrance appearing to the upper right. Christ is carried on a linen cloth, head high with his naked body facing square on to viewers, supported under the arms from behind by an older, balding, bearded figure of Joseph of Arimathea, and also by two younger, muscular, and well-defined figures—Saint John on the left in red and a distinctly female-looking, but probably male figure, most likely Nicodemus, on the right—who are holding a linen strip under his hips, with their upper bodies curving away from the corpse's upper body. Two women flank these figures: the first, Mary Magdalene, in the lower left corner, on her knees; and the second, another Mary, in the upper right corner, standing and facing out of the composition to the right. To the lower right is the space for the Virgin, a part of the painting that was not even begun by the artist.

Of the faces of the figures completed, only Mary Magdalene shows an emotion, sadness, on her face; the others look 'either neutral, self absorbed or even a little bored' (so McCouat).[61] The overall composition itself also lacks realism, though A. Graham-Dixon's suggestion that visitors to the National Gallery should kneel before the image and see it from the perspective of the viewer of the high altarpiece as was originally intended, does improve matters (though it also brings such keen students some attention from the gallery's ever-watchful staff).[62] For unexplained reasons, some online reproductions also stretch the composition height-wise, giving a broadly similar effect. Even so, it is not an easy painting to appreciate in aesthetic terms, and Graham-Dixon has speculated that the painting's abandonment was related to the imbalances—all set to be worsened by the addition of the Virgin—created by the framing.[63] Whatever the reason, the painting remained unfinished and, during the artist's own lifetime at least, unmentioned.

The figure of Joseph is placed at the top of the stairs, head bowed forwards and close to the head/hair of the dead Christ, his hands placed under the arms of the corpse. Dwarfed by the pale corpse and the two outwardly curving figures at Christ's hips, and further distanced from viewers by the viewing position presupposed by its placement as a high altarpiece, the Joseph of the *Entombment* is a much diminished figure. (A comparison of this composition with van der Weyden's *Descent* or Botticelli's *Milan Pietà* makes this abundantly clear.) Viewers look up over Jesus' dead body into the distant, downwards but ultimately evasive eyes of the man from Arimathea. This effect is further enhanced by the fact that he was left unfinished; apart from the flesh tones of his face, the burnished bald dome of his head, and the hair of his beard and his (friar's) fringe, there is no body or clothing detail, but only a blank where they should have been; even had they been finished, however, his garments would struggle to compete visually with the shiny red silkiness of St John's clothing. While retaining his position at the head of the body, leading the way in manoeuvring the corpse to the tomb, and being the embodiment of age and experience among the scene's figures, Joseph has lost his centrality to the event.

When entombment scenes were presented sideways on, the compositional shape kept a balance between Joseph and Nicodemus as they held the body aloft. But as the group rotated feet towards the front, as with Michelangelo's *Entombment*, Joseph tended to recede and even on some occasions to disappear altogether. In Caravaggio's *The Entombment of Christ* (*c*.1601–04), for example, Christ's body is slightly turned feet towards the front, with the legs held by Nicodemus, the torso by St John (single-handedly!), and with three female figures (the Virgin, and two Marys) standing behind the carriers. Joseph no longer even appears, his position at the head of the corpse disappearing into the darkness of Caravaggio's background. Central and active as Joseph is in the burial scenes of the Synoptic Gospels, he could be easily marginalized by an artist's choice of composition. One part of the development of the Joseph tradition that must be acknowledged then is his occasional absence from scenes in which he has, at other times, played a central role.

Political Allegory and Simon Marmion's *Ducal Lamentation*

Before leaving the paintings of Joseph of Arimathea, a recent discussion of one additional painting requires our attention. The painting is the so-called *Ducal Lamentation*, attributed by some art historians to Flemish painters such as Hugo van der Goes or Simon Marmion and by others to later copyists of such painters, and the discussion is that of 'scholar and collector' A. Soudavar in his *Decoding Old Masters: Patrons, Princes and Enigmatic Paintings of the 15th Century*, published in 2008 by I. B. Taurus.[64]

Soudavar has argued from the history of the painting and its copies, the portraiture of the four figures around the Virgin and Christ, and the interaction between the two men carrying the body, that the image is not just another lamentation scene.[65] His summary bears full quotation:

[T]his Lamentation allegorically represents Duke Philip the Good of Burgundy who is dressed in black and is trying to lift Christianity after the fall of Constantinople in 1453. The Duke is soliciting the help of the Holy Roman Emperor Frederick III, as his son Charles the Bold, depicted as St John, is looking on, along with his wife Isabella of Portugal, depicted as Mary Magdalene, who is in mourning. It was painted by Simon Marmion, the most celebrated illuminator of the age, and by the order of Bishop Guillaume Fillastre (1400–73), who was the most ardent supporter of Philip in his oath—pronounced at the famous Feast of the Pheasant—to recapture Constantinople. While the composition obviously depicts a Lamentation scene, its underlying theme—and main purpose—was to blame Philip's aborted crusading efforts on the noncooperation of Emperor Frederick III.[66]

Many scholars will have experienced an intervention into their area of specialism by an outsider, often well qualified in a cognate field, who offers a startlingly different perspective on a long-standing problem or issue. Such offerings occasionally draw positive responses, but often they languish without discussion. Though Soudavar is certainly better known for his publications on Persian/Iranian Art,[67] it is not yet apparent that his book on *Decoding Old Masters* qualifies as such an offering, though it is fair to say that the book's claim of 'innovation', combined with an absence of scholarly reviews, is not encouraging. It is clear, however, that this present writer is not qualified to either confirm or refute Soudavar's general thesis. Fortunately, this volume is concerned only with Joseph and what has been done with the Arimathean through the centuries. If Soudavar is right, then what follows shows the role that Joseph of Arimathea could take in the high politics of fifteenth-century Europe. If he is wrong, however, we can instead see how Joseph has helped generate a modern political allegory that has been attributed—if unsuccessfully—to a little-known painting from that period.

On 17 February 1454, near Lille, Philip the Good, the Duke of Burgundy and one of the most powerful men in Europe, had taken a conditional oath—should his health allow!—that he would go on crusade with the King of France, a task then understood as freeing Constantinople from the Turks rather than taking Jerusalem and the Holy Land. When Pope Pius II vowed in 1463 to lead the crusade personally, Philip's arrangements were set in train, but then collapsed a year later with the pope's sudden death.[68] By the time the new pope, Paul II, tried to push Philip into resuming the crusade, the general indifference of Emperor Frederick and the other European princes and the increasing weariness of Philip himself left him reluctant to fulfil his oath. With the Pope's incessant badgering as the backdrop, Fillastre wrote a letter to Paul II defending Philip and attacking Frederick's inaction. Following that communication, Soudavar argued, the Bishop commissioned a painting from Marmion that would 'illustrate his main argument in a more vivid way':[69]

The Duke had indeed tried to 'lift' Christianity and had solicited the help of the Emperor and his princes, but to no avail; if blame there was, it was on Frederick and not on Philip. Thus a painting in which Frederick was avoiding the solicitations of Philip would indeed complement Fillastre's written argument.[70]

Patronage has so far played little role in our discussion of the portraits of Joseph in the paintings of the European Renaissance. Indeed, it has been noted that it was Nicodemus who tended to be the subject most often rendered with a patron's portrait, with Joseph often conforming to a 'type' derived from a prominent painting such as van der Weyden's *Descent*. In the *Ducal Lamentation*, however, Soudavar claimed that the patron Fillastre had required the painter to base the various figures, not on himself or on members of his family, but rather on his political ally, Philip the Good (and his wife and son), and his political opponent, Frederick III. Soudavar's identification of these two historical figures according to their facial features—with the man at the head as Philip the Good and the man at the feet as Frederick III—is further supported by specific details of their clothing. The black Burgundian garments of Philip match the garb that the Duke typically wore following the assassination of his father, John the Fearless, in 1419, and the firestone on the sword hilt, hanging from a golden belt, was his symbol.[71] Similarly, the jewelled medallion worn on the red hat of the lower figure was a symbol of the Habsburg emperors, and appeared on the coinage of Frederick III.[72] The respective positions of these powerful and wealthy individuals in the composition was dictated by Fillastre's politics, with an earnest Philip looking down upon a largely indifferent Frederick as he tried, without success, to lift the body of 'Christianity'.

Soudavar was eventually unable to decide which of the two figures, Philip or Frederick, represented Joseph and which represented Nicodemus, however. He pointed out that the Arimathean was usually clad in rich garments, but had to note that this feature applies to both men in the painting. The sombre garments of the Philip figure may not be the ornate clothes of some painted Josephs, but historical reasons demanded that the Duke of Burgundy's wealth be recorded in different fashion, through a gold belt and a sword. It was also noteworthy that although the political message seen as imprinted upon the painting by Soudavar required that these two biblical characters be separated into categories of 'political ally' and 'political opponent', their biblical portrayals are not especially amenable to being identified in that way. Nicodemus and Joseph are not so distinct in character that Soudavar was prepared to identify either as being the 'ally' figure or the 'opponent' figure. Once again the figure of Joseph had been rendered as ambiguous, as effectively being interchangeable with Nicodemus, with the tone of 'opponent' now possibly being attributed to the man from Arimathea. While it continues to seem likely that the Philip figure is Joseph, one cannot be sure and that is enough to introduce a new Joseph into the discussion.

Visualizing the biblical Joseph

Though something of the creativity of the earlier literary sources can be seen in the images examined, it is fair to say that the dominance of these four image-scenes in Renaissance art tended to restrict the Josephs portrayed to those preached by contemporary ecclesiastical traditions. The scriptural tensions noted in chapter one were by and large minimized by the dominant versions of the Church's passion story: Joseph was portrayed as a figure of substantial wealth, power, and influence, as a man of age, experience, and courage, as a publicly revealed believer in Christ (the Nicodemite advocacy of secrecy being absent from pictorial representations as far as I am aware), as a man of occasional emotion but consistent and conspicuous piety, as appealing in supplication to Pilate, as one grouped with the mournful saints and the Virgin, and as a near-constant companion to Nicodemus in burying Jesus.

For all their general consistency, however, these portrayals of Joseph could also reflect the more discrete mores of surrounding society. The deep emotion attributed to Joseph by Botticelli in the *Milan Pietà*, for example, reflected the fashionable religious fervour of a late fifteenth-century Florence under the reforms of Savonarola. Yet the restriction of artworks to those who could pay well for their production—rich dynasties, the Church—meant that Joseph's portrayal as a wealthy man was unlikely ever to fade away as an image. In fact, he was far more likely to disappear altogether than he was to appear in the garb of a common man (the Bouts portrait of a pious Joseph at prayer clothed plainly being the exception that proves the rule). The unadorned black garments of the *Ducal Lamentation* reflect the long-standing grief of a patron's friend and ally, and not any renunciation of wealth. Rather it was the golden belt and sword of Philip the Good as Joseph/Nicodemus that served to emphasize the deep connection between wealth and political power, with Joseph readily available to become the visible and legitimizing embodiment of the wealth and status of the dukes, princes, kings, and emperors of Europe.

As was the case with the influence of a Chrysostom, an Augustine, and a Jerome in chapter two, so it was also with the influence of the paintings of a van der Weyden or a Botticelli. Of the works examined here, the works of those two men have had extensive histories of influence while the works of Bening and Michelangelo have had a more restricted impact. The former's illuminated prayer book was the possession of a single man for much of its early existence and the latter's unfinished *Entombment* languished unknown for centuries. The types that each of these paintings represent continued to promulgate the image of the pious rich Arimathean across Western Europe, however. As this method of transmission developed over time, it would not only have illuminated the scriptural portraits within the Gospels and their reception, it would also have interacted with and enhanced the status of the post-biblical Joseph, whose influence was already beginning to loom large in medieval Europe, especially—as we shall now see—in the historiography of the British Isles.

The Glastonbury Joseph

How did Joseph of Arimathea come to visit Britain?

The popularity of the *Vulgate* Gospels and of the *Gospel of Nicodemus*, combined with the increasing prevalence of paintings of Joseph in Renaissance art, do much to explain how the man from Arimathea became familiar to the peoples of Western Europe. They do nothing at all, however, to explain how the man himself physically came to visit the West, and especially Britain's southwest. D. K. E. Crawford has noted the appearance of Joseph in *The Book of the Bee*, a thirteenth-century compilation of traditions of the Eastern Church collected by Mar Shlimon, who was appointed Bishop of Basra (now in Iraq) in 1222. Within, Joseph is described as one of the 70, as owning the upper room, as preaching in Galilee after Jesus' death, and as eventually dying in his hometown of 'Ramah';[1] it is certainly not the case, therefore, that all the oldest traditions about Joseph of Arimathea agree in seeing him departing for Somerset and Glastonbury. With the establishment of the Latin Kingdom of Jerusalem in 1099, such Eastern traditions might conceivably have become known to churchmen from the West. There would have been little incentive for them to 'export' stories about his post-burial life and death in the Holy Land to their own homelands in Europe, however, and virtually none at all for them to have claimed that he physically went there. So why did Joseph end up travelling to Britain?

Two answers have been suggested. For some, the impetus for the link was provided by Glastonbury Abbey, either as part of an authentic tradition about an actual visit or as a creative invention of the monks, most likely generated by their financial interest in developing the lucrative pilgrim trade after the disastrous abbey fire of 1184 which destroyed most of its buildings. For others, the link was created within the continental Grail romance traditions and only transferred secondarily to the abbey. We will consider each in turn.

The earliest mention of Joseph at Glastonbury dates to around 1247, in what is accepted by scholars to be one of a number of revisions introduced into William of Malmesbury's *De Antiquitate Ecclesie Glastonie* by a copyist (his work was completed in the 1130s).[2] The insertion reads:

... St Philip, as Freculph [Bishop of Lisieux] attests in the fourth chapter of his second book [*c*.830], came to the land of the Franks where he converted many to the faith by his preaching and baptised them. Desiring to spread the word further he sent twelve of his disciples to Britain to teach the word of life. It is said [*ut ferunt*] that he appointed as their leader his very dear friend Joseph of Arimathea, who had buried the Lord. They came to Britain in 63AD, the fifteenth year after the assumption of the blessed Mary and confidently began to preach the faith of Christ... [I]n the thirty first year after the passion of the Lord, the fifteenth after the assumption of the glorious Virgin, they completed the chapel as they had been instructed, making the lower part of all its walls of twisted wattle, an unsightly construction no doubt, but one adorned by God with many miracles. Since it was the first one in that territory, the [S]on of God dignified it with a greater honour by dedicating it in honour of his mother.[3]

A later hand towards the end of the thirteenth century added the following: 'The Book of the deeds of the famous King Arthur bears witness that the highly-born [*nobilem*] decurion Joseph of Arimathea, together with his son named Joseph and very many others, came into greater Britain, now called England, and ended his life there.'[4]

Arriving at Glastonbury Abbey in the wake of the appointment in 1126 of its new abbot—the powerful Norman figure, Henry of Blois (1101–71), soon-to-be Bishop of Winchester and the younger brother of King Stephen (*c*.1095–1158)—William had attempted to produce an account of its many traditions, both written and oral, in a volume which would increase its standing in the recently established Norman kingdom. He noted that the place was a spiritual centre of long standing, with many saints resting there (St Patrick, St Bridget, and St Indracht), and that its little wattle church, the '*vetusta ecclesia*' (old church), dedicated to the Virgin Mary, was originally built in the second century by unnamed missionaries sent from Rome at the request of a British king, Lucius (*c*.166). A later editor was to add the names of Phagan and Deruvian to William's account of the missionaries.[5] In a second work, *The Chronicle of the Kings of England* (the final revision of which took place *c*.1140), William noted that if St Philip had preached in Gaul, as 'Freculphus relates in the fourth chapter of his second book', then missionaries might have been sent onwards to Britain. But this was a mere possibility, he felt: 'But that I may not seem to balk the expectation of my readers by vain imaginations, leaving all doubtful matter I shall proceed to the relation of substantial truths.'[6] J. A. Robinson spoke for critical historical scholarship generally when he concluded that the 'general method of his work makes it practically certain that [William] had never heard the name of Joseph of Arimathea in connexion with Glastonbury'.[7]

Though Joseph's place in the abbey's origin narrative was well established by the mid-fourteenth century—royal permission to search for his body at Glastonbury was granted by Edward III to a vision-led 'John Blome of London' in 1345—little public capital was made from his 'presence' there until the long abbotship (1375–1420) of John Chinnock; something that is inexplicable if the story of Joseph's visit to the West Country was created to attract late-twelfth/early-thirteenth-century pilgrims. Even the 1247 insertion into William's *De Antiquitate* was tentative in claiming that Joseph came to Glastonbury; 'It is said' hardly suggests great confidence. In fact, the monks focused their attention post-fire of 1184 on developing the legends of King Arthur as a way of attracting pilgrims, claiming to have uncovered the bodies of Arthur and Guinevere in 1191 and subsequently gaining royal patronage through their possession of these Arthurian relics. The wattle church destroyed in the fire and the identity of its builder(s) played no role in their early attempts to attract pilgrims.

The history of Glastonbury Abbey's use of the Joseph tradition hardly seems to demonstrate the outburst of creativity that would have been required to bring such an unusual visitor to Britain in the first place. Instead, Glastonbury seems to have been, in Crawford's words, 'the hesitant recipient rather than the originator of the link between Joseph and Britain'.[8] His presence there appears to have been only an afterthought.

The second answer proposed is that Joseph came to Britain via a detour through the Arthurian Grail legends, initially popular in continental Europe. Dominating the early French romance tradition was Chrétien de Troyes' *Perceval: Le Conte du Graal* (*Percival: The Story of the Grail*), a work based on a variety of earlier texts and legends, and written around the mid 1180s. (Its author's untimely death meant that it remained unfinished.) Produced for Chrétien's patron, Count Philip of Flanders, this work takes Britain as its narrative setting, and tells the story of Perceval, a young man born in Wales who becomes a knight under British King Arthur. While staying in the castle of 'the Fisher King', Perceval sees a procession of precious objects, including a bleeding lance and a golden jewel-encrusted Grail. Significantly, however, the Grail of the *Perceval* is not a cup or a chalice. When its use to serve as a host is described, the foodstuff that it is said to be improperly used in serving is fish, and not the liquid that might be expected of a cup.[9] In Chrétien's story, the Grail is more akin to a platter or dish, with no literal connection to the bloody events of Christ's passion. It should come as no surprise that Joseph is absent from Chrétien's *Perceval*.

The incomplete *Perceval* was soon receiving widespread attention, and a number of works were produced to conclude it. It was with this surge of activity at the close of the twelfth century that the work of the Burgundian poet, Robert de Boron, appeared. Though some have wondered if Robert knew *Perceval*, the consensus is that he must have been aware of it, given its popularity.[10] Combining his knowledge of Chrétien's romance with his knowledge of the canonical Gospels, and of apocryphal works such as the *Gospel of Nicodemus* and the *Vindicta Salvatoris* (which tells of a cloth bearing Christ's image curing an emperor's son, Titus), Robert produced a linked trilogy of prose romances, *Joseph d'Arimathie*, *Merlin*, and *Perceval* around 1200, with each work perhaps being based on an earlier poetic version.[11] Each became an influential work in its turn.

A single interpretive move made in Robert's *Joseph d'Arimathie* offers the likeliest explanation as to why Joseph eventually came to Britain. In developing Chrétien's images of the bleeding spear and the platter-Grail, the writer apparently decided to turn the Grail into a 'blood relic' of the cross, dropping the spear altogether. Moreover, this relic was not to be just a random container of liquid; it was to be the vessel used by Christ at the Last Supper (not, as we shall see, the easiest of story adjustments to make). Once this choice had been made, a further alteration to Chrétien's story became necessary. The *Perceval*'s largely incidental use of Britain as the backdrop for a romance about a chivalrous knight and his adventures was inevitably foregrounded in the *Joseph d'Arimathie*. Robert now needed to explain how Christ's cup had come to be in that country.[12]

Two minor figures in the passion story, Joseph of Arimathea and Nicodemus, were the most obvious candidates as the collector(s) of the blood of the crucified Christ. The appearance of Jesus' cup at the foot of the cross required a narrative mechanism by which the cup used at the Last Supper could have passed into the hands of one of these men, however. Robert's solution is perhaps not especially convincing to modern readers (or even to all medieval ones, as we shall see), but it certainly does the job in his narrative: Jesus is arrested in the upper room, not Gethsemane; the cup is taken by one of the Jews involved in the arrest and passed to Pilate, who passes it on to Joseph of Arimathea when he requests the body, as a reward for his devotion to 'that prophet', Jesus; it is thus in his possession when he takes the body from the cross and is available to him for use as he collects the still-flowing blood of Christ. Subsequently, as a response to his faithfulness, the risen Christ declares Joseph to be the guardian of the Grail with its precious cargo of blood. He thus becomes the one destined to ensure the arrival of the Grail in Britain, through his descendants (he himself dies in the land of his birth), both in literary terms in the text of Robert's *Joseph d'Arimathie* and its descendants, and in historical terms in the future traditions of the British Isles.[13]

Robert de Boron's *Joseph d'Arimathie*

Robert de Boron's *Joseph d'Arimathie* (*c*.1200) contains three major sections: the crucifixion and Joseph's subsequent imprisonment; the healing of Vespasian and his releasing of Joseph; and the story of Joseph's family until the time of his death.

The first section begins with an indication of Christ's purpose in coming into the world, the redemption of the world from the sin of

Eve first and Adam second, followed by a brief sketch of Jesus' ministry.[14] Pilate and Joseph of Arimathea are introduced, with the latter being described as follows: 'This Pilate had in his service a soldier named Joseph, who followed Jesus Christ to many places and loved him deeply in his heart, but dared not show it for fear of the other Jews. . . . ' (Joseph later suggests another reason for his silence— his fear that Christ would not trust him because of the company he kept.)[15] Judas's decision to betray Jesus leads him to Caiaphas's house, where a group are discussing the capturing of Jesus. Joseph is present and is grieved by their 'sinful' words, but when Judas offers to sell Jesus to them, though it 'weighed heavily up on his heart . . . he dare do nothing.'[16] Jesus is captured in the upper room, and his 'vessel' is taken by an unnamed Jew. The Roman governor Pilate tries, but cannot save him, and when he washes his hands as the Jews take Jesus away to crucify him, the Jew gives Pilate the vessel taken from the upper room.[17]

Filled with anguish at Jesus' death, Joseph asks Pilate for his body as payment for the long service of himself and his knights. Pilate assents, but when his further request that the governor himself give orders for the corpse's release is refused, Joseph hesitates. His fear that the Jews wll not hand over the body to him is proved right when he tries to take it; they would rather kill Joseph, they say. On Joseph's return to Pilate, the governor orders Nicodemus to accompany Joseph to the cross. As they depart, however, Pilate recalls the vessel in his possession: 'Joseph, you love that prophet dearly', he states more than asks. On hearing Joseph's 'yes', Pilate continues: 'I have a vessel of his, given to me by one of the Jews who was present at his capture, and I've no wish to keep anything belonging to him.' Joseph takes possession of the Grail.

At the cross, Nicodemus's forcefulness leads to success, and the Jews go to Pilate to protest as the body is removed. Cradling the body 'tenderly' and washing it 'gently', Joseph sees blood flowing and collects it in the vessel before wrapping the body in a sheet for burial. Following the burial, he departs. The Jews are worried that the body might yet come back to life, however, and set guards over it. When the body disappears, they panic and decide to kill Joseph and Nicodemus secretly so that they can be blamed for the body's disappearance. Nicodemus is forewarned of their intent and escapes, but Joseph is caught, interrogated (without success since he does not know where the body is), badly beaten and then entombed without the Grail, seemingly forever. Pilate, aware that Joseph is missing, is described as 'most distressed and heavy-hearted, for he was the best of friends to him'. The narrator concludes with the observation that 'Joseph was missing for a long time'.

Soon after the imprisonment has begun, Joseph is visited by the risen Jesus. Initially, Joseph sees only a great light and fails to recognize Jesus, who then explains who he is. Assured that Jesus of Nazareth and Jesus Christ are one and the same, Joseph pleads for mercy, explaining that, though imprisoned for Jesus' sake, he 'never dared to speak to you, for I feared, Lord, that you wouldn't trust me because of the people I conversed with, keeping company as I did with the ones who meant you harm'. For Jesus, however, having a friend among enemies meant that Joseph could come to his aid on the cross when no one else could. What Jesus then terms the 'secret love' between the two, a love unknown to the disciples, will be revealed to all because 'you shall have the sign of my death in your keeping', the Grail. He then produces and gives the cup to Joseph, instructing him that it must be guarded by no more than three keepers, in the 'name of the Father, the Son, and the Holy Spirit', the 'three powers [who] are one and the same being in God'. Jesus explains this reward for Joseph's service; the vessel of the sacrament and all of the details of the altar will remind all of what Joseph has done. Other words are spoken—secret words—recorded in a high book to which the narrator does not claim access, thus continuing the 'creed of the great mystery of the Grail'. As Jesus leaves, he encourages Joseph and promises him that he will eventually be released: 'Show love for the one who will come to free you and tell him of the three powers [the Trinity] just as the word comes to you, for the Holy Spirit will be with you and will teach you things of which you know nothing.'[18]

At this point Robert inserted an intriguing explanatory note, framed with two further statements which emphasize Joseph's long entombment:

And so Joseph remained in prison: Of his imprisonment nothing is said by the apostles or those who established the scriptures, for they knew nothing about Joseph except that, because of his affection for Christ, he had asked to be granted His body. Some of the apostles did hear of Joseph's disappearance, but they did not speak of it since they committed nothing to the scriptures except what they had seen or heard themselves; and having seen and heard nothing of Joseph they had no wish to write about him—and they did not want his disappearance to make people uneasy about the faith, but such fear is wrong, and Our Lord says why when he speaks of the false glory of the word. *Joseph stayed imprisoned a long time.*[19]

Here we see Robert's explanation for Joseph's absence from the canonical texts after the burial, and his justification for the apocryphal tale that he was telling.

Robert's second section introduces the one who will release Joseph. It relates the story of a wandering pilgrim—an eyewitness to Jesus' miracles—who travels to Rome. On finding the emperor's son, Vespasian (not Titus), stricken with leprosy and shut away, the pilgrim gives an account of Jesus' life and death to his host. Taken to the emperor, the pilgrim retells the story, with the added detail that even an item belonging to Jesus is able to cure the emperor's son;[20] he is then held as a hostage to the truth of his claim while the emperor sends messengers to Judaea. Pilate admits the truth of the pilgrim's claims to the messengers, but initially finds himself under investigation for murder, and appeals to the Jews to back up his account. The pilgrim is vindicated when a woman, Veronica, is found to possess a cloth with the image of Jesus upon it, a cloth which, when taken to Rome, heals Vespasian completely.[21] (The story is adapted by Robert from an earlier text, the *Vindicta Salvatoris*, in which Titus is healed by Veronica's cloth.) The emperor's son sets off for Jerusalem to avenge Jesus. After hearing the accounts of the Jews for himself, he acquits Pilate and begins to execute those whom he considers guilty of murdering Jesus. One of them, however, offers knowledge of the whereabouts of Joseph in exchange for the lives of himself and his family. Miraculously, Vespasian finds Joseph still alive, and is instructed by him as to the identity of the one who has healed him in Rome and who has sustained Joseph during his long imprisonment. With that Joseph converts Vespasian 'to a firm belief in the true faith'.[22] The Jew and his family are cast adrift in a boat, at the mercy of Christ, and the others are all sold as slaves;[23] the Roman emperor's son Vespasian thus avenges Jesus' death.

In the third section, the focus is on Joseph's family. His sister Enigeus and her husband Bron are delighted to see him still alive and willingly accept the tenets of the faith that he relates to them. Robert's *Joseph d'Arimathie* concludes with Joseph's death in his own land, but not before three separate 'parties' are sent into the West: Bron (eventually to be known as the 'rich Fisher King') and all of his family but one; Petrus, a disciple; and Alain Li Gros, the only one of Bron's 12 sons who remains unmarried. They are all to go to the 'vales of Avalon', described as 'a lonely place in the West' there to eventually meet up once more. The vessel, now named by all involved as the 'Grail', is to travel with Bron, a miraculously delivered letter is to go with Petrus, and, after many adventures, it is to be the son of Alain who will one day appear in Avalon, read and interpret the letter entrusted to Petrus, and thus allow the Grail story to resume once again.[24]

Responses to Robert de Boron's *Joseph d'Arimathie*

The popularity of Robert's trilogy was immediate. Alongside Chrétien's earlier work and a few other contemporary writings such as what is known as the *First Continuation*, Robert's work helped form the basis for the *Lancelot-Grail Cycle*, also known as the *Vulgate Cycle*, a series of five independent works—*Lancelot*, *Queste del Saint Graal*, *Morte Artu*, plus two slightly later works, the *Estoire del Saint Graal* and the *Estoire Merlin*—which together describe the events that occur during the Grail's time on earth.[25] In the *Lancelot*, *Queste del Saint Graal*, and the *Estoire del Saint Graal*, Robert's depiction of Joseph of Arimathea as a 'knight, apostle, and grail guardian' who died in his homeland and passed the Grail to Britain through his sister's husband is developed into one in which he becomes 'the founding father of Britain' (so Chase).[26]

Commentary about Joseph appears throughout the *Lancelot*. An apostle, a miracle-worker, and the one who removed Jesus' body from the cross, he is described in chivalric terms as the first Christian knight, a man-at-arms who is sent to Britain—with the Grail—by God in order to conqueror it, an achievement which seems to have been understood as proceeding by way of conversion to his faith. His son Galahad is described as both a knight and as the first Christian

King of Wales. Joseph is also described as a distant ancestor of Arthur's Lancelot who, through his lineage back through Joseph, is also said to have King David as his ancestor.[27]

The *Queste* concentrates on Joseph's missionary activity rather than any military prowess. He is described as not being Lancelot's ancestor (echoed in the *Estoire del Saint Graal*), an otherwise unexplained alteration that serves to highlight his explicit role as the ancestor of every other Grail knight. His son Galahad appears only by allusion, but another son, Josephus, appears and is included in a number of 'flashback' scenes.[28]

In the *Estoire del Saint Graal*, those flashbacks are renarrated as they happen, once again placing the focus on Joseph's religious role. Though the *Estoire* notes that he had served Pilate as a soldier for seven years, it is also clear the battles won against infidel foes in Britain are fought by converted kings and not by Joseph as a knight. After the events of the crucifixion, his miraculous long imprisonment, now said to be 42 years in length, and his release by Vespasian, Joseph is tasked by God with leading his people from the East to the West (a commission explicitly compared with Moses's role in delivering Israel from Egypt). He is first baptized by St Philip in Jerusalem and then departs with his son Josephus to 'preach, work miracles, convert and baptize' in the West.[29] While Josephus eventually becomes the celibate head of the British Church and takes on the guardianship of the Grail, Joseph has another son, Galahad, who becomes the King of Wales and is the ancestor of all of the Grail knights, Lancelot excepted, putting Joseph at the centre of both spiritual *and* political life in Britain.

The Grail traditions grew dynamically, with variations arising from the beginning. In one addition to the story of the knight Gawain in the *First Continuation*, for example, Joseph is described as having filled the Grail with the blood of the crucified Christ, taken the body down, buried it, been imprisoned and exiled, and as having travelled to Britain with the Grail *and Nicodemus!*[30] In the fourteenth-century *Joseph of Arimathea*, an alliterative poem in vernacular English based on the *Queste* and the *Estoire de Saint Graal*, the Grail was seen as a sacred object, but as no more than that. Seemingly disinterested in any of the chivalric activities associated with the Grail quest, this version of the Joseph story was interested only in what D. A. Lawton terms 'the conversion of heathen potentates', its writer's themes primarily being 'literary and devotional' ones.[31] Intriguingly, in this text written in English there appears to be no interest about Joseph's activities in Britain. Glastonbury and the specifics of its claims about Joseph are mentioned nowhere, and its inclusion of the story about Joseph's release by Vespasian after 42 years of imprisonment seems to deny the possibility of his arrival in the West Country by the traditional Glastonbury date of 63 CE. This author clearly had some other purpose in mind in writing than validating the abbey's story.

Robert's account of Joseph of Arimathea was not received uncritically by everyone, however. In the late thirteenth century, a Dutchman, Jacob van Maerlant, was busily writing numerous works in his own language, some of which were heavily reliant upon French romantic works. In producing his own Grail story (*Historie van den Grale*), however, he had harsh things to say about Robert's *Joseph d'Arimathie*. W. P. Gerritsen has outlined three of his major disagreements to serve as examples which *typify* rather than *constitute* the sum of Jacob's objections.[32] First, Jacob took issue with Robert's portrayal of Joseph as a soldier in Pilate's service:

[A]bout his being [Pilate's] knight I do not say I've ever read in any other story than only in this one. The truest story I've read about this tells that Pilate was a pagan, as were all his knights. All those belonging to his retinue were uncircumcised men. Joseph was a Jew, and very wealthy. . . .[33]

Second, he objected to the story's depiction of Jesus being seized by his enemies in the upper room and not the Garden of Gethsemane, the change in location, of course, being the literary mechanism by which Robert was able to explain how Jesus' cup from the Last Supper came to Pilate and thus to Joseph. Jacob's response was scathing: 'But this is surely a lie and an absurdity.'[34] Third, he objected both to the portrayal of Joseph's imprisonment as being 42 years long—'altogether a lie'— and to what he regarded as an obvious inaccuracy in the *Joseph d'Arimathie*: its mistaken claim that it was Vespasian who was cured by the image of the Lord on Veronica's cloth, and not Titus as recorded in the *Vindicta Salvatoris*. In response to these egregious errors, Jacob turned to what he considered an altogether more trustworthy source,

the *Gospel of Nicodemus*, using its account of a short overnight imprisonment to 'correct' the portrayal in Robert's flawed story.[35]

Jacob's irritation at Robert's story and his willingness to dismiss its
contents in favour of his own views was not an attitude shared by
everyone, however. As we have already seen in chapter two, p. 42,
Jacobus de Voragine had included a summary of the *Gospel of Nicodemus* in volume 1 of his *Legenda aurea*. In volume 3 of the *Legenda
aurea*, however, we find a long imprisonment story which is almost
identical to that found in Robert's work, explicitly juxtaposed with
the short imprisonment account of the *Gospel of Nicodemus*:

We also read that when Titus entered the city, he noticed one particularly
thick wall and gave orders to break into it. Inside the wall they found an
old man, venerable in age and appearance. When asked who he was, he
replied that he was Joseph, from Arimathea, a city of Judea, and that the
Jews had had him shut in and immured because he had buried Christ. He
added that from that time to the present he had been fed with food from
heaven and comforted by divine light. In the *Gospel of Nicodemus*, however,
it is said that though the Jews had walled him in, the risen Christ broke
him out and brought him to Arimathea. It could be said that once released
he would not desist from preaching Christ and therefore was walled in a
second time.[36]

Rather than adopt Jacob van Maerlant's views and dismiss one or
other of the accounts, Jacobus instead imagined a second imprisonment for Joseph that did not actually exist in either version of the
story in circulation in order to reconcile the two accounts.

With Sir Thomas Malory's highly influential translation into
English of the *Vulgate Cycle* and other Arthurian materials (including
some of his own) as *Le Morte D'Arthur*, compiled around 1470,
and with the widespread reproduction of these stories and many
others in other European languages, Joseph of Arimathea had now
become part of a major European medieval literary phenomenon.
Embedded deep within the mass of literature focused upon '*La
Matière de Bretagne*', 'the Matter of [Arthurian] Britain', he had
indeed become the founding father of literary Britain! He had not
as yet been brought to the attention of the people of the British Isles,
however. But that was about to change.

The history of Glastonbury Abbey to the mid thirteenth century

With the Grail now on its way to the West and with Joseph and his descendants firmly established as its guardians, it is time to return to Glastonbury, in the West Country of England, the place where the story would eventually find its primary home.

Set about 5 miles from the waters of the Bristol Channel on the Somerset Levels, the town of Glastonbury and its abbey face westwards at the end of an inland peninsula crowned by the Tor, surrounded by wet moors on three sides and joined to the higher ground to the east by a narrow strip of raised ground, always at least 10 metres above sea level.[37] Periodic flooding could reproduce the impression of an island; combined sea and river flooding in 1606, for example, reached St John's Church in the town, leaving many Glastonbury streets under water.[38] Despite its richness in natural resources such as spring water, peat, clay, and stone, P. Rahtz and L. Watts have nevertheless suggested that the location was particularly adopted as suitable for habitation because of its striking setting below the Tor, visible up to 25 miles away.[39] Settlement after 4000 BCE is evidenced by pits and hearths, arrowheads, animal remains, pottery, and trackways, with religious activity being demonstrated by numerous nearby barrows and stone circles. In the centuries just before Christ, 'marsh-edge settlements'—the so-called 'Lake villages'—appeared at Glastonbury and nearby Meare.[40]

With the Romans came exploitation of the area's mineral resources—lead and silver ores—enabled by the construction of the Fosse Way, the main road between Exeter and Lincoln, but with little other development.[41] Evidence for Christianity around Glastonbury in the Roman period is sparse and for its continuation after the fall of Rome virtually non-existent; Rahtz and Watts could only offer the suggestion that the origins of Christian Glastonbury were likely to be found in one of three sources, the Celtic churches to the West, the Mediterranean via trade routes, or the English church established in Kent by Augustine at the end of the seventh century.[42] Regardless of its origins, however, it is with the rise of Anglo-Saxon England that the area really began to take on its particular Christian hue. The list of early abbots reconstructed from grave markers (called 'pyramids' in literary sources) contains both British and Anglo-Saxon names, leaving open the possibility of a British origin for the abbey. A period of relative stagnation in the ninth and tenth centuries was brought to a close by the abbotship of Dunstan (b. *c.*910), appointed in 940 and responsible for the development of both buildings and technological skills at Glastonbury, before becoming Archbishop of Canterbury. By the time of the Domesday Book of 1086, created by the Norman conquerors to calculate the worth of the country for tax purposes, Glastonbury Abbey was the wealthiest in England.[43]

When the second Norman abbot, Henry of Blois, inspected his abbey in 1126, however, he was unimpressed with its state of repair. Though he himself was to be occupied by his many roles elsewhere and the status bestowed on him as King Stephen's brother—when Stephen was imprisoned for a while, Henry could legitimately claim to be the most powerful man in Britain—his period as abbot revived Glastonbury's fortunes. He gave valuable gifts to the abbey and also built 'many new buildings including a bell tower, chapter house, cloister, lavatory, refectory, dormitory, the infirmary with its chapel, a castellum (a princely "castle"-like structure within the grounds), an outer gate, a brewery, and stabling for houses'.[44]

Unfortunately, on 25 May 1184, not long after Henry's death in 1171, many of the buildings of the abbey were destroyed by a major fire. Though rebuilding began immediately—the Lady Chapel was quickly finished—the funding required to rebuild the whole was substantial. The initial spur towards rebuilding provided by the generous interest of Henry II faded with his death in 1189, and the accession of Richard I (also known as Richard the Lionheart), a king altogether more interested in events elsewhere, meant that rebuilding funds were scarce. Unlike other religious foundations in Britain with their well-known patron saints—Durham had St Cuthbert, Canterbury had St Augustine of Rome and, after his martyrdom in 1170, St Thomas Becket—Glastonbury's claim to a saintly patronage was weak. Though the bones of its former abbot, St Dunstan, had long been claimed at Canterbury, the Glastonbury monks produced them after the fire and built a shrine for them, arguing—to Canterbury's annoyance—that they had been recovered when the Kentish church had been sacked by the Danes in 1012 and hidden in the West Country.[45] It was with the discovery of the bones of King Arthur and his queen, Guinevere, in 1191, however, that the right note was struck and the abbey's fortunes began to recover.

This choice of 'patron' was an easy one for the monks to make. In his *Historia Regum Britanniae* (*c*.1136), Geoffrey of Monmouth (1100–55) had recounted the Arthurian legends as part of a much larger collection of stories about British history. In so doing, he had explicitly linked Arthur's Avalon to the West Country; the King, fatally wounded in battle near the river Cambula in Cornwall, was then carried away 'to the isle of Avalon for the healing of his wounds'.[46] In a Welsh work, Caradoc of Llancarfan's *Life of Gildas* written contemporaneously with Geoffrey's *Historia*, the abbot of Glastonbury is described as intervening in events with St Gildas to deliver a kidnapped Guinevere without bloodshed, thus bringing both king and queen to the town, but without identifying Glastonbury explicitly as Arthur's Avalon.[47] Though criticized by contemporaries as lacking any basis in history, Geoffrey's *Historia Regum Britanniae* was translated into vernacular languages and disseminated widely across Britain and continental Europe. (It is, in fact, credited by some with having a significant influence on the growth of the French romances.)[48] For Glastonbury's monks, Geoffrey and Caradoc's works not only offered them a high-profile patron, the great success of such works offered them 'free advertising' as well. As yet, however, no explicit literary link between Arthur and Glastonbury existed.

The first writings to make that connection would be two accounts from Gerald of Wales, both of which post-dated the discovery of the bodies of Arthur and Guinevere in 1191 (*Liber de Principis instructione*, *c*.1193; *Speculum Ecclesiae*, *c*.1216). Born in Pembrokeshire of Norman stock but with a blood connection to Welsh royalty, Gerald was well acquainted with the powers and authorities of his day, turning down several bishoprics, before becoming Archdeacon of Brecon. In 1193, he found himself in Glastonbury, a witness at one step removed from the events which followed the monks' search for Arthur's body. The search was said to have taken place at the prompting of a Henry II inspired by bardic tales about a hollowed-out oak buried 16 feet down (to avoid Saxon despoiling) and between two inscribed pyramids (*piramides*) in Glastonbury Abbey's graveyard.

Henry had died two years earlier, so the monks had certainly not rushed to follow any such prompting; indeed another account, that of Ralph of Coggleshall around 1194, suggests that the discovery had only occurred because a monk had requested that he be buried in that area.[49] Nevertheless, the abbot told Gerald that the monks had recovered the bones of a tall man (whose skull bore ten wounds— nine mended and one fatal—and whose shin bone was three inches longer than the tallest man present) and a woman with yellow hair (according to Gerald's later retelling, the hair was snatched out of the grave by a depraved monk and became dust). Beneath the bodies, a slab was found with a lead cross underneath it, bearing an inscription which read: 'Here in the Isle of Avalon lies buried the renowned King Arthur, with Guinevere, his second wife.' Gerald concluded his 1216 account by noting that the abbot had provided a fitting marble tomb for the bodies. Glastonbury thus had its principal shrine; that of a long-dead king whom some Britons still believed would return to lead them in battle. Aided by Dunstan's bones and the relics of other minor saints, the recovery of Arthur and Guinevere provided worthy relics for visitors to see, money began to flow into the abbey's coffers, and reconstruction began. Joseph of Arimathea, however, still did not figure in any of these tales of Glastonbury.

Described by J. Scott as the most notorious of Glastonbury's forgeries,[50] the *Charter of St Patrick* (*c.* late twelfth century) supplied two names, Phagan and Deruvian, for the preachers sent by Pope Eleutherius to King Lucius and expanded upon St Philip's brief appearance in William's *Chronicle of the Kings of England*. In the *Charter*, Patrick arrives in Glastonbury and discovers a chapel dedicated to the Virgin, which was built by 12 unnamed disciples sent by St Philip and St James to England, underlining Glastonbury's preeminence in the early evangelization of the British Isles. These disciples, the *Charter* claims, were given 12 pieces of land—the 'twelve hides'—by three unnamed pagan kings. Nevertheless, they failed to establish a vibrant church and its decline was only halted by the arrival of the pope's men. Climbing the Tor, Patrick finds an 'old oratory' constructed by Phagan and Deruvius 'at the inspiration of our Lord Jesus Christ in honour of St Michael the Archangel'. Despite this level of inventiveness, the *Charter* did not mention

Joseph of Arimathea either. Neither did any relics attributed to the man play a role in the period.[51]

By the 1230s–40s, however, a complication had clearly arisen for the monks. They began to respond, hesitantly, to the stories about Joseph that were contained within the *Vulgate Cycle*; presumably these texts (or news of them at least) had begun to reach England. In the *Estoire*, for example, Arthur and his story were prefaced by the account of Joseph's baptism in Jerusalem by St Philip, his divinely sanctioned journey to Britain, and his role in converting the country to Christianity. The French story's similarity to the Arthur narrative adopted by the abbey as a significant part of its self-presentation effectively forced the monks to respond. What they did was to incorporate a number of the *Vulgate Cycle*'s elements into their own 'origins' narrative. William of Malmesbury's *De Antiquitate*— too valuable to be replaced and already implicitly augmented by *St Patrick's Charter*—was altered by the addition of the tentative 1247 claim discussed earlier, that Joseph of Arimathea was the leader of 12 disciples sent by St Philip as missionaries to Britain and that he personally came to Glastonbury and preached the gospel there in 63 CE. The man from Arimathea was thus finally inserted into the abbey's story and with minimal fuss.[52]

These Grail texts were not wholly acceptable to the monks, however. The Grail is noticeably absent from the 1247 insertion. While an acceptance of the *Cycle*'s Arthurian elements was necessary because of the abbey's claim to have unearthed King Arthur and Queen Guinevere in 1191, the Grail itself had no such relevance. Indeed, wider Church suspicion of its literal Christ-blood imagery and a failure to officially sanction the stories in which it appeared would become the most commonplace ecclesiastical response to such traditions. The literal idea of Christ's blood would later be turned by the Glastonbury monks into a very different kind of treasure, however: two relics in the form of silver cruets, one filled with Christ's sweat, the other with his blood. The *Cycle*'s chronology was also apparently problematic for the monks. By dating Joseph's arrival in Glastonbury to 63 CE, the 1247 copyist effectively forced his readers to ignore its account of a 42-year imprisonment in favour of an account with a much shorter imprisonment. For John of Glastonbury (d. 1360–77), writing his *Chronicle of Glastonbury Abbey* in the mid fourteenth

century (1340–42), this involved exchanging the *Cycle*'s long imprisonment for the short imprisonment of the *Gospel of Nicodemus*; he
named the latter text explicitly, reproducing it almost verbatim in his
account of the abbey's history. That the same thought was in the
mind of the 1247 copyist is made probable by the 63 CE date, but it
cannot be proven. Nevertheless, the earliest surviving manuscript of
the *Gospel of Nicodemus* in Old English was donated to Exeter
Cathedral by a Bishop Leofric (d. 1072),[53] and this would suggest
that the *Gospel* was easily available to the monks by the mid
thirteenth century. Whatever the 1247 copyist was thinking, however,
the end result of his work was a Joseph uniquely tailored to Glastonbury's own requirements.

John of Glastonbury's *Cronica sive Antiquitates Glastoniensis Ecclesie*

With the *Cronica sive Antiquitates Glastoniensis Ecclesie* of John of
Glastonbury, completed around 1340–42,[54] we can see the shape of
the Joseph story as it was known during the abbey's greatest years
between the mid fourteenth century and its destruction in the early
sixteenth century. Not all of what is now considered essential by some
to the Glastonbury story is included in his work, however; there are
no references to the planting of Joseph's staff on Weary-all Hill and
its growth as the Glastonbury Thorne, or to the Chalice Well, or to
the appearance of the young Jesus in the West Country at the side of
his rich tin trader uncle Joseph. These later additions would serve
different purposes. With John's selection and use of sources, however,
the version which was to be trumpeted nationally and abroad by the
abbots of Glastonbury at the peak of their power can be seen.

The *Cronica* was produced in a very different political and financial
world to that of William of Malmesbury or that of the 1247 copyist.
The abbey was enjoying a more secure financial position, a fact which
perhaps also explains the limited public development of the Joseph
tradition; Glastonbury had less need to attract new pilgrims. It opens
with a brief introduction about the abbey's early history, which ends
with a set of liturgical prayers, some of which are addressed to Joseph
as a saint and imply (some of) his characteristics and attributes:

Hail, glorious Joseph (*Ioseph gloriose*), who take your name from Arimathea, who saw with grief Christ who suffered for humankind, and who fervently and virtuously asked his body of the governor Pilate, that it might be buried on the day of preparation. Help us mightily in our struggle, that we may rise after him with grace. Amen.

Joseph, be a benevolent soldier (*miles… benignus*) for all who pray to you, that we may be turned from unworthy into worthy ministers.[55]

In the prologue, it becomes clear that John was dependent upon an augmented version of William's *De Antiquitate*, one containing an account of Glastonbury 'from the coming of St Joseph' to the time of Henry of Blois.[56] He outlines the location and extent of the 12 hides, before listing the saints interred at Glastonbury. Top of his list are Joseph of Arimathea, his son Josephes, and their companions. John admits that he is unsure about Phagan and Deruvian before moving on to St Patrick next and many others. He concludes:

I confess that I have by no means listed the names of all the saints who rest in the church of Glastonbury. Even if there had been no fire, so much time has passed that the persistence of any human being would be unable to investigate all of the saints who rest there; the knowledge of God alone comprehends how many saints bodies lie there.[57]

A list of Glastonbury's relics follows.[58]

John then reproduces the short imprisonment tradition of the *Gospel of Nicodemus* almost verbatim, under the heading: 'Here begins the treatise of St Joseph of Arimathea, taken from a book which the Emperor Theodosius found in Pilate's Council Chamber in Jerusalem'. He relates the story of how the apostle John left the Virgin Mary in the charge of Joseph, with Philip, when he departed Jerusalem for Ephesus, and how the man from Arimathea was present at her assumption, an account drawn from traditions echoing the fifth-century *Transitus Mariae*.

Next John describes St Philip's mission to the Franks (from William's *De Antiquitate*), before recounting an adapted version of the *Estoire*'s account of Philip's sending of Joseph, with his son Josephes, to Britain to preach the good news. More than 600 men and women came with him 'as is read in the book called the Holy Grail', though only 150 actually made it (due to the effects of sin), all miraculously flying to Britain on Josephes' shirt. Held captive by the King of

Wales, Joseph and his people are freed by a foreign king, Mordrain, and led to their rescue by a vision of the Lord. Joseph, his son, and ten others then travel through a Britain ruled by King Arviragus, in 63 CE, preaching the gospel, but to no avail. The pagan king is unwilling to convert, but gives the 12 men somewhere to live, an island at the edge of his kingdom, Ynswytryn, or 'the glass island'. John records a brief verse about this gift:

> The twelvefold band of men entered Avalon,
> Joseph, flower of Arimathea, is their chief.
> Josephes, Joseph's son, accompanies his father.
> The right to Glastonbury is held by these and the other ten.[59]

Combining material from the enlarged *De Antiquitate* and the *Charter of St Patrick*, John describes how a vision of the Archangel Gabriel leads the 12 to build an unsightly wattle church at Glastonbury, dedicated to the Virgin Mary and completed the same year that they had been sent by Philip to Britain, 15 years after Mary's assumption, and 31 years after Jesus' death.[60] As they serve their Lord there, the disciples receive gifts of more hides of land, resulting in their possessing 12 altogether. When the time comes for the disciples to be released from the 'workhouse of the body', they are buried on their land, with Joseph himself being buried on a *linea bifurcate* near the church (literally 'a divided line', though the meaning ascribed to that phrase is now unclear). The area is then given over to wilderness, to await the pope's missionaries in the second century. The thirteenth-century insertion to the *De Antiquitate*, which referred to the testimony of the 'Book of the deeds of the famous King Arthur' is then repeated: that the *nobilem decurionem* Joseph of Arimathea, together with his son Josephes and many others, came and died in Britain.

John next reproduces a pseudonymous Latin work attributed to a seventh-century Celtic bard named Melkin. J. A. Robinson described the poem as 'a queer piece of semi-poetical prose, intended to mystify and hardly capable of translation into English';[61] J. Ussher described it as being 'wholly unworthy to be read'.[62] Here is Robinson's valiant attempt:

Avalon's island, with avidity
Claiming the death of pagans,
More than all in the world beside,
For the entombment of them all,
Honoured by the chanting spheres of prophesy:
And for all time to come
Adorned it shall be
By them that praise the Highest
Abbadarè, mighty in Saphat,
Noblest of pagans
With countless thousands
There hath fallen on sleep
Amid these Joseph in marble,
Of Arimathea by name,
Hath found perpetual sleep:
And he lies on a two forked line
Next the south corner of an oratory
Fashioned of wattles
For the adoring of a mighty Virgin
By the aforesaid sphere-betokened
Dwellers in the place, thirteen in all,
For Joseph hath with him
In his sarcophagus
Two cruets (*duo fassula*), white and silver,
Filled with the blood and sweat
Of the Prophet Jesus.
When his sarcophagus
Shall be found entire, intact,
In time to come, it shall be seen
And shall be open unto all the world:
Thenceforth nor water nor the dew of heaven
Shall fail the dwellers in that ancient isle.
For a long while before
The day of judgement in Josaphat
Open shall these things be
And declared to living men.[63]

In this supposedly early version of the Joseph story, the ecclesiastic-ally problematic Grail associated with the Arthurian tales has become a valuable historical relic of both Jesus and Joseph, the cup being exchanged for two white and silver cruets (*fassula*) containing the blood and sweat of Jesus respectively. Carley has suggested that its features suggest a post-Crusade origin for the prophecy, however; the use of the title 'Prophet Jesus' would have been unusual in a Christian work and occurred in John's *Cronica* elsewhere only in the context of an account of a captured knight's time with Muslims in the Holy Land. The confusing introduction of the noble pagan 'Abbadarè', said to be 'mighty in Saphat', is therefore, he concluded, likely to be a 'garbled rendition of some pagan name' combined with Glastonbury's traditions about the long-standing sanctity of its burial grounds. The whole, Carley dated to the second half of the thirteenth century. Melkin's poem is therefore yet another part of the abbey's tradition that was created to support and extend the Joseph at Glastonbury story.[64]

By this point, the contours of the story that the abbey was telling about itself are clear, but what did it do with that story in the years of its greatest influence?

The Great Western Schism, the Glastonbury Joseph, and fifteenth-century Europe

By the mid fourteenth century, Glastonbury Abbey had finally begun to use the Joseph of Arimathea tradition to enhance its power and influence. A visit in 1331 by Edward III and his queen, Philippa, appears to have rekindled royal interest in Arthur and Joseph. The king vowed to re-establish the Round Table with 300 knights in 1344, and, as already noted (under 'How did Joseph come to visit Britain?', p. 74), gave permission a year later for a search for Joseph's body in the abbey grounds. Despite such interest from outside the abbey, however, J. P. Carley noted that the abbot from 1342–75, Walter de Monington, showed no signs of a personal interest in Joseph, perhaps, he speculates, because of the still troublesome question of the Grail for the monks. Not so with his successor, Abbot John Chinnock (1375–1420), however. In 1382, Chinnock dedicated a newly restored chapel in the cemetery to St Michael and St Joseph of Arimathea. On his orders, *Magna Tabula* (Great Tablets) were displayed in the abbey, laying out the story of Joseph of Arimathea for the pilgrims who were visiting an increasingly magnificent set of abbey buildings, worked by a substantial monastic community with an increasingly powerful and wealthy abbot at its head.[65] The authority of the abbey and its abbot was soon to extend far beyond the borders of the West Country, however.

In 1378, the Great Western Schism began, with Pope Gregory XI leaving Avignon for Rome. Following his death soon after, two popes were elected, one in Rome and one in Avignon, a situation which persisted until 1409. With the unity of the papacy compromised, the Councils of the Church became the fora at which possible resolutions of the Schism could be discussed. At the Council of Pisa in 1409, it was agreed by the Council and its members that it represented the universal Church. Having given themselves authority even over the pope, whether it be Rome's Gregory XII or Avignon's Benedict XIII, the Council decided to appoint a third pope, Alexander V, changing but not resolving the situation.

Significant political power was thus being invested in these meetings and in those churchmen who were able to address them. Such Council members found themselves not just speaking as individuals, however; instead they were grouped according to their nations. This practice was well known pre-Schism; in Lyon in 1274, for example, Pope Gregory X had achieved his purposes by consulting with groups of delegates nation by nation. In the fifteenth century, however, that procedure was turned on its head as each nation tried to achieve its political aims through conciliar action. Unsurprisingly, the definition of 'nation' in use became highly contentious, that term's meaning being much more open-ended in the period than its modern usage would suggest. It was this open-endedness that would lead to Joseph of Arimathea being invoked repeatedly at the series of fifteenth-century Councils, beginning in embryonic form at Pisa in 1409, more fully in Constance in 1414–18, and then in Sienna in 1424, and Basle in 1434. Among the English churchmen at each of these Councils were the abbots of Glastonbury, now seen as chief among the churchmen of England, with John Chinnock present at Pisa and Sienna, and Nicholas Frome at Sienna and Basle.[66]

The year 1415 was notable for England's Henry V's victory over the French at the battle of Agincourt on 25 October, one of the series of battles that made up the soon-to-be-lost Hundred Years War (1337–1453). The Council of Constance had already convened to put an end to the schism over the papacy, now being held by three men, and in this it was eventually successful; a single figure, Martin V, emerged as the one true pope, ending the schism. But there was a great deal of skirmishing among the delegates before that conclusion was reached and one such skirmish related to the question of just who could speak and vote at the Council. Unsurprisingly, those involved were the English and their erstwhile opponents, the French. At the heart of the matter was the question of whether the former was a nation at all.

The English position was aided in Constance by the initial absence of the Spanish, who boycotted the Council because of their loyalty to the Avignon pope. The members of the Council began to meet under one of four national banners: the Italians, the Germans, the French, and the English, with a single representative from each bloc speaking at the Council; the English were represented by Robert Hallum, Bishop of Salisbury. These blocs were not comparable in size, however; the English contingent on arrival numbered only 27.[67] Instead what mattered was the power, prestige, and homogeneity of the nation being represented, with the Germans, for example, being joined by the Hungarians and the Scandinavians. To begin with, all went well, but with the departure of the Holy Roman Emperor Sigismund in July 1415 and the arrival of a small delegation from Aragon, tensions began to arise between the French and the English. These culminated in an attack on the latter as a nation by France's Cardinal D'Ailly on 1 October 1416. Agreeing that division of the Council into four nations was both necessary and desirable, D'Ailly argued that the legitimate nations at the Council should be the Italian, the German, the French, and the Spanish, with the English forming a minor part of the German bloc; he cited the contents of a papal bull, *Vas electionis*, issued earlier by Benedict XII on a different matter in support of his position.

Needless to say, the English were incensed at the slight. When a document with five seals reached the English delegate with four already stamped, he defaced the Spanish seal, replaced it with the English one, and added the words 'the same for Spain'. The Aragon contingent was not amused and eventually announced that it would

no longer regard the English as a nation; violence was then threatened among the delegates. The issue continued to rankle until
3 March 1417 when France's Jean Campan tried but failed to read a
formal document attacking the nationhood of the English. Put into
the official records, it argued that England was a particular nation and
not a general one (i.e. it did not include national groups within it as
the other general nations did). It also argued that the small physical
size of England was relevant, as were its inconsequential ecclesiastical
structures and the comparative lack of antiquity of its faith compared
with that of France, dated at the time to the life of St Denis
(understood to be Dionysius, the member of the Areopagus mentioned as a convert of Paul in Acts 17:34); in all of these latter
comparators, Campan argued, England was decidedly inferior to
France.

On 31 March, when the English delegation delivered its response
to the French attack on its nationhood, it was in the form of a
document submitted by the notary Thomas Polton to the Council
clerks, but never read openly. Polton's document argued that Britain
was a general nation, asserting that it represented eight kingdoms
within the British Isles, a region which—in a particularly astonishing
claim—were said to include islands as large as France itself, and five
languages—English, Welsh, Irish, Gascon, and Cornish. That it was
a general nation was also shown by its 'habit of unity', which truly
showed it to be the equal of France. Its physical size was emphasized,
as was the great number of its provinces, dioceses, and parishes. Then
there were Polton's comments on the antiquity of England's faith.
J.-P. Genet helpfully summarizes these:

> The greater antiquity of faith was proved by the fact that Joseph of Arimathea
> himself had come to England with twelve companions; and he converted the
> people to the Christian faith. The King of England gave him the diocese of
> Bath and twelve hides of land, and the saint was buried at Glastonbury, which
> received the twelve hides as its original endowment. France on the other had
> to wait until the time for St Denis to become Christian.[68]

Poulton's arguments were not discussed further at the Council of
Constance, however.

The issue of nationhood may have dropped from the Council
discussions, but Glastonbury and Joseph's appearance in such great

matters raised questions about proof of the English claims; was there something beyond the merely textual? In 1420, Henry V, having heard about an excavation which had taken place at Glastonbury the previous year, enquired after its results. Abbot Nicholas Frome responded with a description of the burials excavated, entangled with an account of the Glastonbury Joseph story. Though he did not claim explicitly that Joseph's body had been recovered, Carley has pointed out that the king could easily have assumed from Frome's letter that such an announcement was imminent; the latter's sudden death in 1422, however, apparently put an end to that possibility. With the appointment of Martin V and the ending of the schism, European interest in conciliar politics was waning, and, as Carley has noted, the need for proof was no longer of such great importance.[69]

Nevertheless, the issue of nationhood arose again at the Council of Sienna in 1424, with Richard Fleming, the Bishop of Lincoln, this time pressing the English case. Again no final resolution took place. At the Council of Basle in 1434, however, what was an increasingly peripheral issue became a bone of contention between the representatives of England and of Spanish Castile. Alphonso Garcia de Santa Maria, 'doctor of laws and Dean of the Churches of Compostella and Segovia', offered a case for the Castilian rejection of the English claim for primacy based on Spain's earlier reception of Christianity. The English claimed that Joseph came to England 15 years after the Assumption of Mary and converted its 'greater part' to the faith of Christ. The Castilian rebuttal of that claim was four-fold.[70]

First, Alphonso denied 'that Joseph came into England. He who asserts it should prove it'. Where was the evidence, he asked? Second, even though the burden of proof lay with the English, the Castilian cleric offered a proof of its falsehood. As we have seen, an account of Titus uncovering a Joseph of Arimathea imprisoned for 42 years was placed alongside the *Gospel of Nicodemus* account of Joseph's release after a single night of imprisonment in volume 3 of Jacobus de Voragine's *Legenda aurea* and explained as a second imprisonment caused by the Arimathean's incessant preaching of Christ (p. 83). If that explanation were true, Alphonso argued, the long imprisonment meant that Joseph could not have gone to England when the English claimed he had done so. Third, even were the English story true (and it most definitely wasn't, according to Castile!), Joseph did not even convert the whole of the land. Finally, Alphonso pointed out that the result of his arguments was that it was Spain which could claim primacy. The deliverer of the faith to the Spanish, James, had been executed during the lifetime of Peter, who had himself been martyred by Nero. Since Nero pre-dated Titus as emperor, the Joseph liberated by Titus could only have reached England around 80 CE, whereas James must have reached Spain years before, around 40 CE.

The English replied in turn to each of Alphonso's arguments. First, it was argued that just as the representatives of the king of England had claimed and as was proved in the 'ancient books and archives' of England, notably in the abbey of Glastonbury, Joseph with 12 companions, fleeing the persecution of either Herod or the Roman governors of Judea, had sailed to England and by his preaching converted many to the Christian faith. He was endowing a church in England at the same time that Peter was preaching in Antioch (in the early 60s), a church that had grown into the great Glastonbury Abbey of the Council's day. Second, the *Legenda*'s account of Joseph and Titus was denounced as a 'very absurd fabrication', and the Castilian was admonished to acknowledge that the reputation of Jacobus de Voragine had been attacked in Spain itself, with Ludovicus Vives and Melchiore Cano asserting that 'the man was brazen of speech and leaden of heart'. Third, since the Spanish were not claiming that James converted the whole of Spain, it was of no consequence that Joseph did not convert all of England. Finally, piqued by the rejection of Joseph's visit to England, the English responded with their own exegetical argument from the Scriptures. They flatly denied that James had visited Spain, quoting the doubts expressed by Rodericus Ximensis, the Archbishop of Toledo, in his argument with the Prefect of Compostello at the Lateran Council of 1215. If the Castilians wanted to argue for James's visit, they should produce compelling evidence of their own, because 'Holy Writ' suggested that he was decapitated under Herod Antipas and never even came to Spain (cf. Acts 12.2).

The Glastonbury rejection of Robert de Boron's long imprisonment narrative and its adoption of 63 CE as the date of arrival for Joseph—explicitly under the influence of the *Gospel of Nicodemus* in the case of John of Glastonbury and most likely under the same influence for the writer of the earlier 1247 insertion into William's *De Antiquitate*—was doing rather more at this point than simply helping to distance him from the Grail and its troublesome theology. It was strongly aiding England's argument about the primacy of its nationhood against the Spanish who were quoting the long imprisonment narrative specifically in order to deny it. Ironically, the Joseph who had been accidentally delivered to Glastonbury and to England by the Burgundian French poet Robert de Boron, had allowed the English 'possessors' of that tradition to assert their own pre-eminence among the great nations of Europe in the four Councils between 1409 and 1436. What would the English have been able to say about their faith's antiquity without Joseph of Arimathea? Very little at all!

The dissolution of Glastonbury Abbey and its modern renaissance

Glastonbury Abbey's earthly power was to prove short-lived. When King Henry VIII planned to dismantle England's monasteries in the aftermath of his dispute with Pope Clement VII about his marriage and to use the funds realized to further his territorial ambitions in France, it was only a matter of time before the wealthy Somerset establishment would draw the attention of his ministers. Richard Whiting, the last abbot of Glastonbury Abbey, was initially arrested on charges of treason, before being tried in Wells in November 1539 on a charge of robbery. Unsurprisingly found guilty, the elderly Whiting was taken through Glastonbury town, dragged up onto the Tor, and executed by hanging. Head cut off and body quartered, his remains were placed on show throughout the region, with his head left to crown the abbey's gateway. Glastonbury Abbey as a powerful material presence in England ceased to exist. Its holdings fell into the hands of the king and were treated accordingly, but following his death in 1547, the ruined remnants were given by Henry's son, Edward VI, to the Duke of Somerset. Decline, destruction, and dismantlement became the norm for the abbey site until the early twentieth-century interest in ancient ruins led to a period of stabilization and development. In 1908, the abbey building and grounds were purchased by the Bath and Wells Diocesan Trust and their conservation began; the abbey began to develop into what it is today.

A small, thriving market town, Glastonbury is a major tourist attraction for Somerset, with one county brochure in 2012 noting that: 'The tradition that Joseph of Arimathea, a Phoenician trader, brought the infant Jesus to Glastonbury two thousand years still lives on'. One abbey leaflet states that 'We are the only continuous sacred site in Britain to claim to have been continuously Christian since the first century CE', before offering a nicely conditional exposition of its legends under the heading of William Blake's opening line from his poetic prologue to his poem *Milton* (see chapter five in this volume, pp. 105–7); 'And did those feet in ancient times walk upon England's mountain green?':

If William Blake was right, Glastonbury can claim to have been one of the places Christ visited, with his uncle Joseph of Arimathea, a trader in tin and lead, credited with bringing sacred relics from the holy Land to Britain in the first century CE. Visit the Holy Thorn Tree, said to be descended from Joseph's staff, which flowers twice each year to recall the birth and death of Christ and the bringing of Christianity to our islands. According to the Somerset legend Christ himself is said to have built the first church on this site. The Old Church now lies beneath the remains of the Lady Chapel, to the west of the Abbey ruins.

In 2007, this kind of claim formed the basis for officially twinning the town with the island of Patmos, Greece. The 'glastonbury-patmos. com' website recounts the attempt of Glastonbury resident, Zoe d'Ay, to forge a link between these 'world famous' places, which:

share the distinction of the presence of men, in St Joseph and St John, who knew the living Christ. These men took with them the same message that Christ had taught from those earliest times; the Christianity that Joseph knew and brought to our Britain was the same that John took to Patmos.... [A]t the ... meeting of the Glastonbury Town Council, on August 7th [2007], [h]er proposal was accepted. Patmos formally accepted the Twinning in March 14th 2008.... [I]t was the very first Twinning between Great Britain and Greece; and for it to be the two places most sanctified by the earliest of Christian saints of each land is truly remarkable. Because of this the Twinning of Glastonbury and Patmos is classified as a Twinning in Perpetuity.[71]

Another Glastonbury attraction which is considered to be related to Joseph is the Chalice Well and Gardens, an iron-rich spring known previously as the 'red spring' or 'blood spring', but associated by legend with the blood of Christ, 'miraculously springing forth from the ground when Joseph of Arimathea buried or washed the cup used at the last supper', a connection by name dated by Rahtz and Watts to the late nineteenth century.[72]

The idea of a miraculous thorn tree first appears in the extant literature in the verse *Lyfe of Joseph of Aramathie*, published by Richard Pynson in 1520, although, as Rahtz and Watts have pointed out, it was not elaborated into the story of Joseph's grounding of his staff, proclaiming his weariness ('weary-all'), and it then taking root—a miracle that has also been attributed to saints elsewhere—until the eighteenth century:[73]

> Thre hawthorns also, that growth in werall [Wirrall/
> Wearyall hill],
> Do burge and bere grene leaues at Christmas
> As fresshe as other in May, . . .[74]

The *Guide to Glastonbury and Street* recounts that: '[i]n December it is a Glastonbury custom for the Mayor to cut a spray of blossom from the Holy Thorn [*Crataegus monogyna*] in St John's Churchyard. . . . [That] blossom is sent to the Queen and is put on the Royal breakfast table on Christmas Day', a tradition believed by some locals to go back to the time of Queen Anne in the early seventeenth century, but certainly revived by the Rev. Lionel Smithett Lewis, vicar of Glastonbury, in December 1929.[75] In 1986, an image of the thorn flowering in the snow was used for the United Kingdom's 12/13p Christmas stamps. The *Guide* also mentions the dispersal of the holy thorn to various cities in North America—New York, Washington, Toronto—and the sending of a 'spray' for the funeral of President John F. Kennedy.

Each of these traditions has its modern defenders and there has been a thriving publishing business in books and pamphlets defending their veracity; for example, the works of Isabel Hill Elder (1999), Ray Gibbs (1988), Glyn S. Lewis (2008), Denis Price (2009), and—especially—the Rev. Lionel Smithett Lewis, vicar of St John's, Glastonbury, in the early to mid twentieth century (7th ed. 1955).

The importance of the Joseph legends to the town of Glastonbury itself was sadly demonstrated when, on 8 December 2010—the day the Queen's blossom was due to be cut from the St John's tree—the thorn tree on Wearyall Hill was badly vandalized, with all of its branches being sawn off. Katherine Gorbing, Glastonbury Abbey's Director, was quoted by Maev Kennedy of the *Guardian* as saying: 'It's a great shock to everyone in Glastonbury—the landscape of the town has changed overnight.'[76] Described by M. Bowman as both a religious and a civic event, the thorn ceremony plays an important role in the modern town's interaction with its older roots; it is tempting to conclude that whoever damaged the tree was probably well aware of the collective dismay that such vandalism would generate.[77]

The town is not just a place to express an orthodox Christian folk spirituality based upon the Joseph legends, however. As Bowman also noted:

Glastonbury's current status as a significant and sacred site for a great range of people is unparalleled in the British Isles, being variously considered the Isle of Avalon, the site of a great Druidic centre of learning, a significant prehistoric centre of Goddess worship, the 'cradle of English Christianity,' the 'New Jerusalem,' a communication point for alien contact, the epicentre of New Age in England, and the 'heart chakra' of planet Earth.[78]

Such notions have made Glastonbury a highly successful centre for alternative spiritualities. Many, such as the Glastonbury Zodiac ideas of Katherine Maltwood and Ross Nichols, are based on the geography of the landscape. The names of the town's shops also give some flavour of the place: 'Portal for the Immortal', 'The Crystal Man', 'Cat and Cauldron', 'Man Myth and Magik', 'Goddess and the Green Man', 'Facets of Avalon', 'The Speaking Tree', 'Yin Yang of Glastonbury', 'The Psychic Piglet', 'Natural Earthling', and so on. Held monthly since 2001, the *Mystic & Earth Spirit Fayre* also offers many options for any interested seeker after spiritual things to investigate: 'dowsing', 'karma release', 'crystals', 'past-life regression', 'psychic questing', 'psychometry', and 'palmistry', for example.

Despite inevitable tensions between some of the churches of Glastonbury and the diverse spiritual approaches of more esoteric traditions, overlaps between the two do occur to varying degrees, with a concert by Robin and Beena Williamson of 'Original, traditional, mystical, and spiritual Folk Music—Unique Indo-Celtic Sound' on 11 August 2012 at the Anglican St John's, Glastonbury, a suitable case in point. But whatever the difficulties that exist between the churches, the alternative spiritual seekers, and the ordinary townfolk, the economic case for Glastonbury as a spiritual magnet for interested visitors/seekers/tourists seems unanswerable in the difficult financial climate that has existed since 2008.

A decisive shift in emphasis: beyond Glastonbury

Clearly, the abbey's story of Joseph of Arimathea did not die out when the wealthy institution fell, but neither did it remain localized to the Somerset Levels. With the dawning of the English Reformation, Joseph was increasingly invoked, not to help define England as a nation, but rather to assert the independence of its Church from Rome. As J. Cunningham has put it, the argument had turned from 'nationalism to confessionalism', with the added twist that the quest for English *equality* as a nation with France, Germany, Italy, and Spain became increasingly an argument for English *superiority* as a national Church over the Church of Rome.[79] The tone is well represented by Queen Elizabeth I's reply in 1559 to pro-Catholic English Bishops, men who were arguing that her father had been led astray by heretics and that she should seek a rapprochement with Rome:

Our realm and subjects have been long wanderers, walking astray, whilst they were under the tuition of Romish pastors, who advised them to own a wolf for their head (in lieu of a careful shepherd) whose inventions, heresies and schisms be so numerous, that the flock of Christ have fed on poisonous shrubs for want of wholesome pastures. And whereas you hit us and our subjects in the teeth that the Romish Church first planted the Catholic within our realm, the records and chronicles of our realm testify the contrary; and your own Romish idolatry maketh you liars; witness the ancient monument of Gildas unto which both foreign and domestic have gone in pilgrimage there to offer. This author testifieth Joseph of Arimathea to be the first preacher of the word of God within our realms. Long after that, when Austin came from Rome, this our realm had bishops and priests therein, as is well known to the learned of our realm by woeful experience, how your church entered therein by blood; they being martyrs for Christ and put to death because they denied Rome's usurped authority.[80]

As Cunningham has pointed out, not only was the English Church said to be ancient in origin, it was also effectively being claimed as '*ex ante* Reformed'.[81] The imposition of Roman orders under

St Augustine heralded the fall of the English Church; that event was not an argument for its need for redemption through the Roman Church of the sixteenth century.

This new form of ecclesiastical and national invocation for Joseph was not to last, however. The ideology of Protestantism had too little long-term use for the Joseph of Arimathea of the relic-laden medieval tradition, with later writers becoming much more dismissive of the truthfulness of the Glastonbury account. The Archbishop of Armagh, James Ussher, offered the following comment in the seventeenth century: 'I do not esteem them more ancient than the coming of the Normans and they are plainly redolent of the superstition of the time'.[82] Perhaps a more concrete symbol of the eventual Protestant rejection of the Glastonbury Joseph is the story of the physical destruction of one of the holy thorn trees by one of Oliver Cromwell's soldiers during the English Civil War!

Despite Glastonbury's renaissance in the twentieth century, the Tudors' shifting of the tradition away from the abbey as its geographical locus towards the crown and the nation as its spiritual locus was a decisive move. This shift was to receive another powerful boost in the early nineteenth century when the story would be repackaged in such a way as to become the underlying myth for a form of thinking that strongly combined both nationalism and confessionalism, beginning with William Blake's poetic work 'Jerusalem' and ending—only temporarily, we can be sure—with the opening ceremony of the London 2012 Olympics.

5

The 'Jerusalem' Joseph

'Jerusalem' and William Blake

Largely unheralded during his lifetime, but regarded today as one of most important English figures of the Romantic Movement, William Blake (1757–1827) used imagery and ideas drawn from what C. Rowland has described as his prime source of inspiration, 'the Bible appropriately read', to express his own radical form of visionary spirituality through engravings, paintings, and poetry.[1] He rejected rationalistic views of the Bible, of its ethics, and of religion in general, preferring to develop what Rowland called a 'complex myth of individual and social redemption', usually embedded within extended epic poems such as *The First Book of Urizen* (1794), *Milton: A Poem* (1804–11), and *Jerusalem: The Emanation of the Giant Albion* (1804–20), with which to critique his contemporary society.

The four stanzas now familiar to us as 'Jerusalem' form part of one such epic, as a poetic section within the preface to some early printings (Copies A and B) of Blake's *Milton*. (The later omission of the preface may reflect a growing appreciation of Milton by Blake and a desire to tone down a work critical of the earlier poet.) Preceding it is a prose call to arms, addressed to contemporary painters, sculptors, and architects. Blasting the suppressive influence of the writings of ancient Greek and Latin writers on the likes of Shakespeare and Milton and their danger to the present as embodied in 'the Camp, the Court, and the University', Blake called for a rejection of the Greek and Roman models undergirding the Enlightenment in favour of the biblical model of 'Christ and his apostles'. Be true to your 'imagination', Blake exhorted his audience of creatives,

an aspiration summed up in the quotation which ends the preface,
Numbers 11.29: 'Would to God that all the Lords People were
Prophets.' The poetic section sits between, and is numbered here
for ease of use:

1. And did those feet in ancient time,
2. Walk upon Englands mountains green:
3. And was the Holy Lamb of God,
4. On Englands pleasant pastures seen!
5. And did the Countenance Divine,
6. Shine forth upon our clouded hills?
7. And was Jerusalem builded here,
8. Among these dark Satanic Mills?
9. Bring me my Bow of burning gold:
10. Bring me my Arrows of desire:
11. Bring me my Spear: O clouds unfold!
12. Bring me my Chariot of fire!
13. I will not cease from Mental Fight,
14. Nor shall my Sword sleep in my hand:
15. Till we have built Jerusalem,
16. In Englands green & pleasant Land.[2]

As Rowland has noted, 'in these famous stanzas, . . . Blake summons
people to be prophets, not expecting them thereby to predict the
future but rather to engage in mental struggle to discern the inad-
equacies of the present and conceive the way to a more hopeful
future.'[3] The strength of such an invocation to prophetic behaviour,
however, must have been predicated on the failings of early nineteenth-century English society and demands that Blake's contemporary audience complete at least the last line of the second stanza with a
resounding 'no'; Jerusalem was certainly not once 'builded here' . . . 'in
England's green and pleasant land'. But what of the opening stanza
and the first question of the second stanza; was Blake also expecting
his readers to supply a definitive 'no' to the other questions posed, of
whether those feet walked upon England's mountains, of whether the
holy Lamb of God had been seen in England, and of whether the
Countenance Divine had shone upon its clouded hills?

Phrasing the question this way, however, presumes that Blake was
himself aware of a tradition that Jesus came to England and expected

his audience to know of it, too. Certainly that is how the situation is most often presented today. On the occasion of the Royal Wedding of Prince William and Kate Middleton on 29 April 2011, for example, *The Daily Telegraph*'s Martin Chilton wrote that: 'The verses are thought to have been based on a legend that Jesus came to England as a young boy and visited the town of Glastonbury, Somerset, where he established a second Jerusalem.'[4] The commonly held belief that Blake was aware of such a tradition is not without its difficulties, however.

Did Blake believe that Joseph of Arimathea brought Jesus to Britain?

In a 1989 edition of the journal *Folklore*, A. W. Smith argued that Blake himself was not aware of a tradition that the young Jesus visited England. Noting that the story had been little studied by academics and was generally dismissed by 'serious writers', he nevertheless found it to be a passionately held belief among some whom he termed 'otherwise quite orthodox Christians'.[5] P. Ashdown has summarized the various versions of the story thus:

Joseph of Arimathea, the wealthy secret follower of Jesus who eventually buried Him in his own tomb (as told in the Gospels) was actually a relative of the Holy Family. He had made his money as a metal-merchant dealing in British tin. In Jesus's youth, in some versions after the death of Joseph of Nazareth, who is last heard of in scripture when Jesus is about twelve, Joseph the Arimathean took Him on one of his mercantile voyages to Britain. In some versions of the story they end their journey at Glastonbury. Jesus is sometimes said to return alone to Glastonbury in His late twenties to prepare in seclusion for His public ministry, perhaps by studying the wisdom of the druids, who are held to have maintained a college there. Joseph of Arimathea returns to the hallowed spot after the Crucifixion, bearing the Grail and perhaps other relics of the passion, to found Britain's first Christian community.[6]

For Smith, the sheer number of these traditions and the broad geographical spread of their local connections were deeply problematic. The repeated connection of the 'Joseph as a tin merchant' story with different tin-mining locations, however, led him to suggest that the basic story may have been a general 'miners' trade tradition' rather than one associated with a specific geographical location (on this, see chapter six in this volume, pp. 133–4).

The next few pages of Smith's article rehearsed the appearance of the story in the works of three early twentieth-century writers— Lionel Smithett Lewis (long-time vicar of the Anglican St John's Church, Glastonbury), H. A. Lewis (vicar of Talland in Cornwall), and C. C. Dobson (vicar of St Mary in the Castle, Hastings)—all of whom tended towards an acceptance of its historical veracity.[7] Their publications included many oral accounts of Christ's visit, they referenced each other heavily, and they eventually came to dominate more recent discussions of the story. Smith found them all wanting evidentially, and noted that one common response to difficulties with verifying the tradition was to fall back on Blake. L. S. Lewis referred to 'Jerusalem' as 'The Glastonbury Hymn', and prefaced his book with its full text. Dobson also began by claiming that Blake was 'quoting the tradition so dear to every native of Cornwall and Somerset, that Our Lord visited these parts as a boy'.[8]

Smith admitted that such views were given a slight credibility by the young Blake's 1773 engraving of 'Joseph of Arimathea among the Rocks of Albion', based upon an 'old Italian drawing' of Michelangelo's,[9] but turned back in his article at this point to the poem itself, well aware that without a plausible alternative explanation for Blake's words he could not successfully win the argument. If the poet had not known of a tradition about a visit to England, he suggested, the verses can only have been meant metaphorically. He then offered evidence to support that position from a poetic segment of plate 77 of Blake's epic poem, *Jerusalem: The Emanation of the Giant Albion*, written and illustrated between 1804–20. The opening page of its chapter four is addressed 'To the Christians' and ends with a poem in an inverted pyramid:

England! awake! awake! awake!　　Thy hills and valleys felt her feet
Jerusalem thy Sister calls!　　Gently upon their bosoms move:
Why wilt thou sleep the sleep of death?　　Thy gates beheld sweet Zion's ways:
And close her from thy ancient walls.　　Then was a time of joy and love.
And now the time returns again:
Our souls exult, and London's towers.
Recieve [sic] the Lamb of God to dwell
In England's green and pleasant bowers.[10]

Smith argued that no one, 'least of all Blake', would understand these stanzas to literally indicate that Jerusalem's feet(?) touched the 'hills and valleys' of England or that—familiar as the wording sounds—the 'Lamb of God' was received by 'London's Towers' or dwelt in 'England's green and pleasant bowers'. Smith further quoted from plate 27, from Chapter Two: To the Jews of *Jerusalem*, the following—also familiar sounding:

> The fields from Islington to Marybone,
> To Primrose Hill and Saint Johns Wood:
> Were builded over with pillars of gold,
> And there Jerusalem's pillars stood.[11]

Closing that part of his discussion with a dismissal of the idea that Blake favoured the Druids—Smith noted that the poet in fact made them represent his hated opponents, the Deists—the remainder of his article explored the carol traditions of the story and the various mis-translations of medieval texts by Lewis et al. before positing that the best way to trace the tradition's origins would be to explore the question of whose ideological world in that period would not only have benefitted from Jesus coming to Britain, but would also have required it. By way of a conclusion, Smith proposed that the 'Jesus in England' tradition most likely originated in the 1840s with the rise of British Israelitism, as propounded by such as Richard Brothers, and was given added verve by the evolving ideological requirements of the colonial project of the nineteenth-century British Empire. A description of one of the three main supporters of the tradition discussed earlier, C. C. Dobson, helpfully made Smith's point:

Cyril Dobson, one of the principal expounders of 'the Holy Legend', was a convinced believer in what is called British Israel Truth, the esoteric key to the Scriptures, always possessed by a faithful few but only in the nineteenth century widely proclaimed. In his pamphlet *The Boyhood and Early Manhood of Christ*, he talks of the lapse of the Jews from God's revealed truth (a common enough theme of the Old Testament prophets) and continues, '(God) therefore selected a new country—Britain. He planted there a new race—the Brits. In them He instilled a religion ... Druidism, possessing the basic principles of Christian truth ... some two thousand years before the birth of Christ.' 'Druidism was Christianity anticipating Christ.'[12]

A few critical responses have been offered to Smith's article, not least from those connected with the southwest of England. P. Ashdown, in his book *The Lord was at Glastonbury: Somerset and the Jesus Voyage Story* (2010), generally contented himself with pointing out minor errors with Smith's argument, while firmly rejecting the British Israel connection as lacking proof—Dobson was merely elaborating the earlier accounts of Harold Jenner and did not develop them himself, he argued—before eventually concluding that the earliest traces of the story came from Somerset and London at the close of the nineteenth century.[13] Dennis Price, in stark contrast, rejected Smith's conclusion completely in his book *The Missing Years of Jesus: The Greatest Story Never Told* (2009); Smith 'missed the point in several respects', he argued:

What is important in these stories is the consistent theme of Jesus visiting Britain in the company of the one person that we know was in a realistic position to provide him with transport to the British Isles. The central and most important element is a named individual being *out of place* and the blunt fact that the individual was notably without a Biblical alibi for the period in question shouldn't be forgotten either.[14]

Further support was culled by Price from the traditions of masons and smiths who prided themselves on traditions going back to Solomon, well before the time of Joseph of Arimathea, and from hints in texts from St Augustine and Gildas referring to a 'church . . . divinely constructed by the hands of Christ Himself' and to the British Isles receiving 'the beams of light, that is, the holy precepts of Christ, . . . at the latter point of the reign of Tiberius Caesar' respectively.[15] Price concluded that he has found 'one tale of demonstrable antiquity that placed Jesus in Britain in the early first century AD'.[16] Needless to say, Price's response would hardly have troubled Smith at all.

The conclusion that the 'Jesus in England' tradition is a late one which was unknown to Blake does not, of course, mean that the poet was unaware of the long-standing Joseph at Glastonbury tradition; the engraving of 'Joseph of Arimathea among the Rocks of Albion' mentioned earlier presumably indicated his acquaintance with that story. But most contemporary English hearers of his poem do think—if they think about it at all—the complete opposite of Smith's argument, that Blake's words do presuppose the presence of both

Joseph and Jesus in first-century Britain. This is perhaps not least because when they hear the opening line 'and did those feet', they do not hear it as the start of a spoken poem, introducing an epic work on Milton, but rather as the lyrics of a short orchestral anthem with deeply nationalistic overtones. Being told by numerous commentators that the Jesus in England tradition stands behind the words that they are singing effectively makes it so for those who hear. As we shall see, the idea of Jesus visiting England offers an even more powerful urge to nationalistic fervour than the comparatively mundane story of Joseph of Arimathea bringing Christianity to England and founding its first church at Glastonbury.

Parry's 'Jerusalem', the Women's Institute, and the British Empire

As the true cost of the war in France became clear to those who remained in England in 1916 and with enthusiasm for the fight consequently on the wane, the poet laureate, Robert Bridges, asked Sir Hubert Parry to set the poetic section of Blake's preface to his *Milton* to music. The intention was to create a rousing anthem for use by Francis Edward Younghusband's recently created 'Fight for Right' movement, which would bolster the nation's weakening resolve to see the war to its end.[17] It would be 'suitable, simple music to Blake's stanza—music that an audience could take up and join in'—and was intended for use at a particular public rally.

Though 'Fight for Right' published a single sheet version for such use, Parry withdrew his permission for the anthem to be used before it could be sung by Younghusband's movement.[18] Instead the anthem was first used by another organization to which he and his wife—an ardent suffragette—were particularly partial, the 'Votes for Women' campaign, in a concert at the Royal Albert Hall on 13 March 1916.[19] With the end of the Great War, the suffrage movement increasingly found the anthem a suitable one for its purposes; one suffragist leader, Millicent Fawcett, wrote to Parry that 'Your Jerusalem ought to be made the women voters' hymn.'[20] (When women gained the vote, however, the anthem became the political hymn of the Labour Party, providing a campaigning slogan during the 1945 election as Clement

Attlee proposed the building of a New Jerusalem in the post-war era, and being sung annually at party political conferences alongside the 'Red Flag'.) Parry's pupil, Walford Davies, took the music to a publisher and soon the song was being used in ways far beyond that of boosting morale in wartime, not least among the churches (for example, *Hymns of the Kingdom* [1923], the Church of Scotland's *Church Hymnary* [1927], *The American Student Hymnal* [1928], and *The Hymnary of the United Church of Canada* [1930]).[21]

The war had also led to the creation in England of the Women's Institute (WI), echoing the Canadian WI founded in 1897, organized under the direction of the Agricultural Organizations Society with the intention of increasing home-grown food stocks to end shortages caused by the submarine menace in the Atlantic; among their specialities were the making of preserves and the pickling of perishables to increase their shelf-life. A letter to *Home and Country*, the WI's journal founded in 1919, from Vice Chairman Grace E. Hadow in December 1923 proposed the adoption of 'Jerusalem' as an Institute anthem, and pointed out some additional opportunities its regular singing would provide.

The attempt cannot be a success unless every delegate is ready to sing whether she thinks she can sing or whether she thinks she can't. Both words and music are simple and dignified and easy to learn. Incidentally the learning would give pleasure to any WI and would afford an excellent opportunity for a short talk either on Blake's poetry, or on poems about England. We have long looked in vain for a national 'Institute Song'. Here is one made to our hand and one which some counties have already adopted.[22]

Some letter-writers objected to the recommendation, with one decrying its allegorical nature: 'What woman nowadays yearns for bows, arrows, spears and chariots of fire? Boadicea might have done, but that was a long time ago.'[23]

Nevertheless, the idea was supported by WI members and their first official rendition of 'Jerusalem' took place in the Queen's Hall London on 20 May 1924 at the Institute's 8th Annual General Meeting. The *Home and Country* of April 1924 described what was to happen thus:

The year's Annual Meeting will have one special feature. The delegates will burst into song. It must be a great inspiring shout of song or the outside world will be in no way impressed. 'Jerusalem' was a happy choice, for as the delegates sing hopefully of the New Jerusalem which every institute member is helping to build, the singers can remember with thankfulness that 'satanic mills' no longer disgrace our land. Blake's protest on behalf of the helpless child victims of those thoughtless days was not made in vain.[24]

So began the long-standing association between the WI and Parry's anthem which has led to the Institute's stereotypical 'Jam and Jerusalem' image, the main title of S. Goodenough's *A Pictorial History of Britain's Greatest Women's Movement* (1977), and echoed in films such as Nigel Cole's *Calendar Girls* (2003) starring Julie Walters and Helen Mirren, and in the 2006–09 BBC TV series *Jam and Jerusalem*, starring Sue Johnston, Jennifer Saunders, and Dawn French.

Alongside the use of Parry's anthem by Christian denominations both home and abroad, and by England's women, 'Jerusalem' had also found a ready home in the musical repertoire of the British Empire. Following political lobbying by Lord Meath (1841–1929), the birthday of the late Queen Victoria, 24 May, had been informally celebrated across the Empire as 'Empire Day' since 1902. As J. A. Mangan has noted, Meath's intention in pushing his imperial agenda was directed towards encouraging the growth of a sense of duty, discipline, sympathy, and patriotism in the Empire's children wherever they were in the world. The creation of a self-sacrificial mindset in the young would, it was assumed, produce a hardy and virtuous stock, well able to ensure the ongoing existence of the British Empire against any potential challenger.[25] The aftermath of the Great War led to the day's recognition as an annual event, celebrated in publicly funded schools across the Empire with festivities and involving public speeches lauding both its civilized culture and its civilizing effect on the globe, the retelling of heroic histories from its glorious past, the offering of obeisance to its symbols (e.g. the Union Flag), and the singing of its songs, 'Jerusalem' among them. The peoples of the various colonies, whether they were descendants of the settlers or of the indigenous, were all to join in and celebrate joyously the ongoing cultural impact of the Empire which dominated their lands.

Music was employed on other occasions to engender and heighten this shared sense of the Empire. J. Richards has described the Empire-strengthening effect of the British Legion Festival of Empire and

Remembrance, held on 11 November 1927, and attended by the Prince of Wales.[26] Broadcast to the Empire, the concert was intended by the *Daily Express*, its sponsors, to renew the ties of friendship that, it was believed, had been forged between the soldiers of the different parts of the Empire during the Great War and also to remember those who were still struggling with its aftermath. The audience were first encouraged to sing songs that were popular during the war, before the second half of the concert introduced a selection of hymns, prayers, and poetry, including 'Jerusalem'. As Richards has put it, the 'musical items all blended in a seamless web of memory, affirmation, regret, pride, and unity'.[27] The devastating experience of the Great War was thus made both sensible and available through an emotionally charged mixture of comradeship and patriotism, all seen through the lens of the British Empire.

Post-World War II, the British Empire began to fade. Empire Day became British Commonwealth Day in 1958, then Commonwealth Day in 1966 (and also eventually moving to the second Monday in March). Though the Coronation of Queen Elizabeth II on 2 June 1953 took place as the old Empire was rapidly becoming the new Commonwealth, it nevertheless retained many of the formal trappings of imperial Britain and its attitudes to the people of its colonies and protectorates, the representatives of whom were invited to attend the ceremony. Richards noted that all bar one of the pieces of music used in the service were composed by British subjects, with G. Handel's 'Zadok the Priest', played as the monarch was crowned, the sole exception. 'Jerusalem' itself was part of the concert played around the Coronation, being performed with the likes of Vaughan Williams' 'Greensleeves', Handel's 'Firework' music, Edward Elgar's 'Nimrod', and Gustav Holst's 'Jupiter'.[28] Combined with the hymns and marches of the Coronation Service itself and the religious components of an event which also set in place a new head of the Church of England, the message of 'Jerusalem' in such a context was clear enough; that this new monarch was a chosen individual, leading a chosen people, not just at home in Britain, but all across the globe as well. As Queen Elizabeth swiftly embarked upon a long tour of Commonwealth countries to great public acclaim, each of the Commonwealth countries began to settle into its own version of an ongoing relationship with the British crown.

The uses of 'Jerusalem' in twenty-first-century Britain will concern us momentarily, but we should first note the ongoing musical presentation of Britishness that has taken place for many years at the annual Last Night of the Proms concert, held in early September in London's Royal Albert Hall. Immensely popular and heavily oversubscribed, the televised concert features a musical overview of the ninety or so concerts that have made up that year's Promenade season, before concluding with a series of patriotic pieces played to a scene of young (and some not so young) concert-goers waving union flags in celebration. Traditionally, Edward Elgar's 'Land of Hope and Glory' (otherwise known as 'Pomp and Circumstance March No. 1 in D major') is followed by Henry Wood's *Fantasia on British Sea-Songs* (including 'Rule Britannia'), before Parry's 'Jerusalem' and the national anthem bring the evening to a close. True, this is not a vision of nationhood appropriate to much of modern multicultural Britain, but it is certainly one that harks back to the imperial/national events of the twentieth century and which doubtless continues to figure in the mind's eye of at least some onlookers from outside the United Kingdom.

'Jerusalem' and English sport

The use of 'Jerusalem' as an anthem for the English people reached new heights (lows?) in the year 2000 when the song—sung by 'Fat Les 2000', a group made up of the pop band Blur's Alex James, artist Damien Hirst, and actor Keith Allen—became the official anthem of the English team for that year's European Football Championship in Holland and Belgium. Allen was quoted by the *Guardian*'s Russell Thomas on 9 May 2000 as saying: 'Everyone has heard Jerusalem, most of us have sung it and all of us know some of the words. Frankly, it's a cracking good hymn.'[29] Thomas's article ended with the approving words of the Football Association's Chief Executive, Adam Crozier: 'We want our fans to leave behind their own club loyalties and join together as England fans. Fat Les 2000 are exactly the right artists to make this happen.' And 'Jerusalem' was clearly thought to be the right song to encourage the country's notoriously tribal football fans to put their local allegiances away—at least temporarily—in support of the English national team. The FA's practice of choosing an official song for each successive tournament, however, would not have encouraged the adoption of the song permanently, and since a dismal England did not progress beyond the group stage, it is highly questionable whether the song fulfilled its intended purpose anyway.

The anthem did soon become the official song of the England cricket team, however. Sung by fans in an ad hoc fashion for years, a campaign was launched by the England captain, Michael Vaughan, to get the entire country to sing 'Jerusalem' at 10.25 am on 8 September 2005, just before the crucial final Ashes test against Australia at the Oval in London. England had not won an Ashes series since 1987, but were leading 2–1 and were favourites for the series win; a draw would be enough to bring the Ashes back to England. The *Daily Mail* published a 'song sheet' on the 6th and exhorted its readers to be ready to sing along—whether 'in pubs, offices, factories, schools or their sitting rooms'. Tory MP Henry Bellingham was quoted as saying that the proposal was a:

superb idea. My singing is not particularly good, but if I am near anyone who is singing I will join in...England's cricketers have inspired the whole country. They are true sportsmen. Not for them the immorality or vulgar behaviour of most football stars. They have done the country proud.[30]

Technical difficulties at the Oval on the day meant that crowd participation was somewhat muted as the anthem played over the public address system, but at the later celebrations for the Ashes winning team in London's Trafalgar Square, opera singer Sean Ruane was joined by both team and crowd in a rousing rendition of English cricket's new 'official' anthem.

In the 2009 series, however, the opening Ashes test was played in Wales, and the choice of songs sung by Katherine Jenkins, the Welsh soprano, became a national concern; 'Jerusalem' was sung but so was the Welsh anthem, 'Land of my Fathers'.[31] The problematic existence of anthems for all of the constituent parts of the United Kingdom, England aside, had been noted for some time, and an 'Anthem for England' campaign had been agitating for an English anthem to match those of the Welsh, the Scots, and the Northern Irish. The issue reached something of a peak when the organizing committee for the England team travelling to the 2010 Commonwealth Games in New Delhi announced on St George's Day that year that a public

vote would choose the anthem to be played at presentation ceremonies whenever the team won a gold medal. A month later, the
results were announced: 'God Save the Queen' received 12 per cent,
'Land of Hope and Glory' received 32.5 per cent, and the winner,
'Jerusalem', received 52.5 per cent.[32] The decision was supported by an
early day motion in the House of Commons sponsored by Liberal
MP Greg Mulholland (on 21 June), which included the following
statement: 'England does not have its own anthem and so looks
forward to other sports and sporting events adopting an English
anthem for occasions when English teams and athletes, as opposed
to British teams and athletes, compete.'[33] As England's first gold
medallists, swimmers Liam Tancock and Fran Halsall, received their
medals on 5 October, a wordless 'Jerusalem' played out for a seemingly
interminable two minutes and twenty seconds, a musical interlude
that would subsequently occur on 35 more occasions.[34] Though
appreciated by some, there seems little doubt that played as a national
anthem without Blake's stirring words, 'Jerusalem' lacked a little
something.

The quest for an English national anthem, for sports or otherwise,
continues to the present day. But we might pause a moment here and
give thought to a sport that has sung 'Jerusalem' at its events for much
longer than the last ten years. Rugby League, the (originally) northern branch of the game that split off from the Rugby Football Union
in the 1890s, has long sung the anthem before its cup final matches.
Australian Greg Mallory recounted online his experience of the 1986/
87 Challenge Cup final between Halifax and St Helens:

Firsly [sic] the players walk out on the filed [sic] about an hour before the
game. They are dressed in their suits with their club ties on and the cheering
made the hairs on the back of my neck stand up. When they have left the field
the community singing starts. Everyone takes part. Traditional Lancashire,
Yorkshire songs, 'Lassie from Lancashire', 'Ilkley Moor by t'at' are sung and
then 'Jerusalem' and 'Land of Hope and Glory'. There is silence and the finale
is 'Abide with Me'.[35]

As Mallory's comments show, however, 'Jerusalem' was not being
sung as a national anthem, but merely as one traditional song
among others. Nevertheless, recent years have witnessed something
of an evolution in which 'Jerusalem' is now being sung in place of the

national anthem at the start of Rugby League cup final matches, and it will be interesting to see how this new practice develops in the medium to long term.

'Jerusalem' and the Church of England

Away from sport, 'Jerusalem's' new millennium continued with something of an old chestnut, its lack of suitability as a Christian *hymn* because of its nationalistic flavour; what made it eminently suitable for singing at an English sporting event or at an event where an English team or individual were competing grated on ecclesiastical ears more concerned with viewing humanity as a whole. *The Daily Telegraph*'s Sophie Borland reported on 9 April 2008 that 'Jerusalem' had been banned from private memorial services held at Southwark Cathedral by its dean, the Very Reverend Colin Slee, an exclusion that had apparently been in place for some time and appeared to mean that even on national occasions the song was rarely sung. Slee was quoted as saying this was because the 'hymn' (as *The Daily Telegraph* pointedly described it) was 'not in the glory of God'. The article noted two other such exclusions—from a 2001 marriage ceremony in Cheadle because, the vicar had said, 'Jerusalem' was a 'nationalistic song that does not praise God' and from St Margaret's, Westminster, because its 'dark satanic mills' were thought to refer to city workers—before adding that it was one of then Prime Minister Gordon Brown's choices on BBC Radio 4's *Desert Island Discs* in 1996.[36]

Having an established national church in England, however, means that the Church of England and the British state must interact. Twenty-six bishops sit in the House of Lords, the upper house of the British Parliament, and senior clergy take their assigned roles in public on State occasions. The long reign of Queen Elizabeth II means that a Coronation Service has not taken place for over 60 years, but—rather ironically given Slee's views—the Church of England has continued to take a prominent role in royal weddings, a number of which have taken place on a very public stage. On 16 November 2010, the engagement of Prince William and Kate Middleton was announced, with the wedding ceremony being set for Westminster Abbey on 29 April 2011. The wedding was soon being described as a 'semi-State' occasion, with the day becoming a national holiday—with Easter the weekend before and May Day just after, just three days out of eleven were thus designated as working days, a fact that was later used as part of the government's explanation for poor national economic results that quarter!—and some expenses of the wedding being paid for out of the public purse. As is typical with such events, the guest list was a combination of family, the great and the good, and the leaders of the nations of the world (one or two uninvited bad apples aside). Officiating at the service was the Dean of Westminster Abbey, Dr John Hall, and solemnizing the wedding was the Archbishop of Canterbury, Dr Rowan Williams. Watching on television was a potential global audience of two billion people.

Following the marriage vows, the lesson (a reading of Romans 12:1–2, 9–18), and the sermon by Bishop of London Richard Chartres, a series of prayers led by Hall and Williams was followed by a rousing rendition of 'Jerusalem', before in turn a blessing was offered and the national anthem sung. The musical accompaniment of two choirs, one orchestra (the London Chamber Orchestra), and two fanfare teams from the Royal Air Force and the Household Cavalry ensured that Blake's words and Parry's music filled the vast abbey space with ease.[37] Described by the *Daily Telegraph* as the most impressive of the 'hymns' (Martin Chilton's headline ran 'Jerusalem triumphant at Kate and Will's wedding'), and chosen by the happy couple with the help, apparently, of the groom's father, the Prince of Wales (who would shortly present a BBC2 TV programme on Parry), the anthem was described by the watching Irish stand-up comedian, Dara O Briain, as the 'Prod's best choon' (helpfully translated by the *Daily Telegraph* as O Briain 'hailing [Jerusalem] as the wedding's best tune')![38] Singing with great gusto, the physical audience included, in one abbey corner, the collected leaders of the Commonwealth countries, many of whose nations had previously sung the song as one of their own. Whatever its suitability for a 'Christian wedding service', there is little doubt that it was eminently suitable for a 'Royal Wedding service' taking place on a world stage, even if it was held to be only a semi-State one!

A further ironic, indeed comic, twist on the potential exclusion of 'Jerusalem' from the wedding services of England's Anglican churches was added soon afterwards by a somewhat tongue-in-cheek intervention in the House of Commons by Labour MP Chris Bryant on 19 May 2011.[39] Bryant, a former Anglican priest who had left the ministry because of its incompatibility with his sexuality, called for a Commons debate, arguing that incoming rules allowing civil partnerships to take place on religious premises meant that a risk of discrimination against straight couples was being introduced into law. Such couples, he said, were unlikely to be able to choose the song 'Jerusalem' in a church ceremony because of the individual vicar's scruples, but would also be precluded from having it in a civil ceremony because it was a religious song. However, under the new proposals, gay and lesbian couples would be allowed to have the song at their civil partnership ceremony. 'So can we just make sure that "Jerusalem" is not just reserved for homosexuals', Bryant concluded, as laughter broke out in the chamber. The Conservative Leader of the Commons, Sir George Young, hesitated, before replying: 'I think "Jerusalem" should be played on every possible occasion'. The subheading of the *Daily Telegraph*'s report of the exchange hinted at the absurdity of the Church-Nation-'Jerusalem' saga: 'William Blake's "Jerusalem", beloved of sporting crowds and Prince William, is in danger of being "reserved for homosexuals", a Labour MP has claimed'.[40]

'Jerusalem' and the XXX Olympiad, or London 2012

The final example of recent use of 'Jerusalem' that should be addressed is its incorporation into the opening ceremony of the London Olympic Games on 27 July 2012. The issue of competing nations, so central to Baron de Coubertin's vision of a revived modern Olympics, produced a complication in the case of the United Kingdom because the four 'home' nations, England, Wales, Scotland, and Northern Ireland, must compete as a single entity (bizarrely called 'Team GB' in 2012, a geographical entity with no legal status; Northern Ireland's argument for a more representative 'Team UK' was unsuccessful). There was thus no possibility of using 'Jerusalem' as an English national anthem during the medal ceremonies themselves. In the opening ceremony, however, the director of proceedings, Danny Boyle, was not so constrained. Rumours before the Games, mixed with aerial photographs of preparations within the stadium, had already given some indication that the Glastonbury story would surface during the opening extravaganza. At one end of the stadium, a sizable model of Glastonbury Tor was built, the level areas of its flanks eventually being used during the ceremony to plant the flags of the nations taking part, set around the two larger flags of the Olympic Movement (the five coloured rings) and the United Kingdom (the Union Flag). On top was not the Thorn of Glastonbury or even the tower that adorns the actual Tor, but an oak tree, an addition which highlighted the hill's symbolic nature throughout the ceremony.

On the evening of the ceremony, Britain's recently crowned first winner of the Tour de France, Bradley Wiggins, stepped forward to ring a specially made bell, the crowd hushed expectantly, and helium-filled balloons soared into the sky. A single voice was heard as 11-year-old Humphrey Keeper from the Dockhead Choir launched into the opening verse of 'Jerusalem'. As the song continued, close-ups of the young vocalist were combined in the TV broadcast with images of rural scenes being enacted on the stadium in-field; as Blake's 'dark satanic mills' line was reached, the scene changed to an aerial shot of the Giant's Causeway on the Antrim coast of Northern Ireland, with the Belfast Philharmonic and Phil Kids Choir singing a verse of 'Danny Boy', the anthem of the province. In quick succession, a Scottish choir, the Big Project Choir, launched into a verse of 'Flower of Scotland' at Edinburgh Castle, before three Welsh choirs—Only Kids Allowed, Only Vale Kids Allowed, and the Welsh National Orchestra Singing Club—sang a verse of 'Bread of Heaven' on Rhossili beach (with—for no obvious reason—rugby tries by each individual nation inserted into the broadcast). This section of the Opening Ceremony closed with a return to the Olympic Stadium for the remaining two verses of 'Jerusalem', sung as actor Kenneth Branagh (dressed as Isambard Kingdom Brunel) climbed the Tor to read Caliban's 'Isle is full of noises' speech from Shakespeare's *The Tempest*, and thus usher in the Industrial Revolution section of the ceremony. The BBC's commentator intoned: 'London's Games, Great Britain's Games, all of the songs from the four countries that make up the United Kingdom.'

Uncommented upon, however, was the fact that only 'Jerusalem' was sung in full, effectively enclosing the diminished songs of the other three nations. As it ended, with Branagh on the Tor, its closing words—'I will not cease from Mental Fight, Nor shall my Sword sleep in my hand: Till we have built Jerusalem, In England's green & pleasant Land'—were also causing some puzzlement among some of the global audience for this Great British (and Northern Irish) Olympiad. Had they had access to the *Opening Ceremony's Media Guide*, however, they would have read these words from Boyle:

The Ceremony will take us through great revolutions in British society—the Industrial Revolution, the revolution of social attitudes that began in the 1960s and the digital revolution through which we're living now. Woven through it all, there runs a golden thread of purpose—the idea of Jerusalem—of a better world that can be built through the prosperity of industry, through the caring nation that built the welfare state, through the joyous energy of popular culture, through the dream of universal communication. We can build Jerusalem. And it will be for everyone.[41]

From Blake's 'Jerusalem', continued the *Guide*, comes the 'phrase "chariots of fire", the title of one of the films to best capture the Olympic spirit'; Vangelis's theme from Hugh Hudson's *Chariots of Fire* (1981) appeared as a Mr Bean backdrop later in the Opening Ceremony and was used to precede every Games medal ceremony.[42] It was not just the three other nations of the United Kingdom that the Ceremony was attempting to enfold within this English 'Jerusalem' ideology, expressed as 'British' by Boyle, therefore. Rather the whole world was to come under Boyle's intellectual 'wing' through his fusion of the home nation's essentially local achievements— for example, the Industrial Revolution and the National Health Service—with a tone of global aspiration set amid the wider Olympic vision of humanity.

Responses from the British papers to the Ceremony ranged from the rapturous to the rancorous. The *Daily Mirror's* Alison Philips wrote:

This Olympic opening ceremony was showing a great Britain [sic] with its head held high. We recounted our history with pride and unashamed accept-ance that it has made us the country we are today, a country still able to put on such an extraordinary event with style and to welcome visitors from around the world with open arms and, importantly, with open minds.[43]

Others added a broad variety of suitably 'English' adjectives, with the *Guardian* excelling—'madcap, surreal and moving', 'irreverent and idiosyncratic', 'Serious and silly, subversive and mainstream, high and low', 'extraordinarily bonkers', with that paper's Marina Hyde concluding that 'Boyle's banquet felt as deliciously indigestible to global tastes as Marmite or jellied eels. I loved it'.[44]

Not everyone did so, however. Echoing the sentiments of a critical tweet from Tory MP Aidan Burley, decrying the ceremony's 'leftie multicultural crap', an opinion piece by the *Daily Mail*'s Rick Dewsbury argued that '[t]he NHS did not deserve to be so disgracefully glorified in this bizarre spectacle of left wing propaganda', citing recent *Mail* reports of the unpleasant death of Kane Gorney in an NHS hospital as evidence of its failings.[45] Burley was roundly castigated by his Tory colleagues and publicly recanted, while Dewsbury's article was subsequently taken offline. The importance of the Games to London and a nation under significant financial pressure meant that such criticisms brought a weighty opprobrium upon the heads of those making them.

Meanwhile, attempts were being made to gauge the reaction of watching nations. A Reuters News Agency report was headlined: 'Are we the same species? World agog at British Games opener', and began with the following lines: '"Strange", "baffling" and "surreal" was how director Danny Boyle described his Olympic opening ceremony. The rest of the world largely agreed.' The report's title quote was taken from *El Mundo*, a Spanish newspaper, and while the praise of other newspapers was noted, a critical note was registered with a prominent quote from Hansel Cereza, the choreographer of the Barcelona Olympics of 1992: 'Of course it was a very British ceremony and it had to be like that, but for me it lacked a certain universality'.[46] The tension between the local and the universal was generally resolved in favour of the local, such critics argued, largely ignoring or at least missing any possible elements of universality within Boyle's message.

The local impact of the Opening Ceremony was critically developed in one of the more politically focused early responses to the event, by Richard Seymour, a British Marxist writer, on his blog *Lenin's Tomb*, on 29 July:

Whatever the creators' intentions, whatever people now do to appropriate elements of this spectacle for their own agendas, the fact is that it's major achievement was to induce people to forget temporarily what a disgrace the Olympics are; how hated they are in the East End where the Olympics Green Zone has been implanted, protected by rooftop missiles that residents don't want; how poor people have been drive out of their homes as they always are when the Olympics comes to town; how much our civil liberties have already been attacked in the name of suppressing criticism of this ugly metro-plasty, as legislation and police exercises have been framed in the assumption that protest during these events is a potential terrorist plot; how preposterous it is that the 'security' for this montage of pointless exercises is being supplied by thousands of soldiers fresh from hunting shepherds in Afganistan [sic]; how fucked up it is that the major sponsors of this debacle, their names glowingly referenced all over the city's billboards, are corporations like McDonalds (which specialises in heart disease, bowel cancer and obesity), and Atos (which specialises in throwing disabled people off benefits and will no doubt have a special role in the Paralympics); and above all the fact that this is sports, pointless, boring sports, and the only reason anyone really wants to watch someone else swim forty lengths or jump over sandpits is because they're doing so on behalf of the nation.[47]

Only slightly less happy about the London Olympics were website producers who saw the coming event as an elaborate occult event. One, the person or persons behind 'Groundzeromedia.com', connected the events to come with the activities of the 'Priory of Zion' and its desire to create a 'One world religion' based on Christ's hidden blood line, a conspiracy group and scenario rather similar to that found in Dan Brown's novel *The Da Vinci Code* (2003, the 'Priory of Sion').[48] Another prognostication of doom came from 'Lawfulrebellion.org':

Danny Boyle's friends, Underworld, will be the musical directors for the opening ceremony…Essentially he has opted to symbolise the green and pleasant land of Brtain/Jeusalem [sic] in a superficial sense with the countryside, sheep & cows, village cricket and rain clouds common in albion [sic]. Overtones of Shakespeare and Peter Pan have been found, as a huge model of Prospero the Magician waving a huge wand and a giant Hook and Pirate were photographed by helicopters. William Blake offers a clear connection to Zion via the word Jerusalem as they are essentially interchangeable [sic] as spiritual homes. The Glastonbury Tor does not feature the legendary St Michael's tower, which dominates the Tor, is completely absent from the models presented to the public by Boyle recently. In the place of the tower stands what appears to be an Oak tree, which is the sacred tree of Jupter [sic] again resonating the same theme. Of particular interest is that opposite the Tor will be the worlds' largest harmonic bell directly above a 'posh pit' of people embued [sic] with 'the spirit of the promenaders' [sic]. The opening ceremony certainly has many surprises in store, but what has already been revealed officially is enough to put together a distinctly manipulative, contrived, satanic ritual.[49]

The introduction of the idea of 'Jerusalem' was clearly intended to achieve much at the London Olympiad, but there was clearly little consensus among the watching commentators as to exactly what that achievement was supposed to be. Nevertheless, most of them eventually seemed to believe that 'Jerusalem' had done its job, whatever it was.

Responses from the colonies: Irish and Australian views on the English Joseph story

In 2011, the Irish band U2 gave its first performance at the Glastonbury Music Festival since the 1980s. Playing in the pouring rain, Bono and the band performed a set of songs from the last 20 years of their back catalogue. Mixed in with their own sounds, however, were a small number of curious Glastonbury-related insertions. The *Guardian* reviewer, Dorian Lynskey, subsequently wrote: 'Aside from an a cappella verse of *Jerusalem*, Bono wisely keeps the Avalon blarney to a minimum. "Could be the leylines," he begins. "Could be the jetlag. But it's a very special feeling being here."'[50] That special feeling was further explicated—or not—when the band was interviewed after its stage appearance by the BBC's Jo Whiley and Zane Lowe.

Jo Whiley: 'Did you enjoy it [playing Glastonbury].'
Bono: 'And you know, that song Jerusalem for an Irish boy to sing that, you gotta admit. And, but you know there's a story about Glastonbury. People don't know that that song that they sung, Jerusalem and England... is all this mythology about Joseph of Arimathea coming to Glastonbury; the oldest Abbey, Christian abbey in northern Europe is here. Everyone talks about "Stonehenge and all that, man." Which I am cool with, but I just, we came, I was, a real pilgrimage for me, and actually got onto that tip (turns to band) then I used some of the lyrics in Bad also...'

Edge: 'I got that'
Bono: 'Were you comfortable with that?'
  [Whiley interrupts and directs the original question to drummer Larry
  Mullen.][51]

Largely incoherent as Bono's doubtless adrenalin-soaked words
were, they provide a clear indication that however much at home
the singer felt himself to be among the festival crowds at Glastonbury, there was still some unease with the words of 'Jerusalem'
themselves: 'that song Jerusalem for an Irish boy to sing that, you
gotta admit....' This distancing from the spatial locatedness of
Blake's 'English' words had also manifested itself during Bono's
performance. That the insertion of Blake's words into two of the
songs, 'Where The Streets Have No Name' and 'Bad', was planned
beforehand is apparent, though guitarist The Edge seemed to be in
the dark about the second insertion at least in the BBC's interview. It
is not clear, however, at what point Bono chose which words he
would sing with which song or when he decided that he would alter
the words of the anthem themselves. In 'Where The Streets Have
No Name' Bono sang the first seven lines of Blake's poem, omitted
the following eight lines, and concluded with its final line (lines 9–12
were added to 'Bad' with unimportant minor changes). Absent
completely from either of Bono's two amended songs were any
mentions of 'dark satanic mills', of ceasing from 'mental fight', of
'my sword shall' not sleep, and of building Jerusalem now 'in England's green and pleasant Land'. Indeed, those last few words had
instead been transposed back into the past in Bono's version of the
lyrics that were inserted into 'Where The Streets Have No Name'.
  For the purposes of comparison, here are the relevant lines of
Blake's original; as we shall see, however, they are not exactly what
Bono sang that day:

   1. And did those feet in ancient time.
   2. Walk upon England's mountains green:
   3. And was the holy Lamb of God.
   4. On England's pleasant pastures seen!
   5. And did the Countenance Divine.
   6. Shine forth upon our clouded hills?

> 7. And was Jerusalem builded here....
> [lines 8–15 omitted]
> 16. In England's green and pleasant Land.[52]

The Irishman's spatial distancing is readily apparent from his swapping of the English 'our' in line 6 and 'here' in line 7 for the outsider's 'your' and 'there' respectively. Similarly the reluctance of a non-Englishman to sing blithely a song about not resting until Jerusalem has been 'builded...In England's green and pleasant Land' is perfectly understandable—at least to anyone who is not an English man or woman singing one of their most popular anthems!

The stand-up comedian Dara O Briain in his book, *Tickling the English: Notes on a Country from an Irish Funny Man on Tour* (2009), a gig-by-gig account of his sellout 2008 tour of the British Isles, opened with a brief statement of how the English had appeared to him as an Irish child: 'I always thought there was something funny about England.' Describing an audience participation technique of building a routine about national traits, he noted that the quickest way to stop the audience cold was to ask about the English. Addressing his book audience he wrote: 'Maybe you just don't have a national identity. Maybe you just don't want to admit to one. We'll see.'[53] In the midst of his musings and wanderings on the tour, O Briain arrived at Basingstoke's Anvil Theatre on 23 April and offered a comparison between the Irish and St Patrick's Day, 17 March—a highly successful global phenomenon and, crucially, he suggested, a day off in the middle of Lent—and the English and St George's Day, 23 April—a damp squib of a day with 'no context, no history, and no purpose'. St George never even came to England, leaving no sites to cherish! This was 'similar', he noted, 'to the never-ending English devotion to the hymn "Jerusalem", despite it being a long feedline to a very curt and obvious punchline':

And did those feet in ancient time/
Walk upon England's mountains green? *No.*

And was the Holy Lamb of God/
On England's pleasant pastures seen? *Nope.*

And did the countenance divine/
Shine forth upon our clouded hills?   *Still a big nooo, I'm afraid.*
And was Jerusalem builded here/   *No. It wasn't. Sorry about*
Among these dark satanic mills?   *that. And it's 'built' by the*
                                         way.[54]

Its comedic value aside, however, it is clear that for O Briain what he had termed the 'Prod's best choon' during the royal wedding in April 2011 remains a work that is highly performative in ways that move far beyond any issues raised by its obvious—to him at least—lack of historicity. After all, there is no possibility that O Briain himself could simply adopt the song's ideology, that he could sing its verses with non-ironic gusto, whether as an Irishman or as an 'atheist' who was 'ethnically Catholic' (his self-description). As Bono's performance at Glastonbury made clear, even the most appreciative Irish speaker of Blake's poetry would probably feel compelled either to justify their decision to speak it out positively as is or to alter its wording to more clearly reflect their distance from the Anglo-centric nature of Blake's vision.

Following Will and Kate's royal wedding, University of Cambridge classicist Mary Beard formulated ten relevant questions for an article in *The Times Literary Supplement* (29 April 2011). Her first question was: 'How come the great and the good of this country don't appear to know the words of "Jerusalem" without looking at their hymn sheets, and even then don't seem to be quite certain of how the words fit the tune?' We are less interested here with the implications of Beard's question itself than with the irate response to Beard's 'stupid' musings from an Australian writer, Hal G. P. Colebatch, in an article entitled 'Blake's Jerusalem—Forget It!' and subtitled, 'What explains the popularity of this ghastly hymn, its words written by a 18th-century free-lance kook and sung at royal weddings?', published in the *New American Statesmen* on 3 May 2011.

For Colebatch, lawyer, author, and one-time Liberal (i.e. an English Conservative-style) candidate for Australia's Parliament, the words of the 'hymn' were written by a barely Christian '18th-century free-lance kook', it was not a hymn, and it was 'not appropriate for a religious (or, I hope to show, any other event) setting'. Unsurprisingly given Colebatch's politics, he also mocked its use as a 'semi official-hymn of the Labour Party', doubting they really knew what it meant. 'It bears', he continued 'as George Bernard Shaw said of its rival the "Internationale", "all the panache of the funeral march of a fried eel".' The answer to the opening stanza, he wrote, 'to anyone with even an elementary knowledge of history and archeology, is "No." The fact that it can be set to a catchy and attractive tune does not prevent it from being rubbish. There is no evidence that Christ ever visited England...' Take that, Mary Beard! The case of the dark Satanic mills was then mentioned and aimed, with some historical justification, at Beard's present employer/s, the university/ies, those contemporary embodiers of Blake's 'particular enemies of humanity, spreading the poison of enlightenment and reason'.

So far, Colebatch's commentary could have been understood as just an internal assault on the song by a conservative Englishman who was not a fan of 'Jerusalem'—there are such around—but he then offered an outsider's dig at the fading country described by Blake.

Anyway, Britain's problem is not now the spread of dark Satanic mills (an abandoned industrial site, well overgrown, can look strangely beautiful), but keeping what mills and other factories it still has open, and, as far as universities go, getting the students to take on hard subjects like chemistry or engineering.

He continued with gusto, broadening his attack:

The poem goes on into the heights of paranoid grandiosity. The late Osama bin Laden, now removed to warmer climes, would particularly have liked that piece about 'chariots of fire', for which he could surely have found a use.... [Bring me my chariot of fire]...Yes, and head it for Ground Zero, maybe. This is the sort of verse one can imagine Charlie Manson concocting if he was a better hand at rhyme, and indeed Blake's poetry was enormously popular in the drug-addled '60s that also tried to make a hero out of Manson...[Nor shall my Sword sleep in my hand]...Oh yeah, and just who is going to get the benefit of the sword? We've seen attempts to build versions of the New Jerusalem, with or without the sword, since Blake wrote, and we've seen what they led to.

Colebatch then returned to the outsider vein, concluding that despite claims that the poem was 'simply lyrical', that will always be ignored by the 'nut-jobs' who choose to act upon them: 'The sooner "Jerusalem" is forgotten the better, and while I lament the loss of many facets of Britain's historical memory and culture, this piece of it is something we can well do without.'[55]

In sharp contrast to Bono's uncomfortable attempt to inhabit the song's space, and O Briain's somewhat mixed response to its enduring power despite its lack of historicity, here we have an outright rejection of its ideology of English/British chosen-ness, an ideology that Colebatch found sufficiently troubling that it was worthy of comparison with those expressed by terrorist Osama Bin Laden and by murderer Charles Manson. Surely one can only pity the Commonwealth leaders made to sing the song in Westminster Abbey, though I would hazard a guess that they at least knew the words far better than the English leaders castigated by Beard!

It is good to be the English!

When the vast majority of the English sing 'Jerusalem' today—and regardless of what they intend to achieve by their performance—what they are actually doing in the eyes of a non-English audience is implicitly testifying to their uniqueness as the possessors of a blessed and chosen land and, in consequence, to their superiority as a nation. Ignorant as so many of the English are about the song that a significant minority would like to see it as the English national anthem, it takes the responses of outsiders such as Ireland's Bono and Dara O Briain and Australia's Hal G. P. Colebatch to show something of the ideological message that is proclaimed abroad when English sportsmen and women receive their gold medals at the Commonwealth Games in New Delhi, when young English folk wave their flags at the Last Night of the Proms in London's Royal Albert Hall, when assembled world leaders are on the receiving end of a gloriously triumphant performance at a royal wedding in the Church of England's Westminster Abbey, or when a national 'signature' event like the opening ceremony of the Olympiad in London 2012 is televised worldwide and features England's 'Jerusalem' bracketing (subsuming!) the discrete anthems of the Northern Irish, the Scots, and the Welsh. No wonder an Irish 'ethnically Catholic atheist' like O Briain finds it easy to both deeply appreciate and yet openly mock such an uninhibited expression of fervent English nationalism. Joseph of Arimathea's gift of chosen-ness to the English people is one that just keeps on giving, no matter how ignorant some of its local proponents are about it or how much its many English and foreign detractors might wish it otherwise.

6

The Twentieth-Century
Joseph

Joseph of Arimathea in other contemporary settings

So far we have looked at the earliest accounts of Joseph of Arimathea, seen how traditions about him began to develop in oral, literary, and visual culture, and examined the developments arising out of his connection with Glastonbury and with England and Britain more generally. In this chapter, we will try to fill out our picture of the extent of the Joseph tradition today, while acknowledging that more could be included. The categories occupying us are sainthood, fiction, film and television, spiritualism, and finally, what we might term 'Joseph myth theory', the discussion about whether Joseph ever existed.

The Church's Joseph

Given Joseph's central role in the events of the passion narratives, his explicit discipleship in Matthew and John, and the potential for imitation supplied by his many extended portrayals down the centuries, it is no surprise to find him also being regarded as a saint in many of the major Christian churches. This may have involved the naming of individual churches after him (examples are: Saint Joseph of Arimathea Episcopal Church in White Plains, New York State; St Joseph of Arimathea Orthodox Church in Whitevale, Ontario; or St Joseph of Arimathea Independent Catholic Church in New Haven, Connecticut); or a seminary (Saint Joseph of Arimathea

Anglican Theological College in Berkeley, California); the celebration of his feast day (traditionally, 17 March in Catholicism, though he now appears on 31 August with Nicodemus; in the Greek Orthodox Church, 31 July); or his taking up of the role of patron saint, in Joseph's case, that of tin miners/tin workers and of funeral directors/undertakers. Interestingly, these two discrete types of workers connect exclusively with either the West Country tradition of Joseph the tin merchant or the biblical tradition of Joseph at the burial of Jesus.

Tin Miners and Tin Workers. Explicit references to Joseph as the patron saint of tin miners and tin workers are quite hard to come by, though he is certainly listed as such on a number of saint-related websites; the *Aquinas & More* website has a Joseph page listing him as 'Patron Of: Tin Miners, Tin Smiths, Coffin Bearers, Funeral Directors, Glastonbury Cathedral, Morticians, Pall Bearers, Undertakers', and sells merchandise ostensibly related to him.[1] Tied into the 'Jesus in England tradition' already discussed in chapter five (see pp. 107–8), the tin mining and tin worker tradition does not seem to be of particularly ancient origin. Of more interest is A. W. Smith's conclusion that the tradition recorded by the Rev. Sabine Baring-Gould in 1899—that Joseph of Arimathea came in a boat to Cornwall and brought the boy Jesus with him, and the latter taught him how to extract tin and purge it from its wolfram; when the tin is flashed then the tinner shouts 'Joseph was in the tin trade'—forms 'something like a very regular "patron saint" story with the Divine Child guiding Joseph to a secret of the tinners' art'.[2]

Smith noted that strong advocates of the historicity of the tin tradition commonly mention a ditty, sung as a refrain by children: 'Joseph was a tin-man, a tin-man, a tin-man, Joseph was a tin-man, and the miners loved him well'.[3] He also repeated an anecdote by Cornish bard Henry Jenner (1848–1934), about a story told at a dinner given by a Mr George Hallam, a master at Harrow School. A friend of Hallam's had visited a firm of organ builders in London to see how organ pipes were constructed. Each workman, before a particular part of the process apparently said 'in a low tone': 'Joseph was in the tin trade'. The foreman's eventual explanation of this comment was reported as follows:

We workers in metal are a very old fraternity and, like other handicrafts, we have old traditions among us. One of these, the memory of which is preserved in this invocation, is that Joseph of Arimathea, the rich man of the Gospels, made his money in the tin trade with Cornwall. We also have a story that he made voyages to Cornwall in his own ships, and that on one occasion he brought with him the Child Christ and His mother and landed them at St Michael's Mount.[4]

This London account, Smith regards as the earliest occurrence of the Joseph and tin-mining tradition. Since some discussions of the story also state that Cornish tin men believed the tradition as late as the 1930s, it would seem that the life of the tradition was a relatively short-lived one. One might also add that since neither tin mining nor tin working are mass industries in the United Kingdom today, the need for such a patron saint is much diminished.

Funeral Workers. Death has always been considerably more commonplace than tin mining or working, of course, and so the more developed 'patron saint' tradition is naturally that of the undertakers and those associated with them. In M. O. McGrath's book, *Patrons and Protectors: More Occupations* (2002), a funeral director, M. T. Higgins, described the exemplary role taken by his 'patron saint':

Joseph of Arimathea prepared Jesus' body for burial and the fact that he is named in the [Gospel] tells of the importance of this merciful, tender act. Christ's resurrection reveals the joyful promise of a new and perfected body, yet our earthy bodies deserve respectful, reverent treatment even in death.

He continued:

Humankind has always gathered in the presence of its dead to ritualise the loss of a loved one, to seek meaning in the face of mystery, and to share community support. Much like a pastor I have discovered the awesome privilege of accompanying people in saying goodbye and helping them plan ceremonies that express thanksgiving and hope. Restoring dignity to the vessels of life and participating in commending them to God is a way of offering a gift to the family and friends of the deceased, and to God.[5]

Involvement with burying the dead under the name of Joseph of Arimathea as a patron has not been restricted to the professionals, however. The website of the St Ignatius High School in Cleveland,

Ohio, described the aims of its St Joseph of Arimathea Pallbearer Ministry, founded in 2002, as being:

> To practice the Works of Mercy by offering pallbearer services free of charge to those in need, especially the poor and the elderly. [The seven traditional corporeal works of mercy are feeding the hungry; giving drink to the thirsty; clothing the naked; sheltering the homeless; visiting the sick; ransom the captive; and burying the dead.]
>
> To affirm the value and dignity of human life.
>
> To represent the community at a person's final commendation.
>
> To commemorate and pray for the dead.[6]

J. Podolak of the *News-Herald* ('Serving Northern Ohio') interviewed some of the 15–17-year-olds involved in another such school society in Munson, Ohio:

> 'It's affected people the most when we're the only ones there,' said Greg Welch, who directs the campus ministry and leads the St Joseph of Arimathea Pallbearer Society at Notre Dame Cathedral Latin High School, Ohio. 'We often serve those with no resources who die alone... Since we serve those without resources, we bring dignity to those who may not have been in good circumstances...' Sophomore Noah Boksansky, 15, said serving as a pallbearer has been an eye-opening experience for him. 'I really wanted to be a part of this ministry,' he said. 'It's a good feeling.' [Unattributed]: 'We make a point of greeting the loved ones with the sign of peace during the mass and at the grave site we tell them we will pray for them.'

Though both girls and boys are members of Notre Dame's St Joseph of Arimathea Pallbearer Society, Welch noted that 'it tends to be something that involves our hockey players and wrestlers.'[7] The all-girl Beaumont School in Cleveland Heights was also said by Podolak to have a pallbearer society, though that school's website contained no mention of it in October 2012.

Fiction

A second area of existence and development for Joseph in the modern world has been in works of literary fiction. There are too many such works to be summarized here, but they can be divided into distinct genres—novels, poetry, and plays—and, more broadly, into types based on their attitude to the chronology and the centrality of Joseph's role.

A Typology of Literary Development—Pre- and Post-Burial. The first broad literary type focuses straightforwardly on Joseph's role in the events building up to and surrounding the passion. For example, in Edward Percy's play *Joseph of Arimathea: A Romantic Morality in Four Scenes* (1920), the action takes place in Jerusalem around the days of the death and resurrection of Jesus; or in the series of poems which made up James Harpur's *The Gospel of Joseph of Arimathea: A Journey into the Mystery of Jesus* (2007), each a reflection on the life and death of Jesus by those who knew him best, sought out and collected by Joseph of Arimathea following the crucifixion. T. Rowland Hughes's Welsh novel *Yr Ogof* ('The Cave'), also entitled *The Story of Joseph of Arimathea* in its English translation, is an extended account of Joseph's actions up until the late blossoming of his confident belief in Christ immediately after his burial of Jesus' body, concluding from the perspective of an eyewitness that: 'The light on [Joseph's] face was not of this world'.[8] At the risk of a sweeping generalization, such works commonly share many of the problems of fictional novels about Jesus; any extended reveries or dialogue on the part of the protagonists are often stilted and the spark which enlivens literary fiction is largely absent.

The second broad literary types are the fictional accounts that may include some pre-crucifixion material, but which are primarily interested in developing ideas about Joseph's post-crucifixion life. Frank C. Tribbe's first-person narrative *I, Joseph of Arimathea: A Story of Jesus, His Resurrection and The Aftermath* (2000), also described as 'A Documented Historical Novel', comprised five sections: 'The Resurrection and the Shroud'; 'My Early Years and My Family'; 'Jesus' Life Ministry, and Crucifixion'; 'The Post-Resurrection Period'; and 'My Exile: Shroud Pilgrimages Begin'. In M. E. Rosson's *Uncle of God: The Voyages of Joseph of Arimathea* (2010), the travels of the man from Arimathea begin before Jesus' birth and form a narrative counterpoint to his life, ministry, and death. Jesus' missing years are spent with Joseph, working and travelling, but the rest of the novel tells of Joseph's life in Britain, where eventually he becomes the repository for 12 scrolls, one from each apostle, given to him by John, the last living apostle.⁹ Sometimes, however, the pre-crucifixion material is reduced almost to a preamble, and the extended focus is on later events, allowing for significant developments to the story of Joseph. In William Boardman's *Sun and Wind: The Legend of Joseph of Arimathea* (2007), the crucifixion takes place on pages 13–14, Joseph has been stripped of his wealth by Caiaphas by page 17, and the rest of the novel shows Joseph living the exemplary life of a devout disciple in Britain. In Frank G. Slaughter's *The Thorn of Arimathea: A Novel of the Days Following the Crucifixion* (1959), a dash of excitement is added to Joseph's often peaceful life in Britain when an attempt is made to burn Joseph and Veronica (familiar from her legendary involvement in the passion, see p. 79) in a wicker cage! The attempted execution is foiled by her veil, and they escape, despite Joseph being speared in the back by one of their captors!¹⁰

The final literary type includes Joseph of Arimathea in some fashion, but presents him largely indirectly; for example, Phil Rickman's *The Bones of Avalon* (2010), subtitled *Being edited from the most private documents of Dr John Dee, astrologer and consultant to Queen Elizabeth*, where the Joseph story is the foil for a complex treason plot involving a search for King Arthur's bones and the intervention of the French seer, Nostradamus, and his earlier novel *The Chalice: A Glastonbury Ghost Story* (1997). Since these novels are free to roam wherever they please, they are potentially the source of the more startling developments in Joseph lore. Indeed, rather than attempt to provide further details here of each of these three categories, the following will simply look at Rickman's *The Chalice*, and examine two very different and essentially discrete responses to the Glastonbury Joseph legend, one with an emphasis on gender and the other with an emphasis on a perverted emulation. To do justice to each, the presence of spoilers is necessary.

Phil Rickman's The Chalice: A Glastonbury Ghost Story. Set in Glastonbury, *The Chalice* (1997) is a ghost story that offers multiple readings of the Joseph myth from the perspective of its characters. The 643-page story revolves around three main characters: Diane Ffitch, the estranged daughter of a rich local family headed by her father, Lord Pennard; Juanita Carey, proprietor of a bookshop selling works on 'Mysticism, Psychic Studies, Earth mysteries, and

Esoterica'; and Joe Powys, an illegitimate descendant (perhaps) of a prominent—and real—Glastonbury author, John Cowper Powys. Against the material backdrop of a proposed new road from Bath to Taunton and the conflict between the ordinary townspeople led by Diane's brother Archer (whose general attitude to the Grail, the Holy Thorn, and the abbey is pithily summarized by printer Sam Daniel as 'it's all bollocks') and Glastonbury's diverse spiritual seekers, both resident and visitors, the three protagonists also experience the rise of a dark spiritual power within the town as the new millennium approaches, the Dark Chalice, described at one point as 'the very opposite' of the Holy Grail[11] and as an 'anti-grail.'[12]

A complex and intriguing story told with many strands and a range of well-observed characters, our focus is on the two discrete versions of the Joseph story mentioned above, and not on the larger ghost story. The version focused on gender is expounded most fully in an extended dialogue between Diane and Domini Dorrell-Adams, the Goddess-seeking owner, with her husband Tony, of a shop called *Holy Thorn Ceramics* on the other side of the High Street from Juanita's bookshop. The version involving perverse emulation of the Holy Grail is the tale of the Dark Chalice itself as related in the unexpurgated diary of Colonel George Pixhill.

An outsider, Domini's attraction to Glastonbury is explained in a conversation with Diane at the end of a very eventful evening. Attracted to religion generally, Glastonbury provided her with the only English spirituality available, she says, a religion older than any of those originating in the Middle East. Alerted to the area's legends as a school kid through hearing Blake's 'Jerusalem', Domini and her husband had arrived in the town and set up their business.[13] But there was always a tension between worship of the Goddess and the ideology of the Holy Thorn, which eventually leads Domini to destroy the shop's stock in the street, an act witnessed by Diane and the catalyst for their exchange on the subject of Joseph (Diane and the narrator's contributions add little and so have been removed here):

The so called Grail quest is a clear-cut male-domination trip, an attempt by armed men to steal Woman's cauldron of wisdom and rape her in the process. Just like the raising of the Abbey, with its great phallic towers—no listen!—

by a male-oriented Roman religion on a spot which just happened to be the holy vagina of the supine Goddess....

In response to Domini's disparaging mention of Joseph's name, Diane recalls favourably the story of his staff on Wearyall Hill. Domini continues:

Isn't it obvious? Sticking his staff into the ground...pulling out his...staff. ... and he pushes it into a sacred landscape formed into the contours of the body of the Goddess. This man Joseph symbolically fucks the Goddess... And...his foul seed germinates into a stunted tree full of vicious thorns. A tree which flowers in the dead of winter against all the laws of 'nature! That's the sick truth behind your pretty little legend."[14]

Later that night, inside Juanita's bookshop, Domini exclaims to Diane that '[t]he Goddess *lives!*' as her husband discovers the heaps of broken ceramics in the street.[15] Set against the Goddess-figure of the local landscape, Joseph's action in planting his staff in the ground is inevitably seen as a penetration and defilement of the feminine by the masculine. Rather than gain credit for placing Jesus' body into the ground/tomb, Joseph's interaction with the earth here brings him only vitriol.

The story of Colonel Pixhill is revealed in segments. An opening scene shows a young woman, Violet Firth, encountering the 'Dark Chalice' in a sexually charged and evil atmosphere in 1919. Cutting back to the present, a censored version of Pixhill's diary has been privately published by Juanita's bookshop, and is characterized by her early on in a letter as containing his 'Nostradamus-like, warnings of impending doom, souls raging in torment, the rising of the Dark Chalice...'.[16] Pixhill, resident since the Second World War at a house called Meadwell, a mile from Glastonbury, had seen a vision of Glastonbury Tor while on active service, and had been despatched to the town to keep an eye on a local spiritual activist Dion Fortune, also known as...Violet Firth. Made aware of the Dark Chalice by Fortune, Pixhill set himself to preparing for its eventual arising, creating a Trust especially to look after Meadwell. Later some missing pages of the diary are sent to Juanita by the last surviving Trust member, and these describe a particular dream of Pixhill's in which he saw the Chalice hovering over the well, the Thorn dead, and cloven footprints left in Avalon by those feet which had 'walked in ancient times.'[17]

The creation of the Dark Chalice is said to relate to the disruption to the 'Spirit of Avalon' that was caused by the hanging and beheading of Abbot Whiting on Glastonbury Tor in 1539. (The subsequent reappearance of the spirit in Avalon is identified by Pixhill's housekeeper as a 'convergence of Goddess worship and the Marian tradition'.)[18] Lord Pennard recounts to Powys a legend that a man named Ffyche (his and Diane's ancestor) betrayed Whiting by planting a gold chalice in his chambers, and, following the abbot's execution, used that same chalice to collect his blood '[i]n deliberate parody of Joseph of Arimathea catching Christ's blood'.[19]

Meadwell, it transpired, was given to Ffyche as a reward, with Pixhill's Trust eventually being revealed as having been created in order to keep the house out of the hands of the Ffytch family. When the Dark Chalice is finally revealed, however, it proves not to be a gold chalice at all. Instead it is described as 'disgusting' by a revolted Powys, being a base of old blackened oak, with skeletal hands raised up to hold the upturned cranium of a human skull![20] Powys's question—'is this the abbot?'—is never answered.

With Pixhill's story in particular, Rickman has offered his readers a stunning retelling of the Joseph tradition. True, as some critics have pointed out, the story is perhaps an overly complex one, but conceptually the Dark Chalice is a masterful and compelling creation. Though the treachery said to lead to Whiting's death is taken by Rickman as the occasion for an inverted re-enactment of Joseph's collection of Christ's blood, however, it is at least arguable that the macabre interest in Christ's blood and the overtly political use made of that interest over the centuries is hardly a faultless paradigm truly opposite to the Dark Chalice. On that issue at least, Domini Dorrell-Adams may well have offered an opinion worth consideration!

Film and television

Joseph of Arimathea has also appeared in numerous films, both in cinematic renderings of Bible stories in a recognizably biblical genre and in films set across a range of genres in which he figures as an essential part of the plot-line. A few examples will be examined before the single most highly developed premise based on Joseph is discussed, Brian Gilbert's *The Gathering* (2003), written by Anthony

Horowitz, author of the popular Alex Rider series of children's books among many others.

Jesus Films. In Piero Paolo Pasolini's *The Gospel of St Matthew* (1964), based primarily but not completely on that text, Joseph—played without words by a technician in his only screen role—is shown observing Jesus from an upper window as he is challenged by the authorities while teaching in Jerusalem. His status is ambiguous, however; he wears a tall hat similar to those of the persecuting authorities and the first challenge to Christ about his source of authority comes from the man standing at his right hand side, but when Caiaphas later orders Jesus' death before the Sanhedrin, Joseph—not a member of the council in Matthew, of course—is absent. Later his appeal to Pilate is omitted by Pasolini, but as (his?) men remove the body of Jesus from the cross, he is shown comforting Mary and leading her to the tomb. The film was widely acclaimed by critics, with the *Chicago Sun-Time*'s Roger Ebert commenting in 1994 that: 'Pasolini's is one of the most effective films on a religious theme I have ever seen, perhaps because it was made by a nonbeliever who did not preach, glorify, underline, sentimentalize or romanticize his famous story, but tried his best to simply record it.'[21] As a result, Pasolini's minimalist Joseph went beyond Matthew's portrayal, but only slightly.

In Franco Zeffirelli's TV mini-series *Jesus of Nazareth* (1977a, 1977b), however, Joseph—here played by James Mason, possibly the greatest actor ever to take on the role—appears much earlier in Jesus' ministry, in Galilee, watching as the gathered crowd are told of God's care for them and the needlessness of their worries. (Though it is tempting to conclude that an actor of Mason's stature had to be given more to say than the zero lines given to Joseph by the four Gospels and by Pasolini, Zeffirelli also extended characters such as Laurence Olivier's Nicodemus and invented others such as Ian Holm's Zerah.) Judas (Ian McShane), looking on, describes Joseph as 'one of the leading Pharisees of Jerusalem'. 'Extraordinary. But isn't that taking it too far', offers one of Joseph's colleagues at Jesus' words, but the Arimathean responds that such things have been said by the prophets, but 'not like this'. A meeting is sought—'such a man must be willing to discuss his ideas with people who are open-minded' says Joseph—and subsequently arranged in the house of Simon the Pharisee. Jesus' 'you will say I am a glutton and drunkard' (Mt. 11.19) opens the scene, but the ensuing discussion turns quickly to the law, debating the legitimacy of healing on the Sabbath. Joseph watches as the discussion develops before openly praising Moses' severity; it is Jesus' lax teachings that worry him most. Separation from sinners is God's way for Israel, he argues, but when Jesus responds by asking about the heart of the law, Joseph offers the first half of what we now know as the Golden Commandment, 'love God'. Joseph, answers Jesus, is not far from the Kingdom (echoing the Markan Jesus' words to the scribe in 12.28–34), but he then adds the second half of the Commandment, 'love your neighbour'. Just who is one's neighbour is illustrated by the abrupt entry of a 'whore', Mary Magdalen; Joseph then watches as Jesus' feet are first anointed by her tears and he in response forgives her sins. Simon objects to the woman, but is firmly put in his place by Jesus (cf. Lk. 7.36–50).

Later, Joseph defends Jesus before Caiaphas (Anthony Quinn), arguing for the practice of humility among Israel's elders and revealing implicitly his own attraction to Jesus' vision. It is Nicodemus, however, who voices the opinion that Jesus really is the Messiah, but he is argued down by Caiaphas, who objects to Jesus' self-designation as the Son of God. Called 'most honest of men' by the high priest and challenged with Nicodemus to declare that they accept that Jesus is equal to God, the two men hesitate, falling back on the legal argument that Jesus must be examined. Both are present when the arrested Jesus subsequently appears before Caiaphas, with Joseph openly opposing the idea of giving him to the Romans. Both appear shocked when Jesus affirms that he is the Messiah, the Son of God, however, and they are unable to prevent his being hustled out and sent to Pilate. Following the removal of the crucified bodies from the crosses and the gifting of Jesus' body to his family by a Roman guard, a Roman administrator tells the enquiring Zerah that a Jew who does not wish to be named has already asked the now-absent Pilate for the body. The entombment is not shown, however, and Joseph himself does not reappear on screen.

Generally well received, the freedoms taken by Zeffirelli with the biblical accounts were often missed or downplayed by critics. In a brief review for the Christian 'Dove Foundation', for example, an anonymous reviewer wrote: 'The film stays closely on track with the gospels although it does vary in some minute ways. One scene in which it strays is when Nicodemus comes to Christ during the day, when the Gospel of John clearly says it was at night.'[22] Joseph's visit to Galilee and his insertion into a number of Gospel stories where he supplements or even replaces those addressed (such as the good scribe of Mark 12—a traditional link seen in chapter one) went unremarked. In a post arguing that Zeffirelli's film is 'terrifically anti-semitic', however, blogger L. Zitzer pointed out that the division of the Golden Commandment 'does not correspond to anything in any of the Gospels. Not only does Jesus in the Gospels not reprove the man like this, but nowhere does he make this point.'[23] Joseph may have gained more screen-time, but he does pay a certain price in characterization for it!

Joseph of Arimathea and Indiana Jones and the Last Crusade. Joseph of Arimathea has also appeared in films that are not biblical in genre terms. In the action adventure film *Indiana Jones and the Last Crusade* (1989), the third instalment in the 'Indiana Jones' franchise, the hero is an American professor of archaeology, Henry 'Indiana' Jones, Jr, with a well-developed sideline in hair-raising and whip-cracking escapades. His opponents from the first film, the Nazis, are once again chasing a weapon of great power, the Holy Grail, a weapon that it turns out is, plot-wise anyway, only available to them via the hands of the erstwhile Joseph of Arimathea. The first few scene-setting minutes of the film show the ending of a lifelong quest to recover the golden Cross of Coronado, but the action begins in earnest with the arrival at Jones's university of a package from Venice containing a notebook belong to his father, Henry Jones, Sr (Sean Connery). As he leaves his office, Jones is picked up and taken to see Walter Donovan, a wealthy contributor to the university's museum. Donovan has a tale to tell, beginning with a damaged stone tablet recovered in a mountainous region of Turkey. The tablet mentions the 'Temple where the cup that holds the blood of Jesus Christ resides forever'.[24] Donovan, in a tone of sincere reverence, fills out the story: 'The Holy Grail, Doctor Jones. The chalice used by Christ during the Last Supper. The cup that caught His blood at the Crucifixion and was entrusted to Joseph of Arimathaea'. The cup, he continues, that would give eternal life, eternal youth, to anyone who drinks from it. Pressing onwards in spite of Jones' doubts both about this 'Arthur Legend' (Indiana's own words) and about locating the cup from the tablet's incomplete description, Donovan recounts another story, told cinematically with a long interjection from Jones:

Donovan: 'After the Grail was entrusted to Joseph of Arimathaea, it disappeared and was lost for a thousand years before it was found again by three Knights of the First Crusade. Three brothers, to be exact.'

Jones: 'I've heard this one as well. Two of these brothers walked out of the desert one hundred and fifty years after having found the Grail and began the long journey back to France. But only one of them made it. And before dying of extreme old age, he supposedly imparted his tale to a—to a Franciscan friar, I think.'

Donovan: 'Not "supposedly," Doctor Jones. This is the manuscript in which the friar chronicled the Knight's story . . . it doesn't reveal on location of the Grail, I'm afraid . . . but the Knight promised that two "markers" that had been left behind would. This Tablet is one of those "markers." It proves the Knight's story is true. But as you pointed out—it's incomplete. Now, the second "marker" is entombed with the Knight's dead brother. Our project leader believes that tomb to be located within the city of Venice, Italy. As you can now see, Doctor Jones, we're about to complete a great quest that began almost two thousand years ago. We're only one step away.'[25]

Given that Donovan's project leader is his father and that Henry Jones, Sr, is now missing, Indiana Jones is recruited to take up the quest for the Grail. Later events in the film effectively verify the historical accuracy of the story expounded by Donovan. Joseph, though never appearing in person himself, proves to have been the essential enabler of this particular 'Last Crusade'. Despite the reference to 'Arthur Legend' by Jones Jr, however, this cinematic version of the tale is a purely Near Eastern one, with no hint that the Grail ever travelled out of that area.

Brian Gilbert's The Gathering. A higher-level conceptual use of Joseph of Arimathea as an enabling figure occurs in Brian Gilbert's *The Gathering* (2003), a film classified as horror/mystery/thriller by the IMDb website;[26] according to Gilbert, 'The Gathering is definitely a genre movie but quite what type of genre is hard to put a finger on.' He continues:

[w]hat really sold me on it was that it was a British Horror film in the same way that The Omen and The Wicker Man were. By that I mean it wasn't just about green smoke or bats flying about but was strongly rooted in ideas about Britain's past, old religions and Christianity.[27]

The Gathering had a problematic post-production period, however, spending five years on the shelf before being released to critical disdain and a swift relegation to a DVD release. Starring Christina Ricci and Ioan Gruffudd, and with a plethora of English acting talent (including Stephen Dillane and Robert Hardy), the film's central premise is that following the gruesome deaths of two Glastonbury festival-goers, a first-century church built by Joseph of Arimathea after the crucifixion is uncovered, its layout bearing witness to a pluralized version of the myth of the wandering Jew, that those who came to watch Christ being crucified were cursed to wander eternally, gathering periodically to look on as people die (for example, at JFK's assassination). Again to do justice to the film's use of Joseph, spoilers are necessary.

As 'art historian' Simon Kirkman (Dillane) works on what he considers to be the church that Joseph built ('probably') at the request of less-convinced ('possibly') churchman Luke Fraser (Simon Russell Beale) and his boss, the bishop (Hardy), he ponders the fact that the cross altarpiece created by an eyewitness faces towards carved figures on the back wall which in turn stare back at the crucified Christ. His wife, Marion (Kerry Fox), in the meantime, accidentally knocks down a young girl, Cassie Grant (Ricci), whom she then brings home to stay with her family—step-children Michael (Harry Forrester) and Emma (Jessica Mann)—to recover from memory loss.

Visions of people she has just met, including young Michael, dying bloodily, and of the Kirkman's home in a dilapidated state haunt Cassie, and strange figures assemble around her during her wanderings around the town. Following an unnerving encounter with a local, Frederick Argyle (Peter McNamara), who stares at Michael, she meets a friendly figure in Dan Blakeley (Gruffudd), who comforts her (and in the extended version, has a sexual encounter with her). They search Argyle's home and find a picture of Michael, but her attempt to warn the police is rebuffed. The Kirkman's housekeeper tells them of the rumours of abuse at the house, a former children's home, and Cassie begins to connect her visions and the events around her to an upcoming outburst of vengeance by the abused Argyle against his tormenters, which will culminate in the (unexplained) killing of the boy.

Meanwhile, Fraser has shared his concerns about the church with Kirkman, recounting some words of first-century writer Aristobulus:

'They came only to see, from the east and from the west, from the city and from the plain. They came not, in holy reverence to the Lord, but in lust'. The church is not, Fraser tells Kirkman, 'about Christ; it is about the people who came to watch'. Presented with Fraser's pictorial evidence about the many historical appearances of the figures on the church wall, the 'Gathering', and with Kirkman's explanation, related earlier, that the church was deliberately buried at the time of the Black Death, over a millennium after it was built, the Church authorities decide to bury Joseph's church. This is not to stop events (they are acknowledged to be 'unstoppable'), but rather to prevent it from becoming a 'centre of superstition and fear'. After all, the bishop states, 'if people become obsessed with evils that might occur, they neglect the present good that they should do'. No explanation is ever offered in the film as to why Joseph of Arimathea would have built his church in such a way, and those familiar with the United Kingdom's legal attitude to archaeological remains will probably be laughing out loud at the earnest but absurd discussions that take place at this point.

Waking from a vision of the young Argyle's abuse, Cassie finds herself comforting Michael, who has been looking at his father's photographs of the excavated church. Interrupted by Simon Kirkman, she tells him that she had seen the people in the photographs in the town, but is then shocked into silence by a final image, unseen by the audience. On his way to tell Kirkman of the bishop's decision, Fraser is killed in a car accident as the 'Gathering' watch from a road bridge. Called to see the bishop, Kirkman is shown Fraser's images, and, recognizing the faces in them, now realizes that his family is at risk and calls to warn his wife, before racing home.

Having taken the children to the village fair, Cassie sees the 'Gathering' all around them, realizes events are coming to a head, and, on meeting the now-alerted Marion, urges her to take the children to safety. Having killed his dog and planted a bomb in his van at the fair, Argyle begins his killing spree. Finding the dog's body, Cassie again tries to alert the police, but finds the duty constable dead, murdered by Dan, whose image she now knows (from the unseen photograph) is on the back wall of Joseph's church; he is one of the 'Gathering'. He revealed to her that she is able to foresee these events because she herself is a member too; she has just forgotten. It becomes clear that the watching of the 'Gathering' has become a fatalistic and enabling involvement in the deaths that they witness.

Rejecting her prescribed role, Cassie fights to stop events, foiling Argyle's bomb by moving his van; Argyle, having killed his older tormenters, however, is after Michael, at that point back at the house, and Cassie arrives just as his initial shot wounds Marion. Cassie and the children flee to the barn. As the 'Gathering' stand around to watch, Cassie is shot dead while defending the children, with Argyle himself then being killed, electrocuted by Simon Kirkman. As the three leave the barn, they see Cassie among the 'Gathering', half-turned away and unable to look them in the eyes. That night, Michael sees a Cassie dressed in white who explains her story to him. The film closes with Cassie, by way of a reward for her intervention, for her taking the 'second chance' offered to her, being freed from her role in the 'Gathering', with her image, broken by an inner light, crumbling from the back wall of the Joseph's church, just as it is being buried in darkness by order of the church authorities.

In 2007, Scott Weinberg described the film 'as a ninth-generation retread of *The Omen*', and asked plaintively '*Who* exactly is the target audience for a horror movie with no horror, a thriller with no thrills, and a movie with no clear focus on what it wants to say?' Though Weinberg was wholly unsympathetic to Joseph of Arimathea's 'eyewitness' church, blogger Dragan Antulov described the idea behind the plot as 'original', before complaining that the film perfectly illustrated 'filmmakers' tendency to waste excellent ideas in mediocre scripts'.[28] While it would not have redeemed the movie's many faults, not least its abject failure to explain Joseph of Arimathea's motivation for ever building such a church, its being categorized and advertised as the story of Cassie's personal redemption would perhaps have found it a different, even appreciative audience. At the very least, the subsequent critical commentary describing it as a non-horror film would have been avoided.

A channelled spirit

The connection between Joseph of Arimathea and practices often considered esoteric or even occult-like was briefly touched on in earlier discussions about the 2012 Olympic Games (pp. 124–5) and stories of Glastonbury such as Phil Rickman's *The Chalice* (pp. 137–40).

Here, however, the focus is primarily on a select body of esoteric literature published by 'The Leaders Partnership', which has grown out of the spiritualist practice of channelling spirits via mediums. An initial volume was compiled by Peter Wheeler (1996; as editor), and a second volume (1997) was authored by medium 'David Davidson', an acknowledged pseudonym.

The Way of Love: Joseph of Arimathea Tells the True Story Behind the Message of Jesus. In the introduction of Wheeler's book, *The Way of Love: Joseph of Arimathea Tells the True Story Behind the Message of Jesus*, an account is given of an anonymous woman who, having lost her mother in 1970, had adopted the belief that her mother now lived in another dimension. Contact with a spiritualist individual led to involvement in a spiritualist church and proof—to her satisfaction at least—that her mother (or at least her 'soul' or 'higher self') was indeed alive elsewhere. Further involvement with a 'psychic development circle' within that church eventually led to the woman entering a deep trance and channelling a 'voice which was unemotional and none too pleasant to listen to for any great period of time'. Following a period of spiritual inactivity due to ill-health, the voice—who wished to be known as 'the Master'—became stronger in her trances, and those who heard its teachings formed a group to question and learn from 'his' utterances. (Wheeler reported a number of tests carried out on the woman in a deep trance including the monitoring of blood pressure [which fell], heart beat [down to 40 bpm], and brain waves, x-rays [which apparently revealed two sets of vocal chords], and the use of an oscilloscope to assign a male gender to the Master's voice.) The woman found that the Master was revealing to individuals within her group that they had had past lives around the time of Jesus, more specifically as members of the family of Joseph of Arimathea, and she soon had a selection of such accounts given through her by the Master recorded and transcribed.[29] Eventually, in 1987, the voice was revealed to be that of Joseph of Arimathea himself, and increasingly the voice talked of Jesus, or 'Yeshua', and 'The Teachings of the Way'. In the early 1990s, the Master asked that the accounts of the past lives of Joseph's family be published, with the book edited by Wheeler being the direct result;[30] those who were talked about by the Master included characters such as Joshua and Abram, Joseph's brothers (a 'past life' given to an 'Anglo-Indian'),[31] Miriam, Joseph's wife (to an 'English woman'),[32] Josephes, Joseph's son (to an 'Englishman', presumably Davidson—a section said to contain extracts from 12 tapes),[33] and Mary Magdalen (to a 'French woman'), included among the group of family members because of her affairs with the men of Joseph's family, including with the man/the Master himself.[34]

This type of revelation is presented in Wheeler's book as a mechanism whereby the Master, representing a 'group of souls who help and guide people on earth', helps specific individuals with problems caused by their karma by revealing details of a past life to them. From the collected accounts and from the previous teachings from the Master himself, it is therefore possible to discern something of the 'historical' Joseph who is being portrayed in Wheeler's book.[35] He is said to come from a wealthy family, trading in tin and timber, and to have visited India and China. Though highly knowledgeable about Judaism, he spent time in India in his youth and was familiar with many religions; he is also said to have visited Britain as a trader. On the death of his father, he inherited the family business, a 'magnificent home in Arimathea', a holiday home on Cyprus, and one on mainland Greece. But a desire to be a rabbi led to his seeking training and eventually joining the Sanhedrin, albeit as an 'opulent' member; his desire to be the high priest, however, was apparently thwarted because of his affair with Mary Magdalen.[36] The Archangel Gabriel is said to have revealed to him that his nephew Jesus, had 'special powers'—'He was descended from the Cosmic God and the Light that shone in him was pure'—and also how he must die, a secret Joseph was said to have kept for 40 years (the reason for this secrecy and its longevity is not specified, however). Responsible for Jesus and his mother following the death of the boy's father, the man from Arimathea took the young Jesus to the Essenes following his return from Egypt after Herod the Great's death, before sending him for a 'long stay' in India—'probably the most important part of Yeshua's educational programme'. His reward for his diligence was to be present at the baptism of Jesus, the last supper, the crucifixion, and the burial. He is said to have taken a special robe from Jesus 'so it could not be rent', and to have 'under special guidance ritually destroyed the cross'.[37]

Preceding the accounts is a long introductory passage attributed to the Master that gives further detail about the type of spirituality which is acclaimed as the 'way of Jesus Christ'. Denying that this is a new Gospel, the Master warns against the dangers of dogmas, and suggests that the passing of 200 years or so will see the final rejection of the creeds that bind 'mankind'; the outcome of a gradual move towards that point will be an increasing willingness of the different religions to come together and share. The religion of Jesus, based on 'Essenic teachings', involves 'spiritual advancement' through the acquisition of 'knowledge', a view rendered as 'love one another'; for '[h]ow can there be any other teaching?' Jesus' words, it is claimed, have been twisted over time, by the transmission process and by doctrines such as original sin, and Jesus' message that life after death is available to all people has been lost. Churchmen have continually twisted his message to imprison, creating scriptures that misrepresent his teaching through the deliberate suppression of genuine texts, a suppression mandated by both a deep fear among the popes and bishops that people would abandon the Church and by their own desire for power; the Koran and 'the teachings of Judaism' are said to contain 'more fundamental truth', however. The accounts of Joseph's family in Wheeler's book demonstrate Jesus' true message, 'enlarge' the portrayal of the Gospels, but play down the miraculous, the magical, the mystical, and the illogical. The Master expresses the hope that the Gospels would eventually be revised, 'possibly by popular request'; one day the Church will be left to walk in darkness as mankind grows into the light.[38] The passage concludes:

The revelations in this book are more than the Gospel story seen through the eyes of Joseph the Arimathean. The source of the knowledge comes from a group of souls which include some of the Apostles and other major figures in those remarkable events of 2000 years ago, revealed through a deep trance medium. This book is therefore for all who seek the Truth and the Light be they Christian, Jewish, Moslem or those with no religious faith.[39]

The Memories of Josephes: Soul Memories of a Cousin of Jesus. In his book, *The Memories of Josephes: Soul Memories of a Cousin of Jesus* (1997), the preface describes how David Davidson vividly recalled memories of life in Palestine during periods of meditation; these were written down, collated, and published.[40] The section in Wheeler's book dealing with Davidson tells a slightly different version, however, confirmed by the Epilogue in Davidson's book; as these memories arose, Davidson checked them with the Master, who confirmed elements of the accounts and added further details.[41] Narrated in the first person is Josephes' life alongside his cousin Yeshua (Jesus) up until the crucifixion. In one passage, at a family meal, 'Josephes' describes his father, Joseph of Arimathea:

I watch my father across the table. He is neither harsh nor oppressive; quite the opposite. He is strong willed and can be forceful but he is no oppressor, he is the patriarch. He provides not just resources but an atmosphere wherein each one has a place and in knowing that they have a place they are able to be fully themselves. This is partly because in our society it is the patriarch who takes responsibility for the misdemeanours of the family. It creates a family environment wherein he is responsible to each and each is responsible to him. It is not a question of two being the same or one being better or worse than another because the foundation stone of the family is diversity, a diversity that is possible because of the degree of belonging that each one feels and my father represents that which we belong to: our faith and the house of Arimathea.[42]

Davidson acknowledges in the Epilogue that many will not be convinced by his account, though he does offer some arguments for its authenticity: the felt experience of meditation on certain events, the confirmation by the Master, the altered tone and wisdom of the words from his own speech and thoughts. He also acknowledges the glamour and intimacy of experiencing 'apparently hallowed personalities', before insisting that he is simply 'an ordinary man with fairly ordinary aspirations'. By 1997, however, he was reporting that his meditation memories had shifted away from those of Josephes towards those of a man named Malachi, the great grandson of Abraham; it is not made clear what role, if any, the Master has continued to play in his life.[43]

The Joseph of Arimathea myth

With Joseph the Master claiming to be a real continuation of the presence of Joseph of Arimathea in the modern world, it is perhaps fitting to return to the question that best befits that world's most

consistent approach to the biblical narratives: did Joseph of Arimathea even exist? With a scholarly acceptance of the view that the
Joseph variants in Matthew, Luke, and John derive from the interaction of their authors' ideologies with the Markan account (see
chapter one in this volume), the next obvious step was for interested
academics to begin to question the earliest canonical Joseph's historicity. Some have now answered that question with a resounding
rejection. F. W. Beare, for example, regarded the Markan Joseph as
a piece of creative hagiography, suggesting that a need similar to
those that pushed the later Evangelists to alter that figure was also
behind his creation by the second Evangelist. The 'mythical' Joseph,
he effectively claimed, was all that has ever existed.[44]

Crossan's Created Joseph of Arimathea.   In the most detailed exploration
of this sceptical approach by biblical scholars, J. D. Crossan has
argued that Joseph was a literary product, designed from scratch
by a highly inventive evangelist to resolve a single problem, that
'[n]obody knew what had happened to Jesus' body'.[45] According to
Crossan, the bodies of those crucified were normally devoured by
wild beasts:

In the ancient mind, the supreme horror of crucifixion was to lose public
mourning, to forfeit proper burial, to be separate from one's ancestors forever,
and to have no place where bones remained, spirits hovered, and descendants
came to eat with the dead. This is how Jesus died.[46]

Accepting the account of the disciples' abandonment of Jesus and
arguing that Jesus' body would not have been returned in a Jewish
context, there being no such Roman policy in place, Crossan concluded that the corpse would have been devoured and its whereabouts
would have been unknown to the early Church.[47]

   Later claims about the resurrection would have made that
unknowing into a significant difficulty, however. According to
Crossan, it was transformed at that point into an account of Jesus'
burial by his disciples through a two-step process. The first step was
the development of a hope that the Jews who had sent Jesus to Pilate
would have retrieved his body and buried it. Crossan argued that this
tradition first appears in the 50s CE, in the so-called 'Cross Gospel', a
text which is not extant in its independent form, but which he has

controversially claimed exists today as a textual strand embedded within the second-century CE *Gospel of Peter*, discussed in chapter two (pp. 21–5).[48] (G. Lüdemann's suggestion that such a tradition might underlie two other New Testament texts offered support for Crossan's argument. In John 19.31, the Jews 'asked Pilate to have the legs of the crucified men broken and the bodies removed' because 'they did not want the bodies left on the cross during the sabbath'. In Acts 13.29 a group—the 'residents of Jerusalem and their leaders' [v. 27]—are said to have taken Jesus 'down from the tree and laid him in a tomb'.)[49] Those with the power to effect the burial were no friends of Jesus, however; as Crossan put it: 'If they had power they were not his friends; if they were his friends they had no power.'[50] The Markan description of Joseph as a councillor waiting for the kingdom was the second step taken, solving the early Church's problem by making him both powerful and friendly, 'a perfect in-between figure'.[51] The brutal destruction and loss of Jesus' body was thus 'sublimated through hope and imagination into its opposite', a body held in constant view from the cross to the grave to the risen Lord.[52]

By solving that one problem, however, Mark created further difficulties which had to be solved in turn by the other evangelists. Straddling the Sanhedrin and disciples, they were left to wonder how this 'perfect in-between figure' related to the circumstances of Jesus' trial and death and to the disciples as a group. Crossan suggested that it was Luke who focused on the former, on the difficulty of his role in the Sanhedrin's deliberations, and tried to exonerate Joseph to ease the tension, whereas Matthew and John emphasized the latter, the tension with the disciples, and converted Joseph into a disciple to ease that difficulty.[53]

Crossan later came to accept that a Joseph-like figure could have existed and could have asked for Jesus' body for reasons of personal piety or communal duty, though he remained unconvinced that anyone did so.[54] To support the view that Mark had invented Joseph, Crossan offered two new arguments. First, he exchanged his previously well-balanced Markan Joseph for an intentionally opaque version. The use of βουλευτής, he suggested, made it 'impossible to know whether Joseph was among the judges of Jesus', and his description as 'one waiting for the kingdom' made it 'impossible to be sure whether [he] was among the followers of Jesus'. Mark's Joseph no longer resolved the issue of power versus discipleship by being a balanced 'in-between figure', but rather by being a deeply ambiguous one; Crossan identified the opacity of the portrayal as 'its Markan purpose'.[55] Second, Crossan suggested that failure to bury all the bodies made it unlikely that a historical figure was acting out of piety or communal duty.[56] Joseph, he concluded (again), was a Markan creation, a myth.

An Argument for a Basic Historicity. According to Crossan's view of the Joseph myth, the early Church had no knowledge about the whereabouts of Jesus' body; the disciples had fled and Roman practice involved the bodies either being left to rot on the cross or being buried unceremoniously by the soldiers. That the disciples fleeing equated to no knowledge of events at all is questionable, however. All four Gospel accounts portrayed Jesus-related figures around the cross, and the sharp contrast between those figures and the fleeing disciples suggests that the early Church could have possessed some knowledge of the trial and crucifixion. Even if the general point is accepted, however, information about the body's fate was likely to be in general circulation.[57]

Crossan's argument that the likelihood of a crucified Jewish body being returned was slim has already been noted in chapter one (pp. 13–14); it is true that the few examples discussed by Crossan are insufficient to prove that a Roman policy of return existed.[58] Alongside those examples, however, we also have an additional five early accounts of the ad hoc existence of the practice that he does not discuss; the four canonical Gospel accounts and Paul's apparently unproblematic statement to the Corinthian church that Jesus was buried (1 Cor. 15.4a). It seems undeniable that Mark's account—traditionally placed in Rome—transcended his immediate context, being utilized by the other three evangelists in different Roman cities/regions. If the occasional returning of a body was as implausible an occurrence as Crossan has suggested, why did the four evangelists, Paul, and their respective audiences not think so? Attempting to replace embarrassment about the body's location with implausible stories about its burial should have failed spectacularly. But it did not.[59]

The balanced Joseph first offered by Crossan eventually proved too historically plausible, and so his second, more ambiguous, version was formulated by way of response. This figure provided a different transition between the enemies who bury Jesus (Crossan's 'Cross Gospel'/ John 19.31/Acts 13.29) and the later traditions of the righteous sympathizer (Luke) or the disciple (Matthew/John). Mark, in Crossan's later view, left the possibility of a friendly burial open, but did not allow a definitive answer to the question. Joseph's dual designation is not as ambiguous as Crossan believes, however. He himself has admitted that only one relevant council/Sanhedrin existed[60] and this—when combined with the interchangeability of the two terms in Jewish texts mentioned in chapter one (pp. 10–11)—would have meant that Mark's audience had little difficulty in seeing Joseph as one of the Sanhedrin members involved in Jesus' condemnation and death. Openness to the kingdom did not, as we have already seen in chapter one (pp. 11–12), indicate discipleship necessarily; rather it was an open-ended category that did not imply acceptance of Jesus' view of the kingdom, but suggested instead a pious Jewish figure.[61] Furthermore, Mark's text had never actually required a powerful friendly figure to take Jesus' burial out of the hands of hostile Jews and place it into the hands of a disciple; continuity regarding the death, burial, and resurrection of Jesus was not supplied by Joseph in Mark (as it is in Matthew and John), but rather by those female followers who were looking on (v. 47: 'Mary Magdalene and Mary the mother of Jesus saw where he was laid').[62]

Crossan's sole remaining argument—that the exercising of personal piety or communal duty would have involved Joseph asking for all of the bodies—is undoubtedly correct. It is less clear why Mark would have mentioned that detail to his audience, however. Had it even been mentioned in the source material that he was using it would most likely have been ignored by the Second Evangelist because it was deemed insignificant or—perhaps less likely given Mark's lax attitude to the supposedly troubling issue of multiple bodies in the tomb—because it was thought to be potentially confusing. Or, as Crossan's 'Cross Gospel', John 19.31 and Acts 13.29 suggest, it might have been a group that removed the bodies. Perhaps Joseph was one of several Jews who interceded with Pilate, and became the one associated with dealing with Jesus' body.[63] Speculative as these two possibilities are, the only alternative is to agree with Crossan that the whole story was fabricated. With so little evidence supporting it, however, that seems the more problematic conclusion.[64]

The Markan account of Joseph can thus be seen as largely historical; it was based on the earliest tradition and strongly suggests both that pious Jews buried Jesus and that this proved no difficulty for Mark's section of the early Church. The continuity between the historical Jesus and the risen Christ was guaranteed for Mark and his audience by the female witnesses without there being any need for a disciple to have handled the body. All mentions of a direct Christian role in the burial were the creations of the later evangelists.

Given the lack of a scholarly consensus on the issue, however, the ironic result of such discussions about whether or not Joseph ever really existed is that even more Josephs have been generated, multiplying his identities exponentially and carelessly scattering them around in scholarly articles and books like so much detritus. Each text in which the 'real Joseph' is presented by the historical critics argues 'here is what he really looks like', adding, if only by implication, that 'he is not like that one, or that one, and certainly not like those two over there'. Anyone persuaded by a specific image in the scholarly domain will inevitably extend the afterlife of that Joseph as they teach/preach/explain it to others, perpetuating it ad infinitum. All of this is the case even before we begin to think about the many Josephs who have been ascribed by historical critics to each of the four individual evangelists over the years. The end-result is that historical criticism has proved no better at limiting the Joseph tradition than any of the other forms of interpretation that have been employed down through the centuries. And needless to say, none of these Josephs has had—or will have—much influence on the wider Joseph traditions. Shadowy figures all, they fade away into utter insignificance by comparison.

Drawing to a close

There is so much left that could, perhaps even should, have been squeezed into this chapter, but these few examples must serve to illustrate something of the variety and the extent of the impact of

Joseph of Arimathea as we now enter the second decade of the new millennium. Since all good things must come to an end, and since word count necessarily limits the content, it is now time to leave the examination of examples behind and turn to a consideration of what conclusions might be drawn from looking at the many, many afterlives of Joseph of Arimathea.

Conclusion

The devil is in the detail

It should be obvious by now that Joseph of Arimathea has enjoyed an extensive reception history, generated in part by the different shapes of the canonical Gospel accounts of the man. Though each contains a similar discrete time-limited episode moving between an approach to Pilate to activity set within a burial tomb, the four are varied in many of their details. This diversity most likely arose as the result of an evangelist's response to an issue within the source that he was using (Luke's concern about the Markan Joseph's guilt) or to his own ideological needs (Matthew's ascription of wealth to the Markan Joseph in order to fulfil a prophecy). Details such as who owned the tomb and the speed and style of the burial could then sit easily within the canonical accounts waiting for the right moment to surface and add difference to later traditions about Joseph. Once such developments began to spill outside the Gospels' limited timeframe, the tradition could begin to expand at an even greater rate. Use of the tradition in myriad settings also offered further opportunities for development, with new traditions breeding yet more opportunities for use, and so on. Finally, along came major opportunities to expand into new territory, here exemplified by the Glastonbury traditions about Joseph and its later outgrowths, especially English nationalism and British imperialism. Not all minor biblical figures would be so fortunate as the man from Arimathea in terms of his 'career' possibilities, though it could always be argued that some were even better served. Joseph nevertheless provides a suitable exemplar for what a minor biblical character could achieve, aided and abetted by his many interpreters, over two millennia.

Taking a broad brush to the Joseph tradition

Trying to examine the patterns of growth of the Joseph tradition is no easy matter, however; its diversity is really quite impressive. One option that I want to try to follow here concerns a basic differentiation that already exists within the four canonical Gospel portraits, that between the broadly active Joseph of the three Synoptic Gospels, a man who approaches Pilate first and alone, who (in Mark and Luke explicitly) removes the body from the cross, and who buries Jesus' corpse in a tomb (both with unimportant help), and the predominantly passive Joseph of the Fourth Gospel, a man who echoes an appeal to Pilate that has already been made by the Jews and whose burial preparations are dominated by Nicodemus and his lavish anointing materials. All later Josephs sit somewhere within the broad spectrum that exists between the two extremes of hyperactivity and hyperpassivity: those nearer the former extreme exhibit his forcefulness, his boldness and bravery, his wealth and status, his piety, his persistence, his masculinity, and his dominance over others, whereas those nearer the latter showcase his guilt, his lack of courage, his secretiveness, and his submissiveness to events and people around him. On a surface level at least, these two extremes are perhaps best exemplified by the contrast between the two alternatives for the historical Joseph discussed in chapter six; the mythical creation is by nature a formless sock-puppet, whereas the pious councillor acts according to his own beliefs and is not beholden to the special interests of others.

Ironically, however, the dominant tendency with the Joseph of Arimathea tradition over the years has not been the activity of the Joseph of the Synoptic Gospels, but rather the passivity of the Joseph of the Gospel of John. In the light of the arguments in chapter one, it is clear that the Matthean and the Lukan Josephs were created precisely in order to assuage the anxieties of the Evangelists and hence their portrayals already exhibit the inherent passivity which was to become one of the dominant features of so many interpreters' remouldings of the Joseph traditions. Compare, for example, the Markan Joseph to the Lukan Joseph, so anxious that the tomb be unused, so concerned about being misunderstood as to his role at the trial of Jesus, or to the Matthean Joseph, so painlessly wealthy, so easily a disciple, so smooth a replacement for the female witnesses. The passive Johannine Joseph would perhaps have swallowed these alterations, but how do they fit in with a dynamic Markan figure who exhibits a certain independence, integrity, and masterfulness? How would such a man have responded to such unforeseen developments of his persona, even those stressing his status as a man of action?

The irony deepens, however. While it remains tempting for the modernity-tainted biblical scholar to try to anchor the tradition in a historical Joseph who broadly equates to the active Markan portrayal, it should be acknowledged that such a historical figure is first and foremost the creation of historical-critical methodologies situated at this end of history; it is in the choices and arguments of the individual scholar that such a figure originates. That those choices have at the same time been deeply influenced—like it or not—by the countless earlier choices made by innumerable biblical interpreters simply emphasizes the inherent circularity of the historical-critical process, all of which leaves the modern historical-critical interpreter with a desire to do the right thing, but with little hope of being able to do so beyond the offering of an assertion of historical plausibility (itself no mean thing). The historical Joseph offered in chapter six mirrors the active Markan Joseph, it is true, but he owes his existence to the multiple arguments that have been used to keep at bay the claim that he is a fabricated entity. The beleaguered Markan Joseph remains an active figure, but at the very least he is tainted by association, both with the historical-critical Joseph and with the altered Josephs of the other Evangelists. With that in mind, we will consider the passive Josephs of the tradition first, before moving on to the active Josephs.

Activity and passivity

The Johannine depiction of Joseph of Arimathea as both subservient to the Jews who first asked Pilate for the bodies on the crosses and to Nicodemus in the burial scene was a substantial imposition on the Markan Joseph. But that passivity was further developed early on in the *Gospel of Peter* when his Markan boldness in approaching Pilate, already set aside in John, was further sidelined by his depiction as a friend of the Roman, with one of the tasks explicitly assigned to him by Mark and Luke—removing the body from the cross—being taken away from him as a result of significant changes made to Pilate's role (see also the *Gospel of Nicodemus* and Robert's *Joseph d'Arimathie* on the relationship between Joseph and Pilate). When Botticelli included Joseph in his *Milan Pietà*, Joseph's necessarily swift movement of the corpse between cross and grave was interrupted and made subservient to a static depiction of an ideological closeness in suffering between the Virgin and the Christ, with the Arimathean kept present as a bystander, as a mere reflection of the grief expected from those viewing the image in its ecclesiastical setting. The Fourth Gospel's description of Joseph as a secret disciple also became entangled with the practices of the Nicodemites, the hiders of their faith, though it is tempting to claim that Joseph's own mixed presentation in the New Testament ultimately led to him being a mere example of the practice rather than him being the one for whom it was named. Nicodemus, for all his actions of visiting Jesus, defending him, and burying him lavishly, and his not being described as a secret disciple, apparently fitted the dithering passive ideal of the 'Nicodemite disciple' envisaged, at least initially, by Calvin far better than Joseph did. One could also add to the list here numerous examples from the Grail and Glastonbury traditions where Joseph was easily subordinated to the needs of the story being told; his very coming to Britain being the prime example of his subservience to a home ideology, albeit one easily set aside when the plot line of an Indiana Jones movie requires that he stay in the Near East. Or, to conclude, we could think of the incoherent Joseph of Gilbert's *The Gathering*, building a church monument to a cursed group of death watchers for no discernible reason other than that the plot requires it.

Ironically, however, many of the things done to Joseph by his interpreters have resulted in his being transformed into a man of action. For example, the depiction of the Arimathean as a soldier, exemplified here by such as Robert de Boron and John of Glastonbury, allowed him to function as an exemplar for a military man of action, and even a 'captain' of sorts, with his translated status of *decurio* for councillor allowing, and perhaps even encouraging, his development into the Christian knight whose militaristic descendants would become the stuff of chivalrous legend as they pursued the

Holy Grail. Much could also be said about the Master, the spirit guide of chapter six, and his controlling influence upon the lives of the individuals involved in channelling his messages. Chrysostom's addition of the character trait of persistence to Joseph's approach to Pilate and his tying of that trait to the need to safeguard the link between cross and resurrection also served to increase the story time focused on the Arimathean's argument for the body; it was no longer a simple quick request. Later expansions such as the fictional accounts of Slaughter (*The Thorn of Arimathea: A Novel of the Days Following the Crucifixion*, 1959) and Boardman (*Sun and Wind: The Legend of Joseph of Arimathea*, 2007) also served to emphasize over and over again Joseph's personal and active piety. Success in recovering the body of Jesus was not just down to his character, however; Joseph's great status and wealth, exemplified in the Renaissance paintings of Simon Bening, Rogier van der Weyden, and Simon Marmion, also explained the ease and naturalness of Pilate's decision to grant his request (and occasionally was used to excuse the failure of the disciples to ask for it themselves). But wealth in this sense, especially when presented with some ostentation, also encouraged a pious emulation of Joseph by the rich and wealthy classes which would then either justify such people in their own eyes (e.g. in Simon Bening's prayer-book for Cardinal Albrecht), in the eyes of their subjects/inferiors (e.g. Rogier van der Weyden's display for those guests visiting Philip II), or in the eyes of Heaven (with both paintings). But status was not to be measured purely in terms of money; Joseph's political role was also affected by the strategic possibilities that became attached to later developments of his life. By taking the Christian faith to Britain, a development that happened purely by chance, remember, Joseph was given the opportunity to support the creation of a number of very powerful structures, for the abbot at Glastonbury, for the English at the Church Councils, and for the British Empire at its last ebb. Even today, the anthem 'Jerusalem' builds upon his presence in England—regardless of what Blake had in mind—in order to keep that peculiar ideology of English chosen-ness alive through sport and pageantry. In being the patron saint of the funeral trade, Joseph also potentially touches the end of all of us, at least in (formerly or nominally) Christian countries.

An ending of sorts

From very small beginnings, the Joseph of today has become an undeniably weighty individual. Given the dire financial situation extending from 2008 up until the completion of this book, it is perhaps fitting to close with a brief consideration of potential responses today to one of the many Josephs that we have examined, the wealthy Joseph created by Matthew. The Joseph who was painted by Simon Bening and Rogier van der Weyden finds deep echoes within the modern world of wealth; Bening's prayer-book resides in the collection of the J. Paul Getty Museum, after all. As the political systems of the late medieval period had their influential wealthy figures, their Cardinal Albrechts and Philip IIs, so the capitalism that dominates the globe today has its rich controlling elites, in the form of the 'billionaires' and their lesser acolytes, the 'millionaires'. The title of Thomas P. Hunt's affirmation of Joseph (and indeed many other biblical characters) in the context of nineteenth-century commerce, *The Book of Wealth; in which it is Proved from The Bible that it is the Duty of Every Man to Become Rich* (New York, 1836), is refreshingly blunt in its unquestioning support of this version of the Arimathean, but slightly subtler affirmations of the economic and political status of the rich can also easily be found in more recent works by, for example, evangelical Christians; here is the United Kingdom's Newton Walkin in 2011:

> Even today this writer hears the pleasant news that the world's richest man Mr Bill Gates...has today given $750million...to charity for the purposes of research that will eliminate many deadly tropical diseases...As intercessors, we pray for God's blessing to rest on Mr Gates and his family giving them health and protection from personal harm, danger and evil...In the New Testament Joseph of Arimathea and Nicodemus were very rich born again Christians who used their wealth for good causes.[1]

In an Easter Sunday sermon in Rio de Janeiro, placed online, the Rev. Canon Stuart Broughton placed Joseph 'in the same league as Bill Gates', and named him as ' Joseph "Bill Gates" of Arimathea' before concluding: '[m]ay God raise up more men and women like him, here and throughout the whole world!'[2]

Ironically, however, Bill Gates was also one of the philanthropic figures described by S. Žižek as 'liberal Communists', as 'the enemies

164 Joseph of Arimathea

of every progressive struggle today', and as 'the embodiment of what is wrong with the system as such'.[3] (Others mentioned by Žižek include 'George Soros, the CEOs of Google, IBM, Intel, eBay, as well as their court Philosophers, most notably the journalist, Thomas Friedman'.)[4] Using their wealth for good causes is not a neutral thing to be regarded as laudable, he argued; instead it is rather an attempt to uphold and prolong a system that is soaked in structural violence. For Žižek, their deserved fate was, and is, best expressed by Bertolt Brecht's poem, 'The Interrogation of the Good' (Žižek's rendering of the German title, *Verhoer des Guten*), which describes such people as the 'enemy', but acknowledges their 'merit' by executing them against a 'good wall' and burying them in the 'good earth'![5]

As one of the Bible's most iconic figures of wealth, and thus as a scriptural-enabler par excellence of capitalism's biggest contemporary figures, Žižek would presumably have also been willing to put—at the very least—the Matthean Joseph and his off-shoots, the Bening and van der Weyden Josephs, against such a good wall. Perhaps, Žižek might even, if pushed, have gone so far as to conclude that it would have been far better had Jesus' corpse been buried with the thieves or been devoured by Crossan's wild beasts than for it to be rescued by such a 'good' man.

Such options can only be contemplated and never achieved, however. Without Joseph of Arimathea much that has been accomplished either would have not taken place or would have had to take a different route towards achieving its actuality. A peculiar mixture of both (passive) achievement and (active) achiever down through the centuries, Joseph provides us with a telling parable of what a minor biblical character can achieve or be used to achieve by his interpreters once he—or she—is abroad in the world. His particular story has certainly not ended, nor is it even near to its ending, however. Extensions to the figure of the Arimathean, even very significant ones, may be just over the horizon. After all, a Joseph who was effectively dead and buried in the Near East for well over a thousand years was resurrected to new life through a remarkable literary accident in de Boron's account of the Grail legend and could do something similar again. We could try to predict the particular avenues in which that might happen, of course, but the very nature of the beast gifts to it a distinctive lack of predictability. Perhaps that is why the reception history of Joseph of Arimathea, and indeed of the Bible itself, remains of such great interest today.

Notes

CHAPTER 1

1. Cf. e.g. M. Goodacre, 2001.
2. Cf. e.g. R. Bauckham (1998:147–71) and J. D. Crossan (1999:23–6).
3. Albright and Mann, 1971:355.
4. Cranfield, 1977:462.
5. The translations here owe much to the *Revised Standard Version*, but do include occasional changes intended to clarify the meaning of certain terms.
6. Cf. e.g. J. Gnilka, 1979:332.
7. Cf. R. E. Brown, 1994:1214.
8. His implied culpability has also led commentators to try to alleviate the Markan Joseph's 'guilt'. Luke's description of Joseph as one who had dissented from their decision in 23.51 is echoed in R. T. France's suggestion that '[p]erhaps Mark's πάντες ['whole'] in 14.64 is not meant to be taken literally' (2002:666). R. Pesch speculates that Joseph had not been present during that particular council meeting (1977:512–13). In a move that does not completely exonerate Joseph, R. E. Brown suggests that he could have been one of those passive members led to condemn Jesus by the High Priest rather than an active agitator for his death (cf. Mk 14.63–64; 1994:1215–16). Each is possible, but does Mark require such apologetic strategies?
9. Lane, 1974:579.
10. Brown, 1994:1215.
11. Senior, 1984:133—emphasis added.
12. Brown, 1994:1224.
13. Black, 1989:45.
14. Brown, 1994:1216.
15. Crossan, 1991:393.
16. Brown, 1994:1209.
17. Lane, 1974:578.
18. Crossan, 1991:553–4; Crossan, 1999:20–1.
19. Brown, 1994:1249–50.
20. W. J. Lyons, 2004; cf. also e.g. M. D. Hooker, 1991:43.

21. Gundry, 1994:580.
22. Gundry, 1994:580.
23. Brown, 1994:1227.
24. Cf. Lincoln, 2000:241–2.
25. Brown, 1994:1267.

CHAPTER 2

1. R. E. Brown, 1994:1317.
2. Cf. Brown, 1994:1337–8.
3. The Greek text appears in F. Neirynck, 1989:171–5; R. E. Brown provides a literal translation of the text (1994:1318–21; cf. also J. D. Crossan's rendering, 1991:462–6).
4. Brown, 1994:1334–5.
5. Brown, 1994:1338–41.
6. Brown, 1994:1341–2.
7. Brown, 1994:1343–7.
8. Brown, 1994:1325–31.
9. Wilken, 1983:7–8.
10. Mayer and Allen, 2000:6.
11. Mayer and Allen, 2000:7–8.
12. Kelly, 1995:203–27.
13. Kelly, 1995:228–85.
14. Most of John's works do not have critical editions or modern translations. The Greek text of the two homilies discussed here can be found in J.-P. Migne, *Patrologia Graeca*, 58,775–82 (Matthew) and 59,459–68 (John); Outdated English translations exist in P. Schaff's *Library of the Nicene and Post-Nicene Fathers* (1886–90).
15. Rebbenich, 2002:5–7.
16. Rebbenich, 2002:7.
17. Williams, 2006:30.
18. Rebbenich 2002:10–11.
19. Rebbenich, 2002:12.
20. Rebbenich 2002:13–20.
21. Rebbenich 2002:21–30.
22. Rebbenich, 2002:32–3.
23. Burton, 2000:3.
24. Jülicher, 1970:155.
25. Jülicher, 1954:268.
26. Tischendorf, 1850; cf. Burton, 2000:6–7.
27. Tischendorf, 1850:88–9,141.

28. Jülicher, 1938:209.
29. Tischendorf, 1850:57.
30. Gizewski, 2011.
31. Gizewski, 2011.
32. Gizewski, 2011.
33. Williams, 2006:29.
34. Pack, 1951:188.
35. Pack, 1951:176.
36. Gilliard, 1984:154–5.
37. Paxton, 2005:235; Latham and Howlett, 1986:582.
38. Paxton, 2005:235.
39. Paxton, 2005:236.
40. Miles, 1997:149.
41. Miles, 1997:150.
42. Miles, 1997:149.
43. Miles, 1997:150–2.
44. Cf. Kannengeisser, 1998:25.
45. Yarchin, 2004:53–5.
46. Harrison, 2004:159.
47. Harrison, 2004:157.
48. The Latin text of the *De consensu evangelistarum* can be found online at the *Patrologia Latin* website: (<http://pld.chadwyck.co.uk/all/fulltext? action=byid&warn=N&id=Z400059631&div=4&sequence=1&file=../ session/1370431919_9000> Accessed on 6 June 2013). A nineteenth-century English translation exists in series 1, vol. 6 of P. Schaff's *Library of the Nicene and Post-Nicene Fathers* (1886–90).
49. Harrison, 2004:157.
50. Cf. Harrison, 2004:159–60.
51. Harrison, 2004:162–3.
52. Izydorczyk, 1997b:3.
53. Izydorczyk, 1997b:17.
54. Izydorczyk, 1997c:73.
55. Izydorczyk, 1997b:14–16.
56. Izydorczyk & Dubois, 1997:25.
57. Izydorczyk & Dubois, 1997:22–3.
58. Izydorczyk & Dubois, 1997:24–5.
59. Izydorczyk & Dubois, 1997:26.
60. Izydorczyk, 1997b:6–9.
61. Izydorczyk & Dubois, 1997:26–8.
62. The commonly available English translation is that of F. Scheidweiller, 1963:449–84. The Latin text on which it is based is the second edition of

Tischendorf's *Evangelica Apocrypha* of 1876. A more recent version is
H. C. Kim, 1973.
63. Izydorczyk, 1997b:16.
64. Ryan, 1993:221.

CHAPTER 3

1. Graeve, 1958:223–4; her comments should also be generalized to include
   the deposition scene.
2. Soudavar, 2008.
3. Hourihane, 2009:204–5.
4. Kren & McKendrick, 2003:456.
5. So Anonymous, 2012a; cf. also Kren & McKendrick, 2003:456.
6. Cf. Kren & McKendrick, 2003:456.
7. Anonymous, 2012a.
8. Luttenberger, 2003:184.
9. Aland, 2004:69.
10. Luttenberger, 2003:185–6.
11. Powell, 2006:542.
12. A. Brown, 2011:136–7, 145–50.
13. D. de Vos wonders if Nicodemus, dressed as a 'contemporary...and
    sumptuously dressed burgher', is based on a patron, but draws no firm
    conclusion about the matter (2002:79).
14. Powell, 2006:542–3.
15. Cf. e.g. O. von Simson, 1953; H. E. Hamburgh, 1981; D. De Vos, 2002:79.
16. Powell, 2006:543–4.
17. De Vos, 1999:31–2.
18. De Vos, 1999:10–11; 2002:75.
19. Powell, 2006:548.
20. De Vos, 1999:12; Powell, 2006:548.
21. De Vos, 1999:35.
22. De Vos, 2002:75.
23. Anonymous, 2012b.
24. De Vos, 1999: 15–16; 2002:77.
25. De Vos, 1999:20.
26. De Vos, 2002:75, 78.
27. De Vos, 2002:77.
28. B. Ridderbos, 2005:27–8.
29. Goldfarb, 1997:6.
30. Goldfarb, 1997:3.
31. Graeve, 1958:224.

32. Graeve, 1958:223–4.
33. Lightbown, 1989:207.
34. Lightbown, 1989:207.
35. Hankins, 1997:17; cf. 14–18; see also Goldfarb, 1997:10–12.
36. Goldfarb, 1997:6.
37. Goldfarb, 1997:7.
38. Lightbown, 1989:209; cf. Goldfarb, 1997:7, 12.
39. Lightbown, 1989:209.
40. Lightbown, 1989:209.
41. Kristof, 1989:163; Shrimplin-Evangelidis, 1989:58–60.
42. Kristof, 1989:170–1; cf. 167.
43. Eire, 1979.
44. Kristof, 1989:172.
45. Kristof, 1989:172.
46. C. M. N. Eire, 1979:45.
47. Kristof, 1989:176.
48. Kristof, 1989; Shrimplin-Evangelidis, 1989.
49. Arkin, 1997:496.
50. C. M. N. Eire, 1979:47.
51. Wabuda, 2007, 47.
52. Snobelen, 1999, esp. 397.
53. Anonymous, 2012f.
54. Zwemer, 1924:120.
55. Zwemer, 1924:121.
56. Zwemer, 1924:105.
57. Zwemer, 1924:109–10.
58. P. McCouat, 2012.
59. A. Graham-Dixon, 1994.
60. McCouat, 2012.
61. McCouat, 2012.
62. Graham-Dixon, 1994; cf. McCouat's approval (2012).
63. Graham-Dixon, 1994.
64. This description of Soudavar comes from the front fly-leaf.
65. Soudavar, 2008:7–36.
66. Soudavar, 2008:8–9.
67. Soudavar, 2008, rear fly-leaf.
68. Soudavar, 2008:26–7.
69. Soudavar, 2008:30.
70. Soudavar, 2008:30.
71. Soudavar, 2008:10–11.
72. Soudavar, 2008:14–15.

CHAPTER 4

1. Crawford, 2001:12.
2. Cf. Scott, 1981:35–6.
3. Crawford, 1993:87.
4. Scott, 1981:47.
5. Scott, 1981:27.
6. Crawford, 1993:87.
7. Robinson, 1926:4.
8. Crawford, 2001:9.
9. Bryant, 2001:4.
10. Bryant, 2001; Crawford, 2001.
11. Bryant, 2001:2–3.
12. So Crawford, 2001:14.
13. Bryant, 2001:34–44.
14. Bryant, 2001:15–16.
15. Bryant, 2001:21.
16. Bryant, 2001:17.
17. Bryant, 2001:18.
18. Bryant, 2001:21.
19. Bryant, 2001:23.
20. Bryant, 2001:23–4.
21. Bryant, 2001:24–9.
22. Bryant, 2001:29–33.
23. Bryant, 2001:33–4.
24. Bryant, 2001:34–44.
25. Dover, 2003:xi.
26. Chase, 2003:69.
27. Chase, 2003:69–70.
28. Chase, 2003:72.
29. Chase, 2003:73.
30. Crawford, 1993:88.
31. Lawton, 1983:xxxiv, xli.
32. Gerritsen, 1981:370–2.
33. Gerritsen, 1981:370.
34. Gerritsen, 1981:372.
35. Gerritsen, 1981:371–2.
36. Ryan, 1993:276.
37. Rahtz and Watts, 2003:11.
38. Rahtz and Watts, 2003:15.
39. Rahtz and Watts, 2003:20.

40. Rahtz and Watts, 2003:22, 26.
41. Rahtz and Watts, 2003:32.
42. Rahtz and Watts, 2003:34–5.
43. Rahtz and Watts, 2003:40–1, 44–5.
44. Rahtz and Watts, 2003:46.
45. Rahtz and Watts, 2003:47.
46. Robinson, 1926:6.
47. Robinson, 1926:7.
48. E.g. Treharne, 1967:85; 'To the writers of the twelfth- and early thirteenth-century who first shaped these romantic stories... the King Arthur of Geoffrey of Monmouth's *History* proved an inspiration beyond price'.
49. Carley, 1985:xlix.
50. Scott, 1981:54–9.
51. Cf. Carley & Howley, 1998:124.
52. So Crawford, 1993:87. For V. M. Lagorio, however, hesitancy was not the issue. Instead she argues that the monks' encounter with the Joseph stories in the Grail material just proved too great an opportunity to claim an original apostolic conversion for them to resist (1971:216).
53. Marx, 1997:208.
54. Carley, 1985:xxix.
55. Carley, 1985:5.
56. Carley, 1985:7.
57. Carley, 1985:19, 21.
58. Carley, 1985:21, 23.
59. Carley, 1985:51.
60. Carley, 1985:53.
61. Robinson, 1926:30.
62. Baker, 1930:29.
63. Robinson, 1926:30–1.
64. Carley, 1985:lviii.
65. Krochalis, 1997.
66. V. M. Lagorio, 1971:223.
67. L. Loomis, 1932:198.
68. Genet, 1984:67.
69. Carley, 1994:132–4.
70. The details here are drawn from Baker's rendering of Ussher's account (1930:33–8).
71. D'Ay, 2009.
72. Rahtz and Watts, 2003:161.
73. Rahtz and Watts, 2003:60.

74. Skeat, 1871:49.
75. Bowman supplies a detailed outline of the recent history and current practice of what she calls 'the Holy Thorn Ceremony' (2006).
76. Kennedy 2012.
77. Bowman, 2006:135–6.
78. Bowman, 2006:123.
79. Cunningham, 2009:253.
80. Elizabeth I, 1559.
81. Cunningham, 2009:254.
82. Cunningham, 2009:254–8.

CHAPTER 5

1. Rowland, 2011:3.
2. W. Blake, 1811; cf. also Rowland, 2011:120.
3. Rowland, 2011:120.
4. Chilton, 2011.
5. Smith, 1989:63.
6. Ashdown, 2010:2–3.
7. L. S. Lewis, 1955; H. A. Lewis, 1939; C. C. Dobson, 1936.
8. Dobson, 1936:10; cited in Smith, 1989:71–2.
9. Smith, 1989:66–7.
10. Blake, 1821(object 77); Smith, 1989:73.
11. Blake, 1821(object 27); Smith, 1989:73.
12. Smith, 1989:79–80.
13. Ashdown, 2010:2, 193–4, 324.
14. Price, 2009:67—his emphasis.
15. Price, 2009:69.
16. Price, 2009:70.
17. Younghusband, 1918; cf. French, 1994:302–3.
18. French, 1994: 308.
19. Fitch, 1990:167.
20. Anonymous, 2012c.
21. Fitch, 1990:168.
22. Anonymous, 2012c.
23. S. Goodenough, 1977:34.
24. Anonymous, 2012c. It is interesting to note that for this writer Blake's target has now become the Satanic Mill owners as harsh employers of children.
25. Mangan, 1986:128–31.
26. Richards, 2001:161–2.
27. Richards, 2001:161.

28. Richards, 2001:119.
29. R. Thomas, 2000.
30. S. Condron and P. Matthews, 2005.
31. R. Kisiel, 2009.
32. 'Gareth', 2010.
33. Anonymous, 2010b.
34. Anonymous, 2010c.
35. Mallory, 2011.
36. Borland, 2008.
37. Anonymous, 2011c.
38. O Briain, 2011. O Briain wrote: 'In summation, then: No, Chewie didn't get a medal; and Jerusalem is the Prod's best choon. Better go now, this Portal 2 won't play itself...'
39. Anonymous, 2011b.
40. J. Kirkup, 2011.
41. Anonymous, 2012d.
42. 'Jerusalem' also appeared in the closing scenes of the film, which was based on the exploits of Harold Abrahams and Eric Liddell in the 1924 Paris Olympics, to illustrate the return of the triumphant athletes to England.
43. A. Philips, 2012.
44. M. Hyde, 2012.
45. R. Dewsbury, 2012—no longer available online.
46. M. Collett-White, 2012.
47. Seymour, 2012.
48. Anonymous, 2012g.
49. Anonymous, 2012h.
50. D. Lynskey, 2011.
51. Anonymous, 2011a—my transcription.
52. W. Blake, 1811.
53. O Briain, 2009:4–17.
54. O Briain, 2009:127–31.
55. Colebatch, 2011.

CHAPTER 6

1. Anonymous, 2012e.
2. Smith, 1989:68.
3. Smith, 1989:67.
4. Smith, 1989:69.
5. McGrath, 2002.
6. Anonymous, 2011d.

7. Podolak, 2011.
8. Hughes, 1961:250.
9. The book has no page numbers.
10. Slaughter, 1959:283–5.
11. Rickman, 1997:525.
12. Rickman, 1997:642.
13. Rickman, 1997:212–13.
14. Rickman, 1997:206–7.
15. Rickman, 1997:212–13.
16. Rickman, 1997:20.
17. Rickman, 1997:475–6.
18. Rickman, 1997:523.
19. Rickman, 1997:537.
20. Rickman, 1997:632–3.
21. Ebert, 1994.
22. Anonymous, 2010a.
23. Zitzer, 2003.
24. Boam, 1989.
25. Boam, 1989.
26. Anonymous, 2012i.
27. http://www.visimag.com/shivers/h95_feature.htm (to Alan Jones's *Shivers* magazine).
28. http://draxreview.blogspot.co.uk/2005/08/gathering-2002.html
29. Wheeler, 1996:6–7.
30. Wheeler, 1996:6–7.
31. Wheeler, 1996:163–5.
32. Wheeler, 1996:166–7.
33. Wheeler, 1996:178–89.
34. Wheeler, 1996:204–7.
35. Wheeler, 1996:160–1.
36. Wheeler, 1996:176.
37. Wheeler, 1996:161.
38. Wheeler, 1996:10–14.
39. Wheeler, 1996:14.
40. Davidson, 1997:8.
41. Wheeler, 1996:17; cf. Davidson, 1997:241.
42. Davidson, 1997:76.
43. Davidson, 1997:241–2.
44. Beare, 1981:538.
45. Crossan, 1991:393.
46. Crossan and Reed, 2001:247.
47. Crossan, 1991:392.

48. Crossan, 1991:392–3, 463–4; Crossan's 'Cross Gospel' has been severely criticized, gaining few adherents (cf. e.g. R. E. Brown, 1987).
49. Lüdemann, 2000:111.
50. Crossan, 1991:393.
51. Crossan, 1991:393.
52. Crossan, 1994:154.
53. Crossan, 1991:393.
54. Crossan, 1999:20–1.
55. Crossan, 1999:21.
56. Crossan, 1999:21.
57. Cf. e.g. Wright, 1996:60–2.
58. Crossan, 1991:393.
59. Lyons, 2004: 47–8.
60. Crossan, 1999:21.
61. Lyons, 2004:48.
62. Lyons, 2004:49–50.
63. Lüdemann suggests that these two traditions—the plural tradition and the Joseph tradition—'perhaps agree in knowing of Joseph of Arimathea'; he 'would have been commissioned to see to the burial of Jesus' (2000:111).
64. Lyons, 2004:48–9.

CONCLUSION

1. Walkin, 2011:375–6.
2. Broughton, 2012.
3. Žižek, 2009:32.
4. Žižek, 2009:14.
5. Žižek, 2009:33.

Bibliography

Aland, K. (2004) *Luther's 95 Theses* (St Louis, MO: Arch Books).

Albright W. F. and C. S. Mann (1971) *Matthew* (Garden City, NY: Doubleday).

Anonymous (2010a) Review of 'Jesus of Nazareth' <http://www.chris tiancinema.com/catalog/article_info.php?articles_id=264#> accessed 30 August 2012.

Anonymous (2010b) 'House of Commons, 21st June 2010: Notices of Motions for which no days have been fixed ("Early Day Motions")' <http://www. publications.parliament.uk/pa/cm/cmedm/100621e01.htm> accessed 3 September 2012.

Anonymous (2010c) 'XIX Commonwealth Games' <http://d2010.thecgf. com> accessed 3 September 2012.

Anonymous (2011a) 'U2 talk to the BBC after their Glastonbury headline set' <http://www.youtube.com/watch?v=sLdvfrikaUQ> accessed 3 September 2012.

Anonymous (2011b) 'MP says hymn Jerusalem "banned from straight weddings"' <http://www.bbc.co.uk/news/uk-politics-13460672> accessed 3 September 2012.

Anonymous (2011c) 'Kate will love, honour (but not obey): The order of service in full' <http://www.dailymail.co.uk/news/article-1381426/Royal-Wedding-Order-Service-Princess-Diana-funeral-hymn-sung.html> accessed 3 September 2011.

Anonymous (2011d) 'Saint Joseph of Arimathea Pallbearer Ministry' <http://www.ignatius.edu/page.aspx?pid=503> accessed 15 September 2012.

Anonymous (2012a) 'Prayer Book of Cardinal Albrecht of Brandenburg', J. Paul Getty Museum <http://www.getty.edu/art/gettyguide/ar tObjectDetails?artobj=1639> accessed 18 July 2012.

Anonymous (2012b) 'Masterpieces of the Prado Museum with Google Earth' <http://www.museodelprado.es/en/the-collection/sueltas/master pieces-of-the-prado-museum-with-google-earth/> accessed 18 July 2012.

Anonymous (2012c) 'FAQs' <http://www.thewi.org.uk/faqs> accessed 3 September 2012.

Anonymous (2012d) 'London 2012 Olympic Games Opening Ceremony: Media guide' <http://www.london2012.com/mm/Document/Documents/Publications/ 01/30/43/40/OPENINGCEREMONYGUIDE_English.pdf> accessed 4 September 2012.

180 *Bibliography*

Anonymous (2012e) 'Joseph of Arimathea' <http://www.aquinasandmore.com/ fuseaction/store.patronsaintpage/saint/539> accessed 25 September 2012.

Anonymous (2012f) 'Third Edition of the *Oxford English Dictionary*' <http://www.oed.com> accessed 9 October 2012.

Anonymous (2012g) 'Playing Games in the Synagogue of Satan' <http://www. groundzeromedia.org/playing-games-in-the-synagogue-of-satan> accessed 5 October 2012.

Anonymous (2012h) 'Be Not Afeared: The Zion Olympics' <http://www.la wfulrebellion.org/2012/07/08/be-not-afeared-the-zion-olympics> accessed 5 October 2012.

Anonymous (2012i) 'The Gathering' <http://www.imdb.com/title/tt0294 594> accessed 5 October 2012.

Arkin, M. (1997) '"One of the Marys . . .": An Interdisciplinary Analysis of Michelangelo's Florentine Pietà', *Art Bulletin*, 79, 493–517.

Ashdown, P. (2010) *The Lord was at Glastonbury: Somerset and the Jesus Voyage Story* (Glastonbury: The Squeeze Press).

Baker, H. K. (1930) *Glastonbury Traditions concerning Joseph of Arimathea. Being a translation of the second chapter of* Britannicarum Ecclesiarum Antiquitates *of James Ussher* (London: Covenant Publishing Co.).

Bauckham, R. (1998) 'John for Readers of Mark', in his *The Gospel for all Christians* (Edinburgh: T&T Clark), 147–71.

Beard, M. (2011) 'A Don's Life: Royal wedding: ten questions', *Times Literary Supplement*, 29 April 2011 <http://timesonline.typepad.com/dons_life/ 2011/04/royal-wedding-ten-questions.html> accessed 22 August 2012.

Beare, F. W. (1981) *The Gospel according to Matthew: Translation, Introduction, and Commentary* (Oxford: Basil Blackwell).

Black, C. C. (1989) *The Disciples according to Mark: Markan Redaction in Current Debate* (Sheffield: JSOT Press).

Blake, W. (1811) *Milton: A Poem* [Copy A: British Museum] <http://www. blakearchive.org/exist/blake/archive/copy.xq?copyid=milton.a&java=no> accessed 20 June 2013.

Blake, W. (1821) *Jerusalem The Emanation of the Giant Albion* [Copy E: Yale Center for British Art] <http://www.blakearchive.org/exist/blake/arch ive/copy.xq?copyid=jerusalem.e&java=no> accessed 20 June 2013.

Boam, J. (1989) 'Indiana Jones and the Last Crusade—Screenplay' <http:// scifiscripts.com/scripts/Indiana3.txt> accessed 30 August 2012.

Boardman, W. (2007) *Sun and Wind: The Legend of Joseph of Arimathea* (New York: Scepter).

Borland, S. (2008) 'Cathedral bans popular hymn Jerusalem' <http://www. telegraph.co.uk/news/uknews/1584578/Cathedral-bans-popular-hymn-Jeru salem.html> accessed 3 September 2012.

Bowman, M. (2006) 'The Holy Thorn Ceremony: Revival, Rivalry and Civil Religion in Glastonbury', *Folklore*, 117, 123–40.

Broughton S. (2012) '"The day God came back to life": an Easter Day Sermon' <http://www.christchurchrio.org.br/cchurch/newscontent.asp?id=7051> accessed 15 October 2012.

Brown, A. (2011) *Civic Ceremony and Religion in Medieval Bruge, c.1300–1520* (Cambridge: Cambridge University Press).

Brown, R. E. (1987) 'The Gospel of Peter and Canonical Gospel Priority', *NTS* 33, 321–43.

Brown, R. E. (1994) *Death of the Messiah, 2 Vols* (New York: Doubleday).

Bryant, N. (2001) *Merlin and the Grail: Joseph of Arimathea, Merlin, Perceval: The Trilogy of Arthurian Prose Romances attributed to Robert de Boron* (Woodbridge: D. S. Brewer).

Burton, P. (2000) *The Old Latin Gospels: A Study of Their Texts and Language* (Oxford: Oxford University Press).

Carley, J. P. (1985) *The Chronicle of Glastonbury Abbey: An Edition, Translation and Study of John of Glastonbury's* Cronica sive Antiquitates Glastoniensis Ecclesie (Woodbridge: Boydell Press).

Carley, J. P. (1994) 'A Grave Event: Henry V, Glastonbury Abbey, and Joseph of Arimathea', in M. B. Schichtman and J. P. Carley (eds.) *Culture and the King: The Social Implications of the Arthurian Legend* (New York: State University of New York Press), 129–48.

Carley, J. P. and M. Howley (1998) 'Relics at Glastonbury in the Fourteenth Century: An Annotated Edition of Bristish Library, Cotton Titus D.vii, fols. 2r-13v', in J. P. Carley and F. Riddy (eds.) *Glastonbury Abbey and the Arthurian Tradition* (Cambridge: D. S. Brewer), 83–128.

Chase, C. J. (2003) 'The Gateway to the *Lancelot-Grail Cycle*: *L'Estoire del Saint Graal*', in C. Dover (ed.) *A Companion to the Lancelot-Grail Cycle* (Woodbridge, Suffolk: D. S. Brewer), 65–74.

Chilton, M. (2011) 'Royal Wedding: Jerusalem triumphant at Kate and Will's wedding', *Daily Telegraph*, 29 April 2011 <http://www.telegraph.co.uk/news/uknews/royal-wedding/8483364/Royal-Wedding-Jerusalem-triumphant-at-Kate-and-Wills-wedding.html> accessed 22 August 2013.

Colebatch, H. G. P. (2011) 'Blake's "Jerusalem"—Forget It!' *New American Spectator*, 3 May 2011 <http://spectator.org/people/hal-gp-colebatch/all> accessed 22 August 2012.

Collett-White, M. (2012) 'Are we same species? World agog at British Games opener' <http://www.reuters.com/london-olympics-2012/articles/2012/07/28/are-we-same-species-world-agog-british-games-opener> accessed 4 September 2012.

Condron, S. and P. Matthews (2005) 'Why Britain should sing Jerusalem on Thursday' <http://www.dailymail.co.uk/sport/cricket/article-361425/Why-Britain-sing-Jerusalem-Thursday.html> accessed 3 September 2012.

Cranfield, C. E. B. (1977) *The Gospel According to Saint Mark* (Cambridge: Cambridge University Press).

Crawford, D. K. E. (1993) 'St. Joseph in Britain: Reconsidering the Legends, Part I', *Folklore* 104, 86–98.

Crawford, D. K. E. (2001) 'St Joseph and Britain: The Old French Origins', *Arthuriana* 11, 1–20.

Crossan, J. D. (1991) *The Historical Jesus: The Life of a Mediterranean Jewish Peasant* (San Francisco, CA: HarperSanFrancisco).

Crossan, J. D. (1994) *Jesus: A Revolutionary Biography* (San Francisco, CA: HarperSanFrancisco).

Crossan, J. D. (1999) 'Historical Jesus as Risen Lord', in J. D. Crossan et al., *The Jesus Controversy: Perspectives in Conflict* (Harrisburg, PA: Trinity Press International), 1–47.

Crossan, J. D. and J. L. Reed (2001) *Excavating Jesus: Beneath the Stones, Behind the Texts* (London: SPCK).

Courcelle, P. (1968) *Recherches sur les Confessions de Saint Augustine* (2nd ed.; Paris: de Boccard).

Cunningham, J. (2009) ' "A young man's brow and an old man's beard": The rise and fall of Joseph of Arimathea in English Reformation thought', *Theology* 112, 251–59.

D'Ay, Z. (2009) 'The Twinning of Glastonbury and Patmos' <http://www.glastonbury-patmos.com> accessed 15 October 2012.

Davidson, D. (1997) *The Memories of Josephes: Soul Memories of a Cousin of Jesus* (London: Leaders Partnership).

Dewsbury, R. (2012) 'The NHS did not deserve to be so disgracefully glorified in this bizarre spectacle of left-wing propaganda' <http://www.dailymail.co.uk/debate/article-2180124/Olympics-opening-ceremony-NHS-disgracefully-glorified.html> accessed 28 July 2012—now removed.

Dobson, C. C. (1936) *Did our Lord visit Britain as they say in Cornwall and Somerset?* (Glastonbury: Avalon Press).

Dover, C. (ed.) (2003) *A Companion to the Lancelot-Grail Cycle* (Woodbridge, Suffolk: D. S. Brewer).

Ebert, R. (1994) 'The Gospel according to St Matthew (1964), 10th March 2004' <http://rogerebert.suntimes.com/apps/pbcs.dll/article?AID=/20040314/REVIEWS08/403140301/1023> accessed 30 August 2012.

Eire, C. M. N. (1979) 'Calvin and Nicodemism: A Reappraisal', *The Sixteenth Century Journal* 10, 44–69.

Elder, I. H. (1999) *Joseph of Arimathea* (Glastonbury: Glastonbury Abbey Shop).

Elizabeth I of England (1559) *Selected Writing and Speeches: On Religion* <http://www.fordham.edu/halsall/mod/elizabeth1.asp#On Religion, 1583> accessed 10 June 2013.

Fitch, D. (1990) *Blake Set to Music: A Bibliography of Musical Settings of the Poems and Prose of William Blake* (Berkeley, CA: University of California Press).

France, R. T. (2002) *The Gospel of Mark* (Grand Rapids, MI: Eerdmans).

French, P. (1994) *Younghusband: The Last Great Imperial Adventurer* (London: Harper Perenniel).

'Gareth' (2010) 'It's Jerusalem for the Commonwealth Games' <http://anthem4england.co.uk/blog_post/its-jerusalem-for-the-commonwealth-games> accessed 3 September 2012.

Genet, J.-P. (1984) 'English Nationalism: Thomas Polton at the Council of Constance', *Nottingham Medieval Studies* 28, 60–78.

Gerritsen, W. P. (1981) 'Jacob van Maerlant and Geoffrey of Monmouth', in K. Varty (ed.) *An Arthurian Tapestry* (Glasgow: University of Glasgow), 368–83.

Gibbs, R. (1988) *The Legendary Twelve Hides of Glastonbury* (Burnham-on-Sea, Somerset: Llanerch).

Gilliard, F. D. (1984) 'Senatorial Bishops in the Fourth Century', *Harvard Theological Review* 77, 153–75.

Gizewski, C. (2011) 'Decurio, Decuriones', in Hubert Cancik et al. (eds.), *Brill's New Pauly Online* <http://referenceworks.brillonline.com/entries/brill-s-new-pauly/decurio-decuriones-e312510?s.num=174&s.start=160> accessed 22 May 2013.

Gnilka, J, (1979) *Das Evangelium nach Markus*, II/2 (Zurich and Neukirchen–Vluyn: Benziger Verlag und Neukirchener Verlag).

Goldfarb, H. T. (1997) 'Sandro Botticelli As Artist and Witness: An Overview', in L. Kanter et al. (eds.), *Botticelli's Witness*, 3–12.

Goodacre, M. (2001) *The Synoptic Problem: A Way Through the Maze* (Sheffield: Continuum).

Goodenough, S. (1977) *Jam and Jerusalem: A Pictorial History of Britain's Greatest Women's Movement* (London: Collins).

Graeve, M. A. (1958) 'The Stone of Unction in Caravaggio's Painting for the Chiesa Nuova', *Art Bulletin* 40, 223–38.

Graham-Dixon, A. (1994) 'Anatomy of a genius: Despite recent claims to the contrary, Andrew Graham-Dixon believes that *The Entombment* is not only a Michelangelo, it is also the perfect expression of the artist's unique synthesis of sensuality and spirituality' <http://www.independent.co.uk/

arts-entertainment/art/art–anatomy-of-a-genius-despite-recent-claims-to-the-contrary-andrew-grahamdixon-believes-that-the-entombment-is-not-only-a-michelangelo-it-is-also-the-perfect-expression-of-the-artists-unique-synthesis-of-sensuality-and-spirituality-1444901.html> accessed 17 July 2012.

Gundry, R. H. (1994) *Matthew: A Commentary on His Handbook for a Mixed Church under Persecution* (2nd ed.; Grand Rapids, MI: Eerdmans).

Hamburgh, H. E. (1981) 'The Problem of Lo Spasimo of the Virgin in Cinquecento Paintings of the Descent from the Cross', *The Sixteenth Century Journal* 12, 45–75.

Hankins, J. (1997) 'From the New Athens to the New Jerusalem: Florence Between Lorenzo de' Medici and Savonarola', in L. Kanter, et al. (eds.) *Botticelli's Witness, Changing Style in a Changing Florence* (Boston, MA: Trustees of the Isabella Stewart Gardner Museum), 13–20.

Harpur, J. (2007) *The Gospel of Joseph of Arimathea* (Glasgow: Wild Goose).

Harrison, C. (2004) ' "Not Words but Things:" Harmonious Diversity in the Four Gospels', in F. van Fleteren and J. C. Schnaubelt (eds.) *Augustine: Biblical Exegete* (Wien: Peter Lang), 157–71.

Hooker, M. D. (1991) *The Gospel according to St. Mark* (London: A&C Black).

Hourihane, C. (2009) *Pontius Pilate, Anti-Semitism, and the Passion in Medieval Art* (Princeton, NJ: Princeton University Press).

Hughes, T. R. (1961) *Yr Ogof (The Cave): The Story of Joseph of Arimathea* (Aberystwyth: Gwasg Aberystwyth).

Hyde, M. (2012) 'Olympic Games opening ceremony: irreverent and idiosyncratic' <http://www.guardian.co.uk/sport/2012/jul/28/olympic-games-opening-ceremony-british?> accessed 4 September 2012.

Izydorczyk, Z. (ed.) (1997a) *The Medieval Gospel of Nicodemus: Texts, Intertexts, and Contexts in Western Europe* (Tempe, AZ: Medieval & Renaissance Texts & Studies; 158), 21–41.

Izydorczyk, Z. (1997b) 'Introduction', in Z. Izydorczyk (ed.) *Medieval Gospel of Nicodemus*, 1–20.

Izydorczyk, Z. (1997c) 'The Evangelium Nicodemi in the Latin Middle Ages', in Z. Izydorczyk (ed.) *Medieval Gospel of Nicodemus*, 42–101.

Izydorczyk, Z. and J.-D. Dubois (1997) 'Nicodemus's Gospel before and beyond the Medieval West', in Z. Izydorczyk (ed.) *The Medieval Gospel of Nicodemus*, 21–41.

Jülicher, A. (1938) *Itala: Das Neue Testament in altlateinischer Überlieferung* (Berlin: W. de Gruyter); vol. 1: Matthäus-Evangelium.

Jülicher, A. (1954) *Itala: Das Neue Testament in altlateinischer Überlieferung* (Berlin: W. de Gruyter); vol. 3: Lucas Evangelium.

Jülicher, A. (1970) *Itala: Das Neue Testament in altlateinischer Überlieferung* (Berlin: W. de Gruyter); vol. 2: Marcus Evangelium (2nd ed.).

Kannengeisser, C. (1998) 'Augustine of Hippo', in D. K. McKim (ed.) *Historical Handbook of Major Biblical Interpreters* (Leicester, UK: IVP), 22–8.

Kanter, L. et al. (eds.) (1997) *Botticelli's Witness: Changing Style in a Changing Florence* (Boston, MA: Trustees of the Isabella Stewart Gardner Museum).

Kelly, J. N. D. (1995) *Golden Mouth: The Story of John Chrysostom: Ascetic, Preacher, Bishop* (Ithaca: Cornell University Press).

Kennedy, M. (2012) 'Glastonbury Thorn chopped down as town rages over attack on famous tree' <http://www.guardian.co.uk/environment/2010/dec/09/glastonbury-mourns-felling-thorn-tree> accessed 18 September 2012.

Kim, H. C. (ed.) (1973) *The Gospel of Nicodemus* (Toronto Medieval Latin Texts 2. Toronto: Pontifical Institute of Mediaeval Studies).

Kirkup, J. (2011) 'Blake's Jerusalem "reserved for homosexuals"' <http://www.telegraph.co.uk/news/uknews/royal-wedding/8524166/Blakes-Jerusalem-reserved-for-homosexuals.html> accessed 3 September 2012.

Kisiel R. (2009) 'Lady in red Katherine Jenkins opens the Ashes with Welsh hymn, before TWO anthems and another hymn' <http://www.dailymail.co.uk/news/article-1197960/Lady-red-Katherine-Jenkins-opens-Ashes-Welsh-hymn-TWO-anthems-hymn.html#ixzz25UMTIFgi> accessed 3 September 2012.

Kren, T. and S. McKendrick (2003) *Illuminating the Renaissance: The triumph of Flemish manuscript painting in Europe* (Los Angeles: J. Paul Getty Museum).

Kristof, J. (1989) 'Michelangelo as Nicodemus: The Florence Pietà', *The Sixteenth Century Journal* 20, 163–82.

Krochalis, J. (1997) 'Magna Tabula: The Glastonbury Tablets (Part 1)', in J. P. Carley and F. Riddy (eds.) *Arthurian Literature XV* (Cambridge: D. S. Brewer), 93–183.

Lagorio, V. M. (1971) 'The Evolving Legend of St. Joseph of Glastonbury', *Speculum* 46, 209–31.

Lane, W. L. (1974) *The Gospel according to Mark* (NICNT; London: Marshall, Morgan & Scott).

Latham, R. E. and D. R. Howlett (1986) *Dictionary of Medieval Latin from British Sources, Vol. 1: A–L* (Oxford: Oxford University Press).

Lawton, D. A. (1983) *Joseph of Arimathea: A Critical Edition* (New York: Garland Pub.).

Lewis, G. S. (2008) *Did Jesus Come to Britain? An Investigation into the Traditions That Christ Visited Cornwall and Somerset* (Forest Row: Clairview Books).

Lewis, H. A. (1939) *Christ in Cornwall* (self-published).

Lewis, L. S. (1955) *St. Joseph of Arimathea at Glastonbury or the Apostolic Church of Britain* (7th ed.; London: James Clarke & Co.).

Lightbown, R. (1989) *Sandro Botticelli: Life and Work* (New ed.; London: Thames and Hudson).

Lincoln, A. T. (2000) *Truth on Trial: The Lawsuit Motif in the Fourth Gospel* (Peabody, MA: Hendrickson).

Loomis, L. R. (1932) 'The Organisation by Nations at Constance', *Church History* 4, 191–210.

Lüdemann, G. (2000) *Jesus After Two Thousand Years: What He Really Said and Did* (London: SCM Press).

Luttenberger, A. (2003) 'Albert of Brandenberg', in P. G. Bietenholz and T. B. Deustcher (eds.) *Contemporaries of Erasmus: A Biographical Register of the Renaissance and Reformation* (Toronto: University of Toronto Press), 184–87.

Lynskey, D. (2011) 'U2 at Glastonbury 2011—review' <http://www.guardian.co.uk/music/2011/jun/25/u2-glastonbury-2011-review> accessed 3 September 2012.

Lyons, W. J. (2004) 'On the Life and Death of Joseph of Arimathea', *JSHJ* 2, 29–53.

Mallory, G. (2011) 'The Challenge Cup: A game I cannot see' <http://www.footyalmanac.com.au/the-challenge-cup-a-game-i-cannot-see> accessed 3 September 2012.

Malory, T. (2008) *Le Morte D'Arthur; The Book of King Arthur and of His Noble Knights of the Round Table* (New York: Signet).

Mangan, J. A. (1986) '"The Grit of our Forefathers": Invented traditions, propaganda, and imperialism', in J. McKenzie (ed.) *Imperialism and Popular Culture* (Manchester: Manchester University Press).

Marx, C. W. (1997) 'The Gospel of Nicodemus in Old English and Middle English', in Z. Izydorczyk (ed.) *Medieval Gospel of Nicodemus*, 208–60.

Mayer, W. and P. Allen (2000) *John Chrysostom* (London: Routledge).

McCouat, P. (2012) 'Michelangelo's disputed Entombment' <http://www.artinsociety.com/michelangelos-disputed-entombment.html> accessed 10 July 2012.

McGrath, M. O. (2002) 'Saint Joseph of Arimathea: Patron of funeral directors', in his *Patrons and Protectors: More Occupations* (Chicago, IL: Liturgy Training Publications), 35.

Miles, M. (1997) 'Augustine of Hippo', in E. Ferguson (ed.) *Encyclopaedia of Early Christianity* (2nd ed.; London: Garland Publishing Inc.), 148–54.

Neirynck, F. (1989) 'The Apocryphal Gospels and the Gospel of Mark', in J.-M. Sevrin (ed.) *The New Testament in Early Christianity* (Leuven: Leuven University Press), 123–75.

O Briain, D. (2009) *Tickling the English: Notes on a Country and Its People from an Irish Funny Man on Tour* (London: Michael Joseph).

O Briain, D. (2011) 'Twitter update on 29 April 2011' <http://twitter.com/daraobriain/statuses/63927262210306048> accessed 30 April 2011.

Pack, R. (1951) 'Curiales in the Correspondence of Libanius', *Transactions and Proceedings of the American Philological Association* 82, 176–92.

Pasolini, P. P. (1964) 'The Gospel of Matthew' <http://www.youtube.com/watch?v=h7ewh5k5-gY> accessed 29 August 2012.

Paxton, J. (2005) 'Lords and Monks: Creating an Ideal of Noble Power in Monastic Chronicles', in R. F. Berkhofer et al. (eds.) *The Experience of power in Medieval Europe, 950–1350* (London: Ashgate).

Percy, E. (1920) *Joseph of Arimathea: A Romantic Morality in Four Scenes* (London: Burnes, Oates & Washburne).

Pesch, R. (1977) *Das Markusevangelium, 8.27–16.20*, II (Freiburg: Herder).

Philips, A. (2012) 'Danny Boyle's history lesson showed a great Britain with its head held high' <http://www.mirror.co.uk/tv/tv-reviews/london-2012-opening-ceremony-opinion-1176886> accessed 4 September 2012.

Podolak, J. (2011) 'NDCL's society of teen pallbearers serves burials for those without anyone else' <http://www.news-herald.com/articles/2011/03/04/life/nh3712750.txt> accessed 14 September 2012.

Powell, A. (2006) 'The Errant Image: Rogier van der Weyden's Deposition from the Cross and Its Copies', *Art History* 29, 540–62.

Price, D. (2009) *The Missing Years Of Jesus: The Extraordinary Evidence that Jesus Visited the British Isles: The Greatest Story Never Told* (London: Hay House UK).

Rahtz, P. and L. Watts (2003) *Glastonbury: Myth and Archaeology* (Stroud: Tempus).

Rebbenich, S. (2002) *Jerome* (London: Routledge).

Richards, J. (2001) *Imperialism and Music: Britain, 1876–1953* (Manchester: Manchester University Press).

Rickman, P. (1997) *The Chalice (Glastonbury Ghost Story)* (London: Pan Books).

Rickman, P. (2010) *The Bones of Avalon* (London: Atlantic Books).

Ridderbos, B. (2005) 'Objects and Questions', in B. Ridderbos et al. (eds.) *Early Netherlandish Paintings*, 4–170.

Ridderbos, B. et al. (eds.) (2005) *Early Netherlandish Paintings: Rediscovery, Reception, and Research* (Amsterdam: Amsterdam University Press).

Robinson, J. A. (1926) *Two Glastonbury Legends: King Arthur and St. Joseph of Arimathea* (Cambridge: Cambridge University Press).

Rosson, M. E. (2010) *Uncle of God: The Voyages of Joseph of Arimathea* (New York: Strategic Book Publishing).

Rowland, C. (2011) *Blake and the Bible* (New Haven: Yale University Press).

Ryan, W. G. (1993) *The Golden Legend: Readings on the Saints, Volume I* (Princeton, NJ: Princeton University Press).

Schaff, P. (ed.) (1886–) *Ante-Nicene Fathers, Nicene and Post-Nicene Fathers* <http://www.ccel.org/fathers.html> accessed 15 May 2013.

Scheidweiller, F. (1963) 'The Gospel of Nicodemus; Acts of Pilate and Christ's Descent into Hell' in W. Schneemelcher (ed.) *New Testament Apocrypha: Gospels and Related Writings, Vol.1* (London: Lutterworth Press), 444–84.

Scott, J. (1981) *The Early History of Glastonbury: An Edition, Translation and Study of William of Malmesbury's* De Antiquitate Glastonie Ecclesie (Woodbridge: Boydell Press).

Senior, D. (1984) *The Passion of Jesus in the Gospel of Mark* (Wilmington, DE: M. Glazier).

Seymour, R. (2012) 'Puke Britannia' <http://www.leninology.com/2012/07/puke-britannia.html> accessed 24 October 2012.

Shrimplin-Evangelidis, V. (1989) 'Michelangelo and Nicodemism: The Florentine Pietà', *Art Bulletin* 71, 58–66.

Simson, O. G. von (1953) 'Compassio and Co-redemptio in Roger van der Weyden's Descent from the Cross', *Art Bulletin* 35, 9–16.

Skeat, W. W. (1871) *Joseph of Arimathie, Otherwise Called the Romance of the Seint Graal or Holy Grail* (London: Early English Text Society).

Slaughter, F. G. (1959) *The Thorn of Arimathea: A Novel of the Days Following the Crucifixion* (London: Jarrolds).

Smith, A. W. (1989) ' "And Did Those Feet...?" The "Legend" of Christ's Visit to Britain', *Folklore* 100, 63–83.

Snobelen, S. D. (1999) 'Isaac Newton, Heretic: The Strategies of a Nicodemite', *British Journal for the History of Science*, 32, 381–419.

Soudavar, A. (2008) *Decoding Old Masters: Patrons, Princes and Enigmatic Paintings of the 15th Century* (London: I. B. Taurus).

Thomas, R. (2000) 'England pick Jerusalem and Fat Les for Euro 2000' <http://www.guardian.co.uk/football/2000/may/09/newsstory.sport6> accessed 3 September 2012.

Tischendorf, C. (1850) *Codex Amiatinus: Novum Testamentum Latine Interprete Hieronymo* (Leipzig: Avenarius and Mendelssohn).

Tischendorf, C. (1876) *Evangelica Apocrypha* (Leipzig: H. Mendelssohn).

Treharne, R. F. (1967) *The Glastonbury Legends: Joseph of Arimathea, The Holy Grail And King Arthur* (London: Cresset).

Tribbe, F. C. (2000) *I, Joseph of Arimathea: A Story of Jesus, His Resurrection and the Aftermath—A Documented Historical Novel* (Nevada City, CA: Blue Dolphin Publishing).

Vos, D. de (1999) *Rogier van der Weyden: The Complete Works* (New York: Harry N. Abrams, Inc.).

Vos, D. de (2002) *The Flemish Primitives* (Princeton, NJ: Princeton University Press).

Wabuda, S. (2007) Review of J. Schofield. *Philip Melanchthon and the English Reformation* (Aldershot: Ashgate, 2006) in *Renaissance Quarterly* 60, 645–47.

Walkin, N. (2011) *Praying for Miracles* (2nd ed.; Maitland, FL: Xulon Press).

Wheeler, P. (1996) *The Way of Love: Joseph of Arimathea tells the true story behind the message of Jesus: Recorded Channelings* (London: Leaders Partnership).

Wilken, R. L. (1983) *John Chrysostom and the Jews: Rhetoric and Reality in the Late 4th Century* (Berkeley: University of California Press).

Williams, M. H. (2006) *The Monk and the Book: Jerome and the Making of Christian Scholarship* (Chicago: University of Chicago Press).

Wright, N. T. (1996) *Jesus and the Victory of God* (London: SPCK).

Yarchin, W. (2004) *History of Biblical Interpretation: A Reader* (Peabody, MT: Hendrickson).

Younghusband, F. E. et al. (1918) *Fight for Right* (New York and London: G. P. Putnam's Sons).

Zeffirelli, F. (1977a) 'Jesus of Nazareth, Part 1' (1.00.00–3.27.42) <http://www.youtube.com/watch?v=ShSerVAKObU> accessed 29 August 2012.

Zeffirelli, F. (1977b) 'Jesus of Nazareth, Part 2' (1.00.00–3.39.55) <http://www.youtube.com/watch?v=zGjIu5DIvG8> accessed 29 August 2012.

Zitzer, L. (2003) 'Zeffirelli' <http://www.historicaljesusghost.com/Zeffirelli T.htm> accessed 30 August 2012.

Žižek, S. (2009) *Violence: Six Sideways Reflections* (London: Profile Books).

Zwemer, S. M. (1924) 'The Law of Apostasy in Islam: Answering the Question Why There are so Few Moslem Converts and Giving Examples of Their Moral Courage and Martyrdom' <http://www.muhammadanism.org/Zwemer/apostasy.pdf> accessed 11 July 2012.

General Index

active 7, 18, 67, 159, 160, 162, 164, 168
Adam 54, 77
Albrecht of Brandenberg/Mainz 47, 48, 50, 162, 163
apostle/apostles 21, 78, 79, 80, 90, 105, 136, 150
Arimathea (town) 10, 18, 30, 40, 41, 42, 44, 48, 66, 70, 72, 83, 88, 90, 91, 136, 149, 151, 158
Arthur, King 5, 74, 75, 81, 83, 85, 86, 87, 88, 93, 137, 143, 144, 173
Augustine of Hippo 5, 21, 29, 32, 33, 34, 35, 36, 37, 43, 71
Australia/Australian 116, 117, 125, 128, 130
Avalon 80, 86, 87, 91, 92, 102, 125, 137, 139, 140

Bening, Simon 5, 46, 47, 48, 49, 50, 71, 162, 163, 164
Blake, William 6, 100, 104, 105, 106, 107, 108, 109, 110, 111, 112, 113, 117, 119, 120, 121, 122, 124, 126, 128, 129, 138, 162, 174, 180
bold/boldness 13, 14, 17, 18, 26, 27, 36, 39, 43, 50, 64, 67, 159, 160
Britain/British Isles 5, 6, 37, 65, 71, 72, 73, 74, 75, 76, 80, 81, 82, 83, 85, 86, 87, 88, 90, 93, 96, 100, 102, 107, 109, 110, 111, 113, 114, 115, 117, 118, 121, 122, 123, 127, 129, 130, 132, 136, 137, 144, 149, 158, 161, 162
Buonarotti, Michelangelo 5, 46, 59, 60, 61, 62, 64, 65, 66, 71, 108
burial 1, 4, 5, 8, 13, 14, 15, 16, 18, 19, 20, 24, 26, 27, 35, 36, 37, 40, 41, 43, 44, 45, 46, 48, 51, 53, 54, 55, 56, 59, 60, 64, 65, 66, 67, 71, 72, 77, 78, 79, 92, 133, 134, 136, 142, 144, 149, 152, 153, 154, 155, 156, 158, 159, 160, 177

Calvin, John 1, 61, 62, 63, 161
canonical 4, 5, 8, 16, 19, 21, 22, 23, 24, 25, 27, 28, 34, 37, 41, 42, 43, 44, 45, 75, 79, 152, 154, 158, 159
Caravaggio 45, 66, 67

Catholic 30, 61, 62, 63, 103, 128, 130, 132, 133
Chrysostom, John 5, 21, 25, 26, 27, 28, 29, 37, 43, 44, 71, 162
Commonwealth 6, 114, 116, 119, 130
councillor 10, 11, 15, 16, 17, 19, 22, 26, 27, 41, 44, 153, 159, 161
crucifixion 1, 6, 12, 21, 24, 26, 35, 37, 38, 76, 81, 107, 136, 137, 143, 145, 149, 151, 152, 154, 162

Decurio 30, 31, 32, 73, 91, 161
deposition 5, 31, 37, 38, 45, 46, 50, 51, 52, 53, 54, 55, 59, 60, 66, 69, 170
descent, see deposition
De Voragine, Jacobus 37, 42, 83, 97, 98
disciple/disciples 9, 11, 12, 14, 15, 18, 19, 20, 26, 27, 35, 39, 64, 73, 78, 80, 87, 88, 91, 132, 137, 152, 153, 154, 155, 156, 160, 161, 162

Elizabeth I 63, 103, 137
England/English 5, 6, 31, 37, 63, 64, 73, 74, 81, 82, 83, 84, 85, 87, 88, 89, 91, 94, 95, 96, 97, 98, 99, 100, 102, 103, 104, 105, 106, 107, 108, 109, 110, 111, 112, 113, 114, 115, 116, 117, 118, 119, 120, 122, 123, 125, 126, 127, 128, 129, 130, 131, 132, 133, 136, 138, 145, 149, 158, 162, 168, 169
entombment, see burial
Evangelist/Evanglists 7, 9, 10, 20, 35, 36, 54, 152, 153, 154, 155, 156, 158, 159, 160
exemplar 12, 59, 60, 134, 137, 158, 161

fear 18, 19, 20, 26, 35, 36, 41, 43, 46, 61, 62, 64, 77, 78, 79, 146, 150
Fourth Gospel, see John, Gospel of
funeral workers 6, 133, 134, 162

Gilbert, Brian 6, 140, 144, 161
Glastonbury 4, 5, 6, 72, 73, 74, 82, 84, 85, 86, 87, 88, 89, 91, 93, 99, 100, 101, 102, 103, 107, 108, 110, 111, 121, 125, 126, 128, 132, 133, 137, 138, 139, 140, 145, 147, 158, 161, 162